The Innocent Killer

Michael Griesbach is a veteran prosecutor in the state of Wisconsin where the events recounted in his book occurred. He wrote The Innocent Killer as a challenge to the system. He hopes to leave readers better informed about the inner workings of the criminal justice system and more concerned about those whose lives it deeply affects. He worked on the case to overturn Steven Avery's original rape conviction and has reviewed all of the evidence in the Teresa Halbach case, to produce a work of non-fiction that will make you think again. He lives in North Eastern Wisconsin with his wife Jody and their four children.

Praise for The Innocent Killer

'The Innocent Killer is a shocking yet effective example of what can happen when our justice system fails. It poses the provocative question – one which those involved in the criminal justice system must ask themselves time and time again: 'What if?' What if the investigation of Steven Avery's alleged crime and its prosecution had gone differently? Would the tragic event that happened eighteen years later still have come to pass? Unfortunately, we'll never know. Griesbach's unflinching page-turner raises all the right questions and brings us closer to the truth.'

Barry Scheck, Co-founder and Co-Director
of the National Innocence Project at the
Benjamin N. Cardozo School of Law

The Innocent Killer

A True Story of a Wrongful Conviction and its Astonishing Aftermath

MICHAEL GRIESBACH

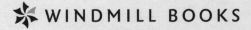

WINDMILL BOOKS

3 5 7 9 10 8 6 4

Windmill Books
20 Vauxhall Bridge Road
London SW1V 2SA

Windmill Books is part of the Penguin Random
House group of companies whose addresses can
be found at global.penguinrandomhouse.com.

Penguin
Random House
UK

A book concerning the same subject matter, titled *Unreasonable Inferences*, was
previously published by Point Beach Publishing, LLC in 2010.

First published in the United States by American Bar Association in 2014

First published in Great Britain in paperback by Windmill Books in 2016

www.windmill-books.co.uk

A CIP catalogue record for this book is available from the British Library.

ISBN 9780099510840 (Trade paperback)
ISBN 9780099510833 (Paperback)

Printed and bound in Great Britain by Clays Ltd, St Ives Plc

For Jody and the kids.

Contents

ACKNOWLEDGMENTS

This book has not been easy to write. Not only is it my first, which means there was a lengthy learning curve, but I am still a prosecutor in the Wisconsin county where Steven Avery's wrongful conviction occurred, and the book is highly critical of the police and the prosecutor responsible for his conviction. Besides, why would a prosecutor write a wrongful conviction book in the first place? They are typically the province of defense attorneys, members of Innocence Projects, or wrongly convicted individuals themselves.

It is with these thoughts in mind that I wish to express my deepest gratitude to the following individuals, without whose wise counsel, encouragement, and support, writing this book would have been a very lonely road to travel.

Thanks first to Penny Beerntsen whose courage and compassion turned what could have been a life-long tragedy into a mission to serve. As an invaluable member of the Wisconsin Criminal Justice Study Commission and the Wisconsin Crime Victims Rights Board in the years following her assault, and as a devoted volunteer for the Manitowoc County Sexual Assault Resource Center, the Wisconsin Restorative Justice Program, and Northwestern University Law School's Center on Wrongful Convictions, Penny has devoted much of her time and considerable talent to helping crime victims and offenders alike get their lives back on track. Thanks Penny, your life is an inspiration!

Thanks also to University of Wisconsin law school professor Keith Findley. Keith is the former director at the Wisconsin Innocence Project and served as lead counsel in the litigation that resulted in Steven Avery's exoneration. From when we first learned about the DNA results until today, I've treasured our conversations.

Thanks to Marquette University law school professor and former Wisconsin Supreme Court Justice Janine Geske. Janine's reputation is unmatched in Wisconsin legal circles, but it was her compassion for her close friend,

Penny Beerntsen, that says the most about her character. Thanks Janine for your support of this project.

Thanks to Milwaukee attorneys Steven Glynn and Walter Kelly, two of the most highly skilled criminal defense attorneys in the state of Wisconsin who represented Steven Avery in his wrongful conviction lawsuit. Generously sharing with me their valuable time, they alerted me to some critical facts surrounding Mr. Avery's wrongful conviction, shedding further light on what I'd already recognized as one of local law enforcement's darkest hours.

A huge thanks to my editor, Jonathan Malysiak at American Bar Association Publishing. This project was on life support until it caught Jon's attention. His enthusiasm and knowledge of all things relating to books could not have come at a better time. It's been my privilege to work you, Jon.

Thanks to Washington lawyer, author, and agent Ronald Goldfarb of Goldfarb and Associates for understanding the importance of the Avery story early on. Working with someone of Ron's caliber was truly an honor.

Thanks to Jody, Mary, Perry, Kerry, Dan, and mom. Reviewing early versions of manuscripts is an unenviable task, but you did it with good cheer. Your comments were thoughtful and your advice was always sound.

Thanks to William Zinsser, whose classic book, *On Writing Well*, about the craft of writing creative non-fiction, helped immeasurably – I marked up more of his book than I left alone.

And most of all, thanks to Jody and the kids. You've put up with an often absent husband and father for three and a half years yet continued with your love and support. Remember, this is our book, not mine.

INTRODUCTION

I've been a prosecutor for twenty-five years, and I thought I'd seen it all. I've been called out to crime scenes in the middle of the night to view victims of gunshot or stab wounds lying mangled in pools of congealing blood. I've comforted overwrought rape victims paralyzed by fear so they could muster the courage to take the stand. I've interviewed victims of armed robberies who stared death in the eyes and knew they were lucky to still be alive. And one time, I even saw tough-guy cops with tears in their eyes and fear on their faces as they scrambled into the night to find the two young hoodlums who had shot and killed one of their own.

I've sat almost comatose through thousands of hours of mindless intake court, listening to the pleas of defendants, "Not guilty, Your Honor," ceremoniously uttered over and over. I've seen my fair share of pompous prosecutors, joined battle with belligerent defense attorneys, and paced courthouse hallways late at night, sweating it out while waiting for a verdict.

But none of that prepared me for the case you're about to read, a true crime story where the good guys are sometimes the bad guys and the bad guys the good. It's a case of violent crime with a mind-numbing twist. But mostly, it's a case about innocence and guilt.

PROLOGUE

Nature's beauty comes not from the spectacular in East Central Wisconsin. There are no thousand foot vertical-drop cliffs, like at Yosemite, or million cubic feet per second waterfalls, like at Niagara. No, the land here owes its beauty to its moderation instead - its balance, its order. In between the extremes of the monolithic vistas of the Great Plains on one hand, and the confining woods of New England on the other, and with rolling farmland sharing the landscape with woods and lakes and streams, the land here seems just right somehow.

But our climate is anything but moderate and is a constant reminder that we are under the governance of a higher and occasionally darker power. Fair and even-tempered one moment, it can turn cruel and contemptuous the next, injudiciously wielding its malevolence, with perfect indifference to the human suffering it leaves in its wake - like some almighty but uncaring pagan god.

Most meteorologists say it's a myth, but some claim Lake Michigan protects East Central Wisconsin from the deadliest of summer storms. The Great Lake's frigid water cools the atmosphere, they say, and robs the beastly storms of the warm, moist air they feed on for their strength. Perhaps there's something to it, but twice in the not so distant past the darker side of Mother Nature ignored Lake Michigan and brewed up storms so powerful that they shattered the balance of the atmosphere and laid waste to parts of the land. This book, in a manner of speaking, is the story of those two storms. The first storm shattered the glass on the courthouse dome, and the second one nearly left the local justice system in ruins.

PART I

ONE

July 14, 1985

It was impossible to identify the man in her room. With the exception of her one-piece bathing suit, which had been hanging on the clothesline but was now wrapped around his head, the intruder was nude. The seventeen-year-old girl thought for a moment she was dreaming, but the knife the man held to her throat was real. This wasn't a dream.

"Say anything and I'll kill you," said the man, sitting on top of her with one hand over her mouth and the other on her breast.

"Take off your clothes," he demanded. "Take off your clothes, or I'll kill you."

The girl, whose parents were up north for the weekend, pointed to the heating pad underneath her and blurted out she was having her period. The man felt the heating pad and then placed the girl's hand on his penis as she squirmed in disgust.

Then he yanked her off the bed, and with the knife to her throat again, he took her by the arm and pushed her to the back door.

"Call anyone and I'll come back and kill you," the man said as he ran into the darkness, leaving as he entered—nude.

For the police, determining the point of entry proved easy. The intruder had dragged a picnic table underneath the kitchen window, popped open the flimsy screen, and let himself in. They had a suspect in mind, but it was too dark for the girl to get a good look at the man; he was around 5 feet 8 inches tall with a solid build, possibly a beard, but that's all she knew. So the investigation led nowhere. There was a predator on the loose, and the police knew he'd strike again—the only question was when.

Two Weeks Later

It was the middle of the summer and like most afternoons over the past few weeks, Tom and Penny Beerntsen went to the beach. The Beerntsens made their home in Manitowoc, Wisconsin—a city of thirty-eight thousand on the western shore of Lake Michigan, seventy miles north of Milwaukee and thirty miles south of Green Bay. A stone's throw from the hallowed grounds of Lambeau Field, the citizens of Manitowoc, whose moods rise and fall with the fortunes of their beloved Packers, are proud to be called "Cheeseheads."

The couple owned and operated Beerntsen's Confectionary on North Eighth Street in the heart of Manitowoc's historic downtown. To step into Beerntsen's is to step into the past. Tom's grandparents opened the old-fashioned candy store and ice cream parlor in 1932, and Tom and Penny were its current caretakers. With homemade chocolates and candies artfully displayed behind glass-paned counters and elegant black walnut booths gracing the parlor, Beerntsen's Confectionary is one of Manitowoc's jewels.

Tom and Penny both grew up in Manitowoc. They met in seventh grade and began dating during their sophomore year in high school. Together, they attended a small liberal arts school in Downers Grove, Illinois, and were married during their third year there. They graduated in 1971—Tom with a Bachelor of Science in Applied Behavioral Science, and Penny with a Bachelor of Arts in Sociology. They spent the first dozen years of their marriage moving from one state to the next—from Illinois to Iowa, then to South Dakota, and later to Minnesota, as Tom accepted various positions at regional YMCAs throughout the Midwest, eventually attaining the position of CEO. Penny gave birth to their two children during this time, a daughter and then a son. She was also a physical fitness instructor and somehow managed to find the time to work part-time as a staff member at a mental health center when they were living in Illinois. Having been on the move for more than a decade, and longing for a more permanent place to call home, they moved back to Manitowoc in 1983 to run Tom's parents' candy store.

Now it was two years later and, as usual, it took a long time for summer to arrive that year on "the Lakeshore," as the local television and radio personalities call east-central Wisconsin, even if nobody else does. And as usual, Lake Michigan was the culprit. For months, forecasters had qualified their predictions of a warm-up with the worn-out phrase, "cooler near the lake," and the patience of local residents wore thin. But the switch flipped in mid-June and the prevailing northeasterly winds mercifully ceased.

With summer now in full swing, the Beerntsens frequently spent late afternoons on the beach at Neshotah Park, a twelve-minute drive from

Manitowoc just north of Two Rivers. In addition to raising the kids and running the confectionary with Tom, Penny was the physical fitness instructor at the YMCA, and now that her summer fitness class was under way, she exercised religiously. A six-mile run, often along the Lake Michigan shoreline, anchored her daily routine.

That Monday was a perfect day for the beach, and with their eleven-year-old daughter and ten-year-old son, Tom and Penny planned to take full advantage of it. Tom pulled their Dodge Caravan into the parking lot and grabbed the cooler while Penny scoped out the beach for a place to set up camp. With sunshine and a mild breeze off the lake, the quarter mile stretch of beach was packed with sunbathers, but Penny found a spot at the edge of the sand and popped open an oversized umbrella to protect them from the sun. She read a few pages from the novel she'd been working on since school let out while Tom kept an eye on the kids who splashed around in the fifty-five degree water.

Penny would testify months later that it was precisely three o'clock in the afternoon when she removed her red and white striped tee shirt and got ready for her run. She knew it was three because a few days earlier she'd struggled against a strong headwind, and Tom and the kids were worried when she was late getting back to the park. This time, she wanted to make sure she was back in an hour, so she checked her watch before leaving— three o'clock on the nose. She said goodbye to Tom and then started jogging north along the smooth wet sand at the edge of the water—barefoot with her swimsuit on.

Penny jogged past the edge of Neshotah Park and crossed into Point Beach State Forest a few minutes later. Lying immediately to the north of the park, Point Beach State Forest transforms Lake Michigan's shoreline into an isolated wilderness. Undulating rows of sand dunes run like waves parallel to the shore and hide from view whatever occurs in their troughs. Towering pines rise sixty feet into the sky at the edge of the forest fifty yards inland and stand guard with an ever watchful and imposing eye over the beach below.

A mile and a half into her run now, Penny gazed out at the sparkling waters of Lake Michigan to her right and the deep forest of Point Beach to her left. With awe, not fear, a sense of utter isolation filtered into her psyche. Bathed in sunlight, with endorphins surging, she felt like she was on top of the world.

Ten minutes earlier she had passed a scraggly-looking man just beyond the public area of the beach, and despite temperatures in the mid-eighties, the man had a leather jacket on. Kind of odd given the temperature, she thought to herself.

"Nice day for a jog," the man said.

"Yes, it's a beautiful day," Penny replied over her left shoulder as she jogged past. Penny wasn't about to let the strange-looking man put a damper on her run.

Fifteen minutes later, she crossed "First Creek," as the locals call the shallow stream that empties into Lake Michigan there, and a half mile further she spied a sailboat running on its auxiliary motor with its sails down. The small craft was traveling in the same direction as she was, so she made a game out of jogging at the same pace.

By the time she crossed "Second Creek" a mile further north she had found her stride and had worked up a considerable sweat. Now at the halfway point of her run, she checked her watch as she made the turn and headed back toward the park. Perfect—three thirty, right on schedule.

She spotted the odd-looking man again twenty minutes later. He'd walked a half mile further north, well into the wilderness now, and he was standing in the midst of a stubby poplar tree ten feet from the water and fifty yards ahead of her. At first, she wasn't afraid—just curious. Why had the man walked so far up the beach with his street clothes on? And why was he hiding in the midst of a poplar tree just thirty feet in front of her now?

A few strides later, she noticed that the man's face looked different this time. It wasn't the odd, but seemingly harmless face of the stranger that she'd come across earlier. No, the man looked determined this time, determined to do something terrible—and he wasn't even trying to hide it. Penny's curiosity rapidly turned to fear. She knew she was in trouble. Each second stretched into what seemed like forever, and her heart began to pound. She didn't change her pace as she approached the man, and she didn't look him in the eye. Maybe he wouldn't do anything if she ignored him—maybe he wouldn't be real somehow.

But the man in the midst of the poplar tree wasn't just her imagination—he was less than ten feet in front of her now. Penny angled into the water. The man lunged at her, but missed. She angled a little further out and considered diving into the deeper water, but she was afraid he'd swim after her and she'd drown in a struggle. It was difficult to run in the waist-deep water and the man was gaining on her, so Penny arched back toward the shore. But she didn't have a chance. The attacker lunged at her from behind and wrapped his arms around her upper body. She tried twisting free, but the man placed her in a bear hug and dragged her to the shore.

"Help, help!" Penny yelled to a sailboat two hundred yards from shore.

But the man tightened his grip and cut off her windpipe.

"Shut up," he grunted. "We're gonna take a little walk up the sand."

With his prey onshore now, the attacker started pushing Penny over the first dune. She dug her feet into the sand and pushed back as hard as she could, but at five foot two and 105 pounds, the man easily overpowered her and manhandled her over the dunes, ripping off her top along the way.

He loosened his grip for a few seconds and Penny almost twisted free, but then he squeezed even harder and dragged her to the edge of the woods. Fifty yards from the beach now, and concealed from view, the assailant had Penny exactly where he wanted her.

He ripped off his belt, unsnapped his jeans, and exposed his penis. Then he pushed Penny a little further into the woods and pulled off the rest of her swimsuit. Face to face for the first time, she got a good look at the man, but he was bearded and it was difficult to make out his facial features.

"Do what I tell you," he mumbled. "I have a knife."

He began fondling Penny's breasts and then he sucked on her right breast, biting her slightly.

"Make me hard," he demanded.

Somehow, Penny kept her wits about her and tried reasoning with the man. "I've been gone too long," she said. "My husband will be worried and he'll come looking for me."

But the man didn't buy it. "Make me hard," he demanded again.

"No!" Penny yelled back in anger and disgust.

Then he reminded her about the knife, and Penny reluctantly placed her hand on his penis.

"Play with yourself," he said, while he fondled her breasts.

Penny removed her hand from his penis and put it on herself, hoping to buy some time.

"Now put your mouth on my penis."

"No!" Penny shot back.

"Put your fucking mouth on my penis. You're really fucking this up."

Penny refused again and then the assailant shoved her to the ground. Anger spewed viciously from his filthy mouth. "Spread your legs. Spread your goddamned legs," he said. "You're fucking this up."

Penny held fast.

And then, he beat her. She heard a crack when he grabbed her face and shoved her head into the ground, jerking her nose to the side. And then he pummeled her face with relentless blows to her eyes, nose, cheeks, and forehead. She kicked him in the groin, but he grabbed her around her neck and began strangling her like a madman.

"Now you're gonna die, bitch."

He shook her so violently that her head pounded against the ground, and she thought that he'd bring out the knife and stab her to death in the sand.

Penny was close to passing out, but the man wanted her alive so he loosened his grip and screamed at her, "Now, are you going to do it or not?"

"Okay, I'll do it," Penny said softly, trying to buy time. "But I'm sure my husband is looking for me. I've been gone too long."

That infuriated him, and the beating resumed until a few minutes later when Penny looked up and saw him inexplicably scramble away and miraculously disappear into the woods.

The attack had taken its toll. Naked, bloodied, and badly bruised, Penny was barely able to move. She rolled onto her hands and knees and tried to get up, but she immediately fell down. Desperate to get into the open where someone could find her, she started crawling instead, but halfway to the water she was too weak to go on. Empty, devoid of emotion, she sat cross legged and stared blankly into the sparkling waters of Lake Michigan—alone among the towering pines. She looked down at her hands and wondered where all the blood came from, and then she gave up and lay back on the sand.

When she came to, Penny summoned up all the energy she could and resumed crawling toward the water. After twenty minutes she finally made it, and then she began washing the blood off her face—the last thing she wanted was for her children to see her like that, all beaten and bloody. Then she saw a young couple walking on the beach. "Help! Help!" Penny shouted as she curled up into a ball to hide her nakedness. The woman ran over and wrapped a towel around her, and with Penny in the middle, the three of them began walking down the beach toward Neshotah Park.

Penny saw a man approaching—it was Tom!

Tom Beerntsen bolted toward his wife and lifted her into his arms. "Oh, my God, what happened?"

"A man tried raping me, Tom, he tried to kill me! Where's Julie?"

"Don't worry, she's with her grandfather," Tom said.

"What about Mike?" Penny asked.

"My mom's taking care of him. Don't worry, honey."

Tom Beerntsen ran down the beach with his wife in his arms. An ambulance was waiting when they made it back to the parking lot, and the EMTs lifted her inside and rushed her to Memorial Hospital in Manitowoc—sirens wailing.

Penny was safe now. Whoever he was, the man who attacked her had chosen the wrong victim. She had kicked and clawed and screamed at him relentlessly, and with his victim showing no sign of surrender, it was the would-be rapist, not the victim, who paradoxically gave in.

TWO

Six days before Penny Beerntsen was assaulted on the Lake Michigan shoreline, Lori Avery gave birth to a pair of healthy baby boys. Memorial Hospital in Manitowoc granted her a five-day stay because the birth was by C-section, which qualified the delivery as "complicated." Besides, it was 1985, and early release for the uninsured was not yet standard operating procedure.

Choosing names for the boys hadn't been easy. After all, most parents have a difficult time coming up with one name—let alone two. Maybe Lori and her husband Steve didn't know that Billy is a nickname for William; maybe they didn't know that tacking "Jr." at the end of a boy's name means his name is the same as his dad's—or maybe they knew both, but just didn't care. But whatever the reason, the names Steve and Lori chose for their two baby boys were William and Billy Jr.

The Averys had three other children; thankfully each had a separate and distinct name. Another boy, at four, was the oldest and two girls, ages one and two, rounded off the family.

On the night Lori was released from the hospital, she and Steve went out to the stock car races at the 141 Speedway. It was a celebration of sorts for the birth of William and Billy Jr. It was also an Enduro race, and Steve wouldn't miss one of those for the world.

The cars in an Enduro race are stripped to the bone. All the glass except the windshield is removed, and only the driver's seat is left inside. Steve had a blast watching the old wrecks crash into each other as they raced around the dirt track. Lori was happy, too. She was excited about the newborns, and so was Steve. Lord knows, he'd put her through enough over the years, but since the incident last January he seemed to have changed—or at least he was trying.

It had started the previous November. Sandy Murphy, the wife of Manitowoc County reserve deputy Bill Murphy, lived right up the road from the Averys. She had to drive past their house on her way to work at five-thirty every morning. Steve would get up early, grab his field glasses, and peer down the road to watch Sandy leaving. Then he'd wait for her to drive past, and depending on how screwed up he was that day, he'd either rub himself on the hood of his truck or jump out into the road, nude. Sandy nearly struck him with her car one time.

The most serious incident happened a little over two months later, on January 3, 1985. Sandy pulled out of her driveway at the usual time and started driving down the road past Steve and Lori's. She had her six-month-old baby in the car that morning, and she planned to drop him off at her parents' house in town. Just past the Avery residence she looked in her rearview mirror and saw lights approaching from behind. The truck seemed to come out of nowhere. It began passing on her left, and then without warning it rammed into the side of her car. Sandy careened back and forth, but somehow managed to maintain control of her car.

Sandy pulled over to the side of the road to inspect the damage, but before getting out of her car she looked up and saw Steven Avery walking toward her. He was pointing a rifle at her head. He ordered her to get into his truck, but Sandy motioned to the backseat and told him her baby would freeze to death if she left him alone. Avery looked inside the car and told her she could go.

Steve had served his fair share of stints in the county jail, but accosting the wife of a deputy sheriff on the road that morning was one of the dumbest crimes he'd ever committed. Sandy Murphy knew who he was—they were practically neighbors, after all—and she called the police immediately to report the incident.

Three deputies arrested Steve within the hour, and when they searched his house, they found a .30–06 rifle stashed under one of the kids' beds with a live round in the chamber. Steve even confessed. Yes, he rammed his Blazer into Mrs. Murphy's car. Yes, he pointed the gun at her. And yes, he planned to force her into his truck.

The district attorney threw the book at him, charging him with two counts of endangering safety by conduct evincing a depraved mind—one count for the mother and one for her child—and one count of felon in possession of a firearm. By virtue of his two prior misdemeanor convictions, Steve was a "habitual offender," so the prosecutor dutifully tacked on the appropriate penalty enhancer, which increased the maximum sentence on each count by six years. He faced a maximum sentence of forty-eight years in prison, but for some reason bail was set at only $2,000, which Steve's mom and dad posted forthwith. He was a free man pending trial.

* * *

But that was seven months ago, and now it is the morning after the Enduro race—the same day that Penny Beerntsen was assaulted on the beach. Lori got up early, but Steve had more beers than he should have the night before and was still in bed at a quarter to nine when she told him to get up and start helping out. They had lots of errands to run and it was time to get moving.

Lori had the kids fed, dressed, and ready to go within half an hour. When Steve was ready, they piled the kids into his 1976 Chevy Blazer and headed into town. First stop was Fleet Farm, where Steve bought a five gallon pail of plaster to repair some cracks in the living room ceiling. According to a receipt received into evidence five months later, the cost of the plaster was $8.29.

Next was Shopko, where exterior paint was supposed to be on sale for $8.99 a gallon. Lori had started to paint the house in mid-June, but she wisely put the project on hold when her due date got closer. The last thing she needed was to fall off a ladder. Steve went into Shopko while Lori stayed in the car with the kids, but the sale was off, and as Steve would later testify, "We sure as hell weren't gonna pay $17.99 for a gallon of paint."

Then they drove up to Two Rivers, or "Trivers," as those of us who live here pronounce it, where they stopped at Wolfe-Snyder Drug Store to fill a prescription for Lori. This time Steve stayed with the kids while Lori went inside. On her way out, Lori remembered they were running low on milk so she ducked into the Red Owl grocery store next door and picked up a few gallons. The sun was getting hotter by the hour, and with five fidgety kids all under five years old in a truck without air-conditioning, it was time to go home. Steve wanted to stop at his mom and dad's place on the way, and Lori agreed, not that she had much of a choice.

Allan and Dolores Avery lived on forty acres of hardscrabble land out on Highway 147, about twelve miles north of Manitowoc. In addition to their home, the property is also the site of the family business—the Avery Salvage Yard—which turned a decent profit back then, and still does today.

Steve's mom pulled into the gravel driveway right behind them and asked Steve if he could help his dad pour a few slabs of concrete—they had a big project going and could sure use the help if he and Lori had the time. As Steve put it later, they "didn't have nothin' to do that day" so he was glad to pitch in.

For Lori, a long morning of running errands in town turned into a long afternoon of visiting family at the salvage yard. Steve's Aunt Rose and his sister Barb were already there, and more family and a few friends of the family arrived as the day wore on. Lori persevered, keeping an eye on the kids and occasionally visiting with her in-laws while Steve went outside.

Allan Avery was putting up a sheep shed. The idea was to graze his sheep in the hilly acres of the junkyard to keep the grass from getting too tall around the cars. He already had the sheep and now needed a shed, so he had ordered a load of cement that day for the foundation.

Steve shot the bull with his brother, Chuck, and the rest of the guys until the cement truck turned off Avery Road and pulled into the driveway a few minutes later. When the truck couldn't squeeze through the gate, Steve hopped into a wrecker and hauled a couple of junked cars out of the way. Then the truck backed into position in front of the foundation for the first shed, and the driver lowered the chute. Steve directed the chute so the cement poured evenly while the other guys spread it around with shovels, and after that, the whole crew went over and poured a second slab for another shed. Steve and Chuck filled a wheelbarrow with the last of the cement and poured a small slab that their dad wanted in front of the garage, throwing in some loose gravel so the cement would rise to the top—not a bad way to stretch a load of cement if you're running thin. With the entire job completed, Steve went inside to tell Lori to get the kids ready—it was time to go home. Lori took longer than she should have to say her good-byes, and when she went outside she couldn't find Steve. She was exhausted, and she wanted to go home. Why would he disappear like that? He knew she'd been caring for William and Billy Jr. nonstop since the moment they were born six days earlier, not to mention the three older kids, who constantly vied for her attention and needed her now more than ever. Sometimes it seemed like he just didn't care, Lori thought to herself, and she was getting tired of it.

It was 4:30 p.m.—approximately thirty minutes after Penny Beerntsen was nearly killed on a beach ten miles away—when Steve finally came back up to the house and said they should get going. Steve later told the police he had taken his sister for a ride down at the quarry on his brand-new four-wheeler, though he didn't tell Lori where he was until much later. They said their goodbyes to his parents and headed out in the Blazer, leaving a trail of dust as they sped down Avery Road.

Lori assumed they were going home, but a few miles down the road Steve said they were going out to eat at R&M's instead, a little burger joint just over the county line. Five minutes later, he changed his mind. Now he wanted to drive all the way up to Green Bay to see if the Shopko there still had the damned paint on sale.

They arrived in Green Bay a half hour later. With five hungry kids crammed into the backseat of the Chevy Blazer, their first stop was the drive-through window at Burger King. After that, Steve pulled into a car wash across the street. The Blazer was covered in mud, and Steve wanted to hose it down before they drove home.

When they got to Shopko, Steve went to the paint section while Lori took one of the girls to the bathroom. It looked like the sale was over, but Steve checked every can in case they had left a price tag on one. No luck. But Lori talked him into buying the paint anyhow. Despite the progress she made before the twins were born, there was still a good chunk of the house left to paint and Lori was determined to get it done that summer. So they grabbed a gallon and proceeded to the checkout lane where they were given a receipt that later established the precise time they were in Green Bay. It was 5:13 p.m., an hour and fifteen minutes after Penny Beerntsen was attacked on the beach nearly thirty miles away.

After they left Shopko, Steve dragged them to an automotive store on Green Bay's west side where he looked at truck accessories for a while. And finally, after stopping at another drive-through restaurant—Hardee's this time—they headed home.

THREE

The staff was waiting when the EMTs rushed Penny Beerntsen into the emergency room at Memorial Hospital. The ER doctor on duty enumerated Penny's wounds: severe bruising and swelling around both eyes; bleeding inside the right eye with a deep cut underneath that took several stitches to close; a fractured nose; scattered bruises on her back and a more pronounced bruise at the base of her neck; and shattered fingernails on her right hand from clawing at her assailant.

Deputy Judy Dvorak was the first officer to respond at the hospital. Following procedure, she started interviewing Penny even before the nurses were finished treating her wounds. Still shaking and struggling to see out of her nearly swollen-shut eyes, Penny told Deputy Dvorak how the man with the leather jacket grabbed her while she was jogging down the beach, how he manhandled her over the dunes, and then pushed her into the woods where he viciously assaulted her.

Manitowoc County Sheriff Tom Kocourek arrived twenty minutes later. The Kocoureks and the Beerntsens knew each other; they attended the same church and were practically neighbors. So the sheriff joined Tom Beerntsen in the emergency room lobby and offered him what little comfort he could.

Kocourek had started his career as a patrol officer, later working as a detective with the Manitowoc Police Department before moving over to the sheriff's department in 1977, where he steadily moved up the ranks. First elected in 1979, Kocourek had to run for office every two years, but he never faced serious political opposition. He was a man of law and order, the kind of man voters trusted, and every two years the citizens of Manitowoc County rewarded him with another term.

The sheriff's large rimmed, rectangular glasses and neatly combed gray hair exuded intelligence and a no-nonsense competence that people admired. He rarely smiled, but when he did, it was thin and expressionless. To some he came off as aloof, but to all he was known as a straight shooter—when Tom Kocourek said something, you could take it to the bank.

He assured Tom Beerntsen that he'd do everything in his power to bring Penny's assailant to justice. Manitowoc County doesn't allow this sort of thing to happen, especially to people like the Beerntsens, and his department wouldn't rest until they apprehended the reprobate who was responsible.

Looking back, it would have been better if Kocourek had backed off and let his detectives handle the investigation instead—but he decided to call the shots on this one. As the administrator of one of the largest agencies in the county, he didn't have time to involve himself in criminal investigations. Mostly, though, it was his personal acquaintance with the Beerntsens that should have disqualified him. Years later, a private investigator recalled that in all the years he practiced in Manitowoc County, he never saw Sheriff Kocourek personally investigate another crime. Not once.

The sheriff joined Deputy Dvorak in the emergency room and listened carefully as she wrapped up her interview of Penny. Although he had to step out of the room during the medical examination, he did ask Penny a few questions—especially about the assailant's description. Penny knew the sheriff was a good man, a man of character and high ideals. His can-do attitude combined with his physical appearance—he was a few inches over six feet tall with strong angular facial features—left Penny convinced that her assailant would soon be apprehended.

She did her best to describe the man: five foot six or seven, stocky build, brown eyes, long sandy hair with a scraggly beard. She said he was wearing long pants and had a black leather jacket on with buttons or snaps down the front. She thought he was about thirty.

Steven Avery immediately came to Deputy Dvorak's mind. Steve had long hair and a beard that would pass as scraggly in some circles, but he was nowhere near five foot six or seven—he's lucky if he's five feet tall. And his eyes aren't brown, they're blue. But it didn't matter to Deputy Dvorak—she knew it was Steven Avery. It just had to be.

Dvorak lived right across the road from Steve and Lori out on Old Highway Y, and she was familiar with some of his antics. She despised him, and she considered him just the sort of lowlife creep that would commit such a heinous crime. A few years earlier, she even saw him tether his two-year-old toddler to a tree to keep the child from wandering off. So that's his idea of babysitting, Dvorak thought at the time. What a piece of work.

She also knew Steve from his frequent stints in the county jail where she'd worked as a corrections officer before moving over to the patrol division. When she was asked at a deposition years later why she suspected Steven Avery so soon, Dvorak responded that he had "a look in his eyes" that made her feel uncomfortable. He was "a dirty man," she continued, and the first thing they did whenever he was placed in the slammer was get him in the shower—"the stench was that bad."

It's no wonder Steven Avery creeped out Dvorak. He had a record that dated back to when he was a juvenile, and some of his crimes were truly despicable. In September 1982, for instance, he and a friend set a cat on fire. The previous year a neighbor's dog returned home half-castrated, and the neighbor suspected Steve was behind that, too. He once threatened to run his former girlfriend off the road and shoot out her car windows. He told her he was going to put sugar in her gas tank, and a week later she found sand in her motor oil. He was so distraught over their break-up that he told her he was going to burn down her parents' house while they were inside.

But it was the crime Steve was out on bail for—the episode where he rammed into Sandy Murphy's car and then held her at gunpoint—that was most on Dvorak and Kocourek's minds. You don't victimize the wife of a deputy sheriff and expect it to go unnoticed; the men and women in blue—or brown, in the case of the Manitowoc County Sheriff's Department—pay close attention when one of their own is the victim of a crime.

There was another reason why Steve might have come so quickly to Deputy Dvorak's mind. Steve's uncle Arland was a deputy at the sheriff's department, and Arland's fellow officers knew that his nephew was firmly planted on the wrong side of the law. So it wasn't surprising that within hours after Penny was attacked, there was "talk among the officers," as Dvorak later put it, that Steven Avery might have been the assailant.

After he and Dvorak settled on Steve as the likely assailant, Sheriff Kocourek promptly called the jail. He wanted a mug shot of Steve brought up to the hospital along with a dozen or so photos of other white males in their early thirties sporting beards. The deputy who answered the sheriff's call could tell he meant business, and the photos arrived within minutes.

Kocourek stuffed the mug shots into his pocket and summoned Chief Deputy Gene Kusche, who was the nearest thing the department had to a police artist. The sheriff wanted him to work up a composite sketch of the suspect. Penny had been moved to a room on the second floor, and after pulling up a chair next to her bed, Kusche introduced himself and did his best to put Penny at ease—something that came natural to the affable, handle-bar mustached chief deputy.

Police sketches are basically head shots—they show what a suspect looks like from the neck up—and while facial hair limits the pool of potential suspects it presents its own set of problems. The most obvious is that the suspect can alter his appearance by simply shaving off his beard. But there's another problem that's not as apparent. Since a bearded suspect's face is partially concealed, the extent to which a victim is uncertain about a suspect's facial features can be higher and the reliability of the police sketch is therefore diminished.

Penny's assailant was bearded, but she did her best to describe him anyhow, and Kusche worked on the sketch until, as he put it at trial, "the victim was satisfied in her mind that it was a reasonable representation of what her memory was." If his testimony sounds convoluted, perhaps there's a reason. Kusche took great pride in his composite sketch of Penny's assailant. For one thing, it was his first. But mostly, it was so darn good. In fact, over the years, more than a few who've seen it have commented that it looks exactly like Steve's mug shot from seven months earlier. Even the trial judge referred to the two depictions as bearing an "uncanny resemblance" to each other.

With Kusche's composite sketch out of the way, it was time for Sheriff Kocourek to conduct the photo array. To hold up in court, a photo array can't be "unduly suggestive." In other words, in addition to the photo of the suspect, the array must include photos of at least six other people who look similar to the suspect—the closer the better. So if the victim describes a bald man with a bulbous nose and three missing front teeth, for example, it won't do to show her one photo of a suspect who meets that description and six others of Matt Damon lookalikes.

The sheriff brought out the stack of mug shots he'd stuffed into his pocket a few hours earlier and assembled the photo array. With Kusche still in the room, he spread out nine photos on a table in front of Penny and asked her if she recognized the man who assaulted her. Penny picked out Steve immediately. She looked over the others just to make sure, and then she told Sheriff Kocourek that the man in the photo she picked was the man who assaulted her. It was that simple. The sheriff had what he needed, and he directed his night shift commander to take "the subject" into custody.

FOUR

It was after ten that night when Steve and Lori finally got home from Green Bay. The kids had fallen asleep in the Blazer and Lori got them into bed after Steve carried them in. They'd been on the go since nine that morning and they were both exhausted, so they crawled into bed a little after eleven.

Having given birth to the twins only six days earlier, Lori was especially tired, but she couldn't fall asleep. Steve's impulsive act of confronting Sandy Murphy on the road last January weighed heavily on her mind and robbed her of a peaceful night's sleep that sometimes comes from exhaustion. Despite everything, she still loved Steve and she and the kids needed him dearly. He was far from perfect, but he'd been trying hard to improve since the incident with Sandy Murphy. He was finally getting on track, not a perfect track, but a track Lori could live with. Neither of them had unreasonable expectations—financially or otherwise. Steve had his truck, and Lori felt welcome in his close-knit family. If only he'd had control of himself last January and not pulled that stunt with Sandy Murphy.

Lori asked him more than once what he had been thinking. Sandy Murphy's identification of him was irrefutable; he did the crime, and now he'd do the time. In a few months, some judge would send him off to prison—the only question was for how long—and she'd be left to raise five young children all on her own. But what Lori didn't know was that a worse nightmare loomed right around the corner, a nightmare that would begin in less than an hour and one that would haunt her for the rest of her life.

* * *

Police exercise extreme caution when they take a bad guy into custody—especially when the man they're after is as dangerous as whoever it was that attacked Penny Beerntsen. Violent offenders are desperate to avoid apprehension since being caught usually lands them in prison. And while cops are committed to making the streets safe for the rest of us, they'd just as soon come home at night alive.

But self-preservation isn't the only thing police must consider when they make an arrest. From petty crimes like disturbing the peace, to more serious ones like sexual assault or murder, the Fourth Amendment's prohibition against unreasonable searches and seizures is the most litigated issue in trial and appellate courts all over the land. If police violate a suspect's constitutional rights, then the evidence that is derived, or as the law metaphorically puts it, "the fruits of the poisonous tree," will be suppressed, and the whole case might fail. And police must tread especially cautiously when it comes to our homes for "a man's home is his castle," or so says the law. The rule is uncharacteristically clear: Absent exigent circumstances, consent of the owner, or a warrant, cops can't arrest a person in his or her home.

Sheriff Kocourek, however, must have missed that section of law enforcement training. As soon as Penny Beerntsen identified Steven Avery as her assailant, he rounded up his officers and sent them to Steve and Lori's house to bring Steve in. In fact, the officers assigned to make the arrest even considered calling in the SWAT team. But, fortunately, the night shift commander, Sergeant Ken Petersen, had a better idea. Maybe Arland Avery, Steve's uncle and a deputy on the force, could get the police in the door. They could make the arrest without incident that way, and everybody could go home alive. So Petersen called Arland, who was off duty but quickly agreed. Arland knew Lori and the kids were home sleeping, and the last thing he wanted was for the SWAT team to storm the house with guns blazing.

So Sergeant Petersen along with Deputies Jim Froelich and Mike Bushman gathered at Arland's house at eleven thirty. The four of them huddled together and formulated a plan. Arland and Froelich would enter from the rear while Petersen covered the front. Bushman and his canine unit "Duke" would float around the perimeter in case Steve slipped past them and tried to escape.

Arland knocked on the back door just before midnight, but nobody answered so he gave a "slight push," and the door magically opened.

"Lori," he shouted, as he and Deputy Froelich walked in. "Where are you?"

Lori had heard the dog barking in the backyard a few minutes earlier and wondered if someone was out there. "Upstairs," she shouted back.

"Where's Steve? I need to talk to him," Arland yelled from the landing halfway up the stairs.

Steve woke up to the shouting and walked warily down the stairs. Froelich had ducked into a closet underneath the stairwell, and as Steve walked past, he sneaked behind and followed him into the kitchen where Sergeant Petersen was waiting. Froelich told Steve to turn around, and then he handcuffed him. According to Froelich's report, Petersen advised Steve he was under arrest for "suspicion of attempted murder"—without mentioning anything about a sexual assault.

Still upstairs, Lori fell onto the bed when she heard someone tell Steve he was under arrest, but she quickly got herself together and went downstairs to find out what was going on. When she walked into her kitchen, she saw two sheriff's deputies standing next to Steve. He had handcuffs on, and someone with a flashlight was reading him his rights.

"Would someone please tell me what's going on?" Lori asked.

Sergeant Petersen told her he was sorry, but he couldn't say anything. Directing her question to her husband this time, Lori asked again, "What's going on?"

According to Froelich and Petersen, Steve looked at his wife and said, "They said I tried to murder some girl." The significance of Steve's response was hotly disputed at trial. The prosecution seized on the comment. The deputies hadn't said anything to suggest that the victim was female, the prosecutor argued, so since Steve Avery knew the victim was a woman, he must have committed the crime. Steve's lawyer, on the other hand, considered the argument pretty thin.

Sergeant Petersen possessed a quality that would serve him well years later when he succeeded Tom Kocourek as sheriff—he doesn't beat around the bush. So he asked Steve point blank in the squad car that night, "Did you assault Penny Beerntsen?" Steve replied with an equally direct "no." Then Petersen asked him if he was on the beach that day, and Steve denied that, too—he said he was pouring concrete at his dad's salvage yard, and then he and his family went up to Green Bay.

The sheriff was waiting for Steve when he arrived at the jail—he planned to ask him a few questions of his own. But Steve stuck to his guns, or as Kocourek put it in his report, "He denied any involvement in the incident, admitting to nothing." Sheriff Kocourek hadn't worked a case in years, but he still had some of the detective in him, and he wanted to make sure the follow-up investigation was done right. He was certain Steve was lying and that his family would lie for him too. So before leaving the jail that night, he instructed the jail staff not to permit any phone calls or visits with Steve. As he put it in his report, "Steve is using his family as an alibi for his whereabouts, and I wish to question them without affording Steve the opportunity of establishing a phony alibi."

* * *

Lori Avery didn't sleep after Steve was arrested that night. There must be some mistake, she thought, he was with her all day. She called Steve's mom and dad at six in the morning and told them how the police had barged in at midnight and arrested their son.

Allan Avery tried calling the jail, but the dayshift commander told him the sheriff had denied all phone calls and visits with Steve until further notice. Undeterred, Mr. Avery called Captain Don Belz. It was seven in the morning, but Allan knew Belz personally, and he called him at home.

"What's going on with my son?" Mr. Avery demanded. "He was working with me all day, pouring cement. They don't have no right taking him out of his house like that—after all, a guy's got some rights."

Captain Belz told Mr. Avery he didn't know anything about it—he works days, not nights—but he'd check it out and get right back to him. But Belz never got back to Mr. Avery. Years later, he told a private investigator that the sheriff told him if he did, he'd be fired.

Sheriff Kocourek called the district attorney first thing in the morning and told him he needed a search warrant. He wanted to search Steven Avery's residence for physical evidence—blood, hair, semen, that sort of thing—and anything else that might be evidence of the crime. He told the DA he was convinced that Avery was the assailant, and he was determined to bring him to justice. The DA made the arrangements with the judge, and by ten-thirty, the sheriff and his deputies were knocking at Lori's door with a search warrant in hand.

The sheriff had a few questions for Lori while the deputies executed the warrant. He wanted to know her husband's whereabouts in the late afternoon hours on the day before. Lori told him Steve couldn't have done whatever they were accusing him of—he was with her all day. They were at his parents' salvage yard for most of the afternoon, and Steve was outside pouring concrete with the guys while she was visiting with her in-laws inside. Lori explained that Steve came in just as *Divorce Court* ended at three-thirty and told her to get the kids ready. Then, as Kocourek qualified in his report, she and Steve "reportedly" drove to Green Bay.

Not a bad alibi, Kocourek thought to himself, but it doesn't prove a thing. She was in the house the whole time while Steve was supposedly outside pouring concrete—he was out of her sight for hours. She doesn't know what he was up to. Besides, she's probably lying.

But Lori wasn't the only one to tell police that Steven Avery couldn't have committed the assault. His parents and almost a dozen family members and friends of the family gave the same account that Steve and Lori did, and even though they hadn't spoken with Steve or with each other, their stories all matched.

As for the search warrant, the sheriff and his men found little that interested them—but they took it anyhow. Their haul included a pair of cutoff shorts, a brown T-shirt, some black socks, black dress shoes, some more T-shirts, and two pairs of blue jeans. They also took the floor mat from the driver's side of Steve's 1976 Chevy Blazer, hoping the crime lab would find some embedded grains of Lake Michigan sand.

Kocourek knew they'd have to prove a time frame to show that Steve had time to commit the assault, and he knew it would be close. Penny Beerntsen had been an excellent reporter of time; it was ten to four when the man first grabbed her, and he scampered into the woods fifteen minutes later at five minutes after four. If Steve really was at the Shopko in Green Bay like his wife says he was, Kocourek knew he'd better find out precisely what time they were there.

So the next day, the sheriff sent his men to do some more digging. Detective Fred Nicholson drove up to Green Bay and spoke with the checkout clerk at Shopko. Sure, she remembered the family with the newborn twins—she couldn't believe they'd bring infants to such a public place, with so many germs and everything. The manager retrieved the sales data: The paint was purchased at 5:13 that afternoon.

That meant that Steve had only sixty-eight minutes—between 4:05 and 5:13—to run the half mile from the crime scene to the beach parking lot—in street clothes no less—drive ten miles back to the Avery Salvage Yard to pick up Lori and the kids, and be in the checkout lane at Shopko thirty miles north in Green Bay. Sixty-eight minutes to do all that, Detective Nicholson thought, there wouldn't be any wiggle room.

So he drove to the crime scene and made a dry run. Intermittently running and walking at a fast pace, it took him thirteen minutes to get from where Duke the police dog found Penny's bathing suit to the parking lot, and another forty-four minutes to drive to the salvage yard and up to Shopko in Green Bay, grab a gallon of paint, and walk to the checkout lane. Fifty-seven minutes in all, so the sheriff had his time-frame—with eleven minutes to spare!

Never mind that Nicholson later testified he "averaged 10 miles an hour over the limit, but never more than 15 over." Or that he didn't account for the time it would take to load five children into a truck, including two infants, stop at a fast-food restaurant and then a car wash, and check the paint section at Shopko for a leftover can of paint on sale. No matter, they had their man. It was Steven Avery—it just had to be!

FIVE

Dressed in bright orange jail garb, Steven Avery was brought before the court commissioner the next day for a bail hearing. District Attorney Denis Vogel informed the court he was charging the defendant with first degree sexual assault and attempted murder. Vogel requested $50,000 cash bail, and the court commissioner agreed—Steve wasn't going anywhere this time.

Denis Vogel had been the district attorney for just over eight years when Penny Beerntsen was attacked on the beach. With his close-cropped mustache, plastered-on hair, and three-piece suits, he looked every bit the part of a young and aggressive attorney, making up for his small stature and tinny voice with a quick tongue and sharp wit.

Nobody has ever known an Avery who could post $50,000 cash bail, but Vogel wasn't about to take any chances. The state legislature had recently added a new crime-fighting weapon to the prosecution's arsenal called a "Petition for Pretrial Preventive Detention." The new law permitted the court to detain an accused awaiting trial without bail if release on bail would not "adequately protect members of the community from serious bodily harm." The statute only applied to a handful of specifically enumerated felonies, however, and first degree sexual assault and attempted murder weren't on the list.

Vogel knew he'd be pushing the envelope if he filed a petition in this case, but it didn't matter to the aggressive young prosecutor. He even called a friend at the attorney general's office who cautioned him that the law probably didn't apply. Vogel apparently recorded his telephone calls and had his conversations transcribed, so there's a record of the call. Here's a portion:

"Hi Mike—Denis Vogel calling."

"Denis, how are you? I'm sorry not to get to you sooner but I've been tied up in a telephone call, a couple of phone calls since 7:30."

"You work harder than I do, Mike."

"I was here at quarter to seven so don't give me that shit, I beat you in."

"Jesus Christ. Say, listen, I got a pretrial detention hearing tomorrow."

"Okay."

"On a fellow that was charged with attempted first degree murder and second degree sexual assault, and I'm wondering what type of evidence you recommend putting in to show dangerousness to the community or whatever it is—hang on, let me get my statute book.

"She's a real respectable lady in town," Vogel continued, "and her husband has a very good business. Basically, she's a very—she comes from a good family, she just happened to be jogging down the beach, gets grabbed, you know, he goes after her and tries to rape her.

"He's tried to establish somewhat of an alibi by claiming he wasn't there. His family members are going to support him, but I think when it comes down to it, it's going to be her word saying it's positively him versus him saying he didn't do it. But I've got him. He's been convicted of burglary before and he's out on bail right now on two counts of endangering safety by conduct regardless of life.

"You see my problem is this," Vogel continued. "The guy doesn't have a prior conviction for a violent crime, as required under paragraph one. But you know—what's the worst thing that could happen?"

"I think you've got trouble with that attempt charge, Denis, I really do," the assistant attorney general said. "I remember at the time they passed this thing they tried to make it as tight as possible because, you know, trying to get something like this through this legislature, which is very liberal by and large—at least the committee chairman and the chairpersons in the right committees are very liberal—and I think everything was tightened up as much as possible. I think that was the intent when I looked at this thing."

"Alright, listen Mike, thanks a lot, I appreciate it," Vogel said. "I got it scheduled for tomorrow. Who knows, it might be a good case to appeal."

As a practical matter, Vogel's petition meant nothing. Steve and Lori didn't have a pot to pee in, and Steve's parents didn't have that kind of money lying around either. But it didn't matter—Vogel smelled blood in the water. He filed his petition and the judge granted it the following day. It was official—Steven Avery was "preventively detained."

To Lori, of course, it didn't matter whether Steve was being detained under some stupid new law or held on high cash bail—either way, he wasn't coming home. She was left alone to care for five young children who were starting to wonder where their dad was, and all she could do was hope and pray.

But hoping and praying didn't seem to be working, so after a while Lori did what many inmates' loved ones do when they don't know where else to turn—she wrote a letter to the judge:

Dear Judge Hazlewood,

I am writing this on behalf of Steven Avery. Steve along with myself, Lori (his wife), and his family and friends do not understand why he cannot be put up on bail. How can the law hold an innocent man when we have witnesses as to his whereabouts and the state only has Penny Beerntsen's word?

I was brought up to believe in the laws and that people have rights, and since my husband has been arrested, I no longer believe in either one. I thought people along with law enforcement officers did not have the right to walk into someone else's home, in this case late at night, without permission and arrest someone without a warrant for that person's arrest.

I am left out here by myself to raise five children who all miss their daddy very much. I don't really believe that there are too many people in the world who could take as much stuff as I have since July 19th. In a brief summary, I have gone from false labor to real labor to emergency surgery (C-section) to getting out with restrictions of no heavy or exerting work to having my husband arrested for something he didn't do to being left alone with our five kids—and no one seems to care.

I am now talking (by phone) to Steve and he would like to say a few words: "Judge, I am innocent and I'm not lying, I'll take a lie detector test to prove it. I like you a lot but I don't understand how they can hold me on such little evidence.... Is there any way the motions can be heard by the end of the month and any chance of me getting out on the motions? Could you please help me and my family? I would really appreciate it. Thank you, Judge. Steve"

I am sorry for taking out so much of your time. Thank you for listening.

Sincerely,

Lori Avery

P.S. Could you please let me or Steve know what you think?

What can a judge do when he or she receives a letter like that—when a woman painfully pleads for justice on behalf of her husband and her children, but doesn't know where to turn? Unfortunately, not much, for the law refers to judges as "neutral and detached magistrates," and as such, they aren't supposed to side with one party or the other. So all Judge Hazlewood could do was forward copies of Lori's letter to the district attorney and defense counsel and hope they'd respond.

SIX

Wounds slowly healing, Penny Beerntsen was at home two days after the assault when the telephone rang.

"Hello ... hello," Penny answered.

"What are you doing?" asked the caller.

"Who do you want?"

"I want you."

Penny hung up the phone, thinking, "Oh my God, he knows who I am, he has our telephone number and he probably knows where we live!" She called Tom and he told her to call the sheriff. He'd be right home.

Sheriff Kocourek immediately stepped up security. He had dispatch send out a teletype to all squad units—until further notice, the sheriff wanted a squad car at the Beerntsens' residence around the clock. He also put a tracer on their phone line in case the suspect called again.

Who called Penny Beerntsen two days after she was attacked? It wasn't Steven Avery—he was in jail under the sheriff's order prohibiting him from making any telephone calls. But if the sheriff or the DA ever asked themselves who might have called Penny Beerntsen if Steven Avery didn't, there isn't any evidence they did. Which begs the question—why not?

Even though she wasn't a detective, Kocourek assigned Deputy Dvorak to do some of the follow-up investigation on the Avery case. Penny would have to recount the embarrassing details of the assault to complete strangers as the case wound its way through the justice system, and the sheriff thought the least he could do was limit the number of officers she'd have to confide in. Besides, as a woman, Deputy Dvorak understood what Penny went through—at least more than a male detective could, and she had been emotionally involved in the case from the start. She even brought some cut flowers from her garden to Penny the morning after the assault, before she was released from the hospital.

The sheriff sent Dvorak out to Penny's home to reinterview her a few days after the assault. Something wasn't adding up. When Penny was asked at the hospital if the assailant's hands were greasy, Penny's answer was clear—no, his hands weren't greasy, they were clean. But Steven Avery's hands were perpetually greasy because he worked on cars so much. Even the clerk at Shopko noticed his hands were greasy when he was in the checkout lane just an hour after Penny was assaulted. So Deputy Dvorak asked Penny again, "Did the assailant have anything on his hands, anything—grease, oil, cement?" But Penny was no less certain this time—"No," she said, "his hands were clean."

After the interview, Dvorak and Penny drove downtown to the Big Boy restaurant where they killed some time before walking over to the Sheriff's Department. The sheriff had organized a lineup to see if Penny could identify her assailant again. Deputy Dvorak escorted Penny into a dark hallway with a one-way glass window that looked into a larger room on the other side. Tom Beerntsen was already there, so were Kocourek and Vogel; an assistant public defender was also there to observe the circumstances of the lineup. Penny slowly viewed the eight men in the lineup, and although it took a long time, she eventually placed a checkmark after No. 6 on the form. She'd picked out Steve again.

The defense later challenged the lineup in court. Asked how long the victim viewed the participants, the assistant public defender testified, "I'd estimate between eight and ten minutes, probably closer to ten." She claimed one of the participants looked at Steve during most of the lineup, and in her opinion, Steven Avery stuck out like a sore thumb: "He was the youngest, the fairest, possibly the shortest—he left a distinct impression." She also testified that she had to ask Tom Beerntsen not to talk to his wife during the lineup procedure and that she wasn't able to see the form after Penny marked it because Penny immediately gave it to the sheriff and walked out of the room.

With another identification of the assailant under his belt, Sheriff Kocourek felt confident about the case. With his wife's assailant locked securely behind bars, Tom Beerntsen wanted to thank the sheriff's deputies and the EMTs who came to Penny's aid. So the sheriff sent him their names, and while he was at it, he included some prudent advice for his friend:

Tom, I realize that you are intending to thank these people individually. I wish to point out that a simple letter acknowledging their professionalism and dedication, to be placed in their personnel file, goes a long way.

Tom Kocourek

* * *

Usually the victim goes to the prosecutor's office, not the other way around, but a few days after the live line-up Denis Vogel interviewed Penny at her home. He asked her how certain she was that Steven Avery was the assailant. Penny answered 90 to 95 percent. But that wasn't good enough for Vogel since any decent defense attorney could turn five to ten percent uncertainty into a reasonable doubt. So Vogel told Penny when he asks her on the stand how certain she was she better say 100 percent.

Penny trusted the Sheriff and the DA implicitly. Why wouldn't she? They were the good guys, the guys with the white hats. They'd never try to convict someone who was innocent. And besides, both of them were so kind to her and seemed so professional. So a week later when she testified at the Preliminary Examination, given how the composite sketch, the photo array, and the live line-up had been presented to her, and with all the other information about Steven Avery the Sheriff and his deputies had shared with her, Penny was one hundred percent certain that Steven Avery was the assailant, and that's what she said on the stand.

A little more than a month later, Penny received another disturbing phone call. But this time it wasn't from some creep who made her wonder if she had misidentified her assailant—this time it was from the District Attorney's office. Wisconsin prosecutors have thirty days from the date of the Preliminary Examination to file an Information, the formal document charging a defendant with a crime. If the State fails to file the Information on time, the case must be dismissed—though it can be re-filed later. It happens, but it shouldn't, especially in a sexual assault case when missing the deadline means the victim will have to testify at another Preliminary Examination and recount the abominable details of the sexual assault for a second time, typically to a predominantly male audience of lawyers, police officers, the judge and, of course, the assailant himself.

But Denis Vogel forgot to file the Information, and the charges were dismissed. He immediately re-filed the criminal complaint and had Victim Witness Coordinator Brenda Petersen call Penny to tell her the bad news. Penny was furious, and she had every right to be. Vogel had told her she wouldn't have to testify again until the trial, which would not be scheduled for another six months or so. And there wouldn't even be a trial if the defendant agreed to enter a plea. Penny knew it would take years to overcome the fear that had settled upon her since the day she was attacked on the beach, but she had taken comfort in knowing that at least for a while she could forget about the court proceedings and leave the prosecution of her assailant to the professionals.

Penny felt helpless. She didn't want Vogel to find out how upset she was. He would be trying the case, and she couldn't risk offending him. What if his heart wasn't in the case and Steven Avery went free? Like many crime victims, at times Penny felt powerless interacting with a court system that she had no prior experience with and that appeared either unwilling or unable to truly appreciate what she'd been through.

SEVEN

Every day, prosecutors, defense attorneys, and judges in county courthouses across the land do the heavy lifting on the front lines of the criminal justice system. Thousands of cases flow through, each with its own set of facts—a few are complicated, but most of them are not. Prosecutors start the ball rolling by summoning offenders to court with criminal complaints, and the ball doesn't stop rolling until the case is resolved. They carry boxes loaded with files to "Intake Court," where scores of lawyers and unrepresented defendants wait patiently for the judge to call their case so they can take their turn at the table and enter their plea—"Not guilty, Your Honor." There are initial appearances, preliminary examinations, arraignments, settlement conferences, motion hearings, plea hearings, pretrial conferences, and the occasional trial.

In the Avery case, Assistant Public Defender Reesa Evans-Marcinczyk was appointed to represent the accused. She would come to believe so firmly in Steven Avery's innocence that she refused to go to the beach to observe where Penny was attacked for fear the assailant might still be out there. She filed eighteen motions in the days immediately following Steve's arrest. There was a motion for everything—to suppress, to exclude, to compel, and, of course, to dismiss. You name it, she moved for it.

But Evans-Marcinczyk became ill a few months into the case, and another attorney was appointed to replace her. As the years went by, though no longer a participant in the legal proceedings, Evans-Marcinczyk never wavered in her belief that Steven Avery was innocent.

Attorney Jim Bolgert from Sheboygan was appointed successor counsel. Bolgert, who went on to serve as a circuit court judge in Sheboygan County, one county south of Manitowoc, promptly requested an adjournment of the motion hearing to allow him time to prepare.

Judge Fred Hazlewood was on intake when the charges were filed. Affectionately known as Judge Fred, Judge Hazlewood liked to keep cases moving along swiftly, but he also knew that Jim Bolgert would need time to prepare for the boatload of motions filed by Evans-Marcinczyk, so he granted a three-week adjournment and set aside a full day for the hearing.

On the day of the hearing, Judge Hazlewood and the parties methodically addressed each of the motions, one at a time. Number one on the docket was the defendant's motion to change venue. Jim Bolgert argued that extensive media coverage of the assault had made it impossible for his client to receive a fair trial in Manitowoc County. The local radio and TV stations had covered the case extensively—even the Milwaukee papers ran a story about the assault.

But concluding that the publicity wasn't so "widespread or salacious or prejudicial" that it would deny the defendant a fair trial, Judge Hazlewood denied the defendant's request to change venue. The trial would be held in Manitowoc County.

Not surprisingly, though, the parties spent most of their time at the motion hearing on the defendant's request to suppress Penny's identification of Steven Avery as her assailant. Jim Bolgert called Deputies Judy Dvorak and Gene Kusche, and Sheriff Kocourek to the stand and painstakingly questioned each of them about the procedures they used to obtain the identification of his client as the assailant.

But Judge Hazlewood didn't buy Bolgert's argument that the identification procedure was impermissibly suggestive and that Penny's identification of the defendant therefore had to be suppressed. In his November 13, 1985, "Memorandum to Supplement Oral Decision," he ruled that "the preparation of a composite drawing prior to showing the complaining witness a photo lineup was particularly appropriate in this case. And as noted, both the sheriff and the deputy who initially interviewed Ms. Beerntsen considered the possibility that the defendant was involved in this assault."

In a sentence brimming with irony given how things turned out, the judge continued: "This additional check, arguably unnecessary, provides an added assurance that Deputy Dvorak and Sheriff Kocourek's initial suspicions did not become a self-fulfilling prophecy when Ms. Beerntsen selected the defendant's photograph." The motion was denied.

Jim Bolgert fought valiantly, but most of the motions filed by Evans-Marcinczyk were perfunctory, and the court granted only two of them: the motion to suppress Steve's statement to Sheriff Kocourek—which didn't hurt the state anyhow since Steve told the sheriff he was innocent—and the motion for access to the crime lab analyst.

* * *

Most prosecutors and defense lawyers—assuming they've been on the job for five or more years—can predict early on with surprising accuracy how a case will be resolved six or nine months later after it's ground its way through the court process. They know whether the state has the goods for a conviction or if there's a realistic defense. They know the parameters of what the judge is likely to do at sentencing, and they know when the other attorney is bluffing. As a result, most criminal cases are resolved by plea bargains, which aren't as tawdry as the press makes them sound. Like making sausage, the process is ugly, but the end product is usually palatable as long as everyone does their job.

Then there are trials, which are animals of a completely different stripe. Amidst the chaos, most lawyers can tell early on which case files are likely to go to trial. They're usually close cases where the charges are serious and the stakes are high. And most lawyers know the feeling—that slight discomfort that begins about six weeks before the trial. It's been months since the charges were filed and the early skirmishes in court have faded from memory, and due to the pressure of other matters, they've neglected the file. Then, depending on the complexity of the case and how much emotional discomfort the lawyer can handle, the increasingly nervous attorney performs a cursory review to spot problems that will be fatal if they're not addressed immediately. Eventually they carve out several hours from their calendar and review the entire file, flagging the most important portions, while continually shrinking the information into a more manageable size. But despite their best intentions to have every detail nailed down early enough to get a good night's sleep on the night before the trial, most of them are invariably still up working well into the night.

A few weeks before the trial, Bolgert and Vogel sparred over whether the defense should have access to records relating to counseling services that Penny Beerntsen received in the weeks immediately after the assault.

Penny diffused the controversy herself by consenting to their release, but in a letter to the court, she relayed her concerns:

Dear Judge Hazlewood:

I didn't want Mr. Vogel to turn over my counseling records without this accompanying comment on the impact of my decision to cooperate in this matter.

I'm not sure Mr. Bolgert fully comprehends the import of his request, though I am sure it was made in good faith and in the spirit of providing Mr. Steven Avery with the best possible defense. Discussions which occur between therapist and client are privileged information, as I'm sure all parties involved in this case are aware. When a person decides to enter into counseling he/she is aware of the confidentiality of all conversations that occur in the privacy of the therapist's office. It is one of the basic tenets of psychotherapy and essential to the establishment of a trusting relationship between client and therapist. Without this fundamental principle there can be no meaningful therapeutic progress.

Additionally, I am concerned that I may be setting a dangerous precedent for future victims of violent crime. I do not want any other victim to delay or rule out therapy due to fear that what is said in the privacy of a psychologist's office may become part of the public record.

But I have made peace with the fact that it is essential to turn these records over to the court; I do not object if you turn them over in their entirety to Mr. Bolgert. I have nothing to hide and want to cooperate fully in order that justice might best be served.

Thank you for your careful consideration of this issue.

Sincerely yours,

Penny Beerntsen

* * *

Denis Vogel had a surprise for the defense on the eve of trial. Penny Beerntsen had told the police on the night she was attacked that her assailant was wearing a worn-out waist length black leather jacket. Up to now the prosecution had given no indication that Steven Avery owned such a jacket; in fact nothing even remotely matching the description had been found when the police executed the search warrant at Steve and Lori's house. But now, just three days before the start of the trial, Jim Bolgert received some bad news.

Dear Jim, the letter started.

In speaking with three witnesses, Deput[ies Jim] Froelich, Judy Dvorak, and Ken Petersen, all three officers have had prior contact with Steve Avery, the defendant, and will be in a position to testify that they have personally seen Mr. Avery wearing a leather motorcycle-type jacket, dark brownish in color, which would be short/waist-length.

They say a criminal defense attorney's worst nightmare is to defend someone who's innocent—what if you lose? Most people charged with a serious crime are guilty. They better be or the prosecutor has no business charging them. But once in a great while, a defense lawyer comes across a client who they're almost certain is innocent. And so it was for Jim Bolgert. He knew the state's case was weak—it relied almost entirely on the victim's identification of the defendant, and eyewitness identifications are notoriously unreliable. If he could effectively attack the identification and present a strong alibi defense, his client stood half a chance.

But while trials aim for objective truth, the influence of emotion is never completely divorced from a jury's decision, and Bolgert knew that the state would own the emotional subtext in this one. With the Avery clan and their salvage yard sheep sheds on one side, and Penny and Tom Beerntsen and their storied candy store on the other, the intangibles were not on his side.

EIGHT

Scheduled to begin on December 9, 1985, just two weeks before Christmas, Steve couldn't have drawn a worse time for the trial. For an acquittal, the jury would have to pay the closest attention, and the defense would have to be nearly unassailable. But with sugarplums and last minute shopping dancing in their heads, the jurors would likely be distracted, and the last thing they'd want to do is revictimize Penny Beerntsen by acquitting her assailant right before Christmas.

The first day of the trial finally arrived. In order to accommodate the large number of people in the jury pool, Judge Hazlewood conducted jury selection in Branch 1, the most spacious of the three courtrooms. The lawyers scurried about down to the last minute, or maybe a few beyond, and if they were like most trial attorneys, they'd probably downed three or four cups of coffee and made their final stop at the restroom just in time.

The clerk assembled the panel of prospective jurors, and Judge Hazlewood addressed them for the first time:

"Ladies and gentlemen, the case we're going to be trying today is the State of Wisconsin vs. Steven A. Avery. Appearing and representing the State is District Attorney Denis Vogel."

The prosecutor stood and greeted the jurors, "Good morning everybody."

"Sitting next to Mr. Vogel is Sheriff Tom Kocourek for Manitowoc County."

"Good morning."

"Representing the defendant is Attorney James Bolgert. Mr. Bolgert?"

"Good morning."

"And seated next to Mr. Bolgert is the defendant, Steven Avery—Mr. Avery?"

"Good morning," the defendant managed a soft reply.

"Are counsel ready for trial?"

"Yes, Your Honor," Vogel and Bolgert answered in unison.

Warning the jurors not to consider the charges, themselves, as evidence against the defendant, Judge Hazlewood read them out loud:

Count 1: On or about the 29th of July 1985, in the Township of Two Rivers, in said County and State, the defendant did unlawfully have sexual contact with another person without the consent of that person and by the threat of use of a dangerous weapon, to wit: by the threat of the use of a knife, contrary to Section 940.225(l)(d) of the Wisconsin Statutes.

The jury gulped, and Judge Hazlewood continued:

Count 2: At the same time and place, the defendant did unlawfully attempt to cause the death of another human being with intent to kill that person, contrary to Sections 940.01 and 939.32(l)(a) of the Wisconsin Statutes.

They gulped again, and then the judge read the final charge—false imprisonment:

Count 3: At the same time and place, the defendant did unlawfully and intentionally restrain another without that person's consent and with knowledge that he had no lawful authority to do so, contrary to Section 940.30 of the Wisconsin Statutes.

If you've ever sat on a jury in a criminal case, you've heard a version of Judge Hazlewood's final instruction, and if you were Steven Avery that day, you hoped like hell they were paying attention:

To the charges I have just read, the defendant has entered a plea of not guilty, which means a denial of every material allegation in the information. The law presumes every person charged with the commission of an offense to be innocent, this presumption attends the defendant;

that is, it stays with the defendant throughout the trial and prevails at its close unless it is overcome by evidence which satisfies a jury of guilt beyond a reasonable doubt. The defendant is not required to prove his innocence. The burden of proving the defendant guilty of every element of the crime charged is upon the state. Before you can return a verdict of guilty, the state must prove to your satisfaction beyond a reasonable doubt that the defendant is guilty.

Thankfully, all but the most jaded jurors actually take that instruction seriously. They might be incensed by the charges, and maybe even put off by the appearance of the defendant, but they also know that the defendant's life, or at least a good portion of it, is in their hands.

❊ ❊ ❊

With Manitowoc County's population at just over 80,000, there's always a good chance that some of the jurors know one of the parties, one of the attorneys, or maybe a witness or two—and the Avery trial was no exception. Several jurors knew of the unsavory reputation of Steve's family, and for those who didn't, they'd soon find out since the entire jury pool was present during the selection process and could hear everyone's answers.

With Bolgert and Vogel holding their breaths, Judge Hazlewood began *voir dire*—French for, "to speak the truth": "Are there any among you who are acquainted with or know either the defendant, Steven Avery, or a member of his immediate family?"

Several jurors raised their hands, and starting with Juror No. 8, Judge Hazlewood explored their potential for bias:

"Ms. R (the author has used initials to protect the identity of members of the jury panel), how long have you known either the defendant or his family?"

"About seventeen years."

"And do you have regular contact with the family?"

"No."

"Or the defendant?"

"Not any longer."

"When was the last time you saw either the defendant or a family member?"

"It would have been quite a while ago; I'm a schoolteacher."

"That's how you happen to know the family?"

"Yes."

"Because of your relationship with the family—we won't probe into that in any detail—do you feel that you would tend to give greater or lesser weight to one side over the other?"

"I would try not to."

"Do you feel it would be difficult for you to judge the case fairly and impartially, strictly on the evidence that is produced at the trial and excluding everything else?"

"I would try not to."

"So do you think it would be possible for you to judge this case fairly and impartially after you have heard the evidence, without bringing any preconceived notions one way or the other into your deliberations?"

"I would hope that would be the case, yes."

"Do you think there's a possibility that you would not be able to do so?"

"I guess I would have some question."

Judge Hazlewood then did exactly what he should have under the law—he excused Ms. R for cause.

Juror No. 10, who'd also raised her hand, was an even easier call:

"Ms. S, do you know the defendant or his family?"

"Yes, I do."

"How long have you known them?"

"Six years."

"Six years?"

"Yup."

"Do you feel it would be difficult for you to judge this case fairly and impartially because of your prior knowledge of the defendant or his family?"

"Yes."

Judge Hazlewood ended the colloquy: "The court will excuse Juror No. 10."

Then Juror No. 26 piped in out of the blue: "It doesn't have anything to do with this, but I do know somebody who's a neighbor of the accused and I've heard that...."

Judge Hazlewood cut him off: "We don't want to know what you've heard. We'll get into that later."

Other prospective jurors knew Denis Vogel, and still others knew some of the sheriff's deputies who would testify—more bad signs for the defense.

Again, Judge Hazlewood: "Are there any among you who is acquainted with or knows District Attorney Denis Vogel?"

Juror No. 2 raised his hand.

"Mr. H, how long have you known Mr. Vogel?"

"About five years."

"Is that a business or a personal relationship?"

"We're neighbors."

"You live right next door to Mr. Vogel?"

"Same block, three doors down."

"Do you feel that because you live on the same block, and Mr. Vogel will have to go home sometime and you'll see him, that there might be cause for you to give greater or lesser weight to one side in this case over the other?"

"None whatsoever, Your Honor."

Juror No. 2 stayed.

Juror No. 5 was a teacher, and Vogel had recently led a discussion for one of her high school classes. But she said she could be fair—so she stayed.

Then there was Juror No. 15:

"Mr. Vogel spoke at a tavern league meeting I was at."

"Do you think that would affect your judgment one way or the other?"

"No, it wouldn't, Your Honor."

Even more jurors knew the sheriff. No. 27 served with him on an advisory panel for Wisconsin Public Service; No. 11 was the Maple Grove town constable; No. 22 knew him since 1979 when they were both Realtors—"We spoke at church just last Sunday, Your Honor."

But each of them professed impartiality so they survived being struck for cause.

One of the jurors knew Chief Deputy Gene Kusche through the VFW: "He's the commander right now."

Another belonged to the same parish as Deputy Froelich—and she went to grade school with his daughter.

Another knew Froelich's wife from working on church committees together, and still another was his neighbor.

Juror No. 10's son was a member of the den where another one of the detectives who worked on the case, Detective Larry Conrad, was the Cub Scout den leader.

But each of them pledged fairness, so they stayed.

Denis Vogel knew he would face an onslaught of alibi witnesses when the defense presented its case, so when it was his turn to address the panel he tried to mitigate the impact:

"Members of the jury—if one side calls more witnesses than the other would you weigh that in favor of that side?

"As an example, if I was to call only one witness to the stand and the defense called fifteen witnesses, would you give the defense more weight than my one witness?"

When it was Jim Bolgert's turn, he knew that with such an awful jury pool for the defense, he couldn't afford to beat around the bush:

"Do any of you think just because Steve is sitting here, the chances are better than not that he's guilty? Anybody think that way?

"As you already know, the charges are serious—attempted murder, sexual assault—are any of those accusations so emotional for any of you that you won't be able to make your decision rationally? Do any of you think those accusations are so serious that you couldn't find anybody charged with them not guilty?"

Nobody raised their hand, but Jim Bolgert had his doubts. True, he could use his peremptory challenges to strike those who were unfavorably disposed toward his client, but each side only gets six strikes, and given the makeup of the panel, he could have used three times that many.

After lunch, Judge Hazlewood, the two attorneys, and the defendant retired to the judge's chambers to conduct individual *voir dire*, that is, they questioned the prospective jurors in private. It's used to ferret out information from each juror, one at a time, about what they've heard about the case from the media or from other sources without poisoning the entire jury pool. It's a tiresome process, and it took all afternoon.

Finally, it was time to select the jury, and with everyone back in the courtroom, the lawyers alternated making their peremptory strikes until they'd each struck six. The panel of twenty-six prospective jurors was winnowed down to fourteen—twelve would deliberate Steve's fate and two alternates would be randomly excused at the end of the trial.

The jury was sworn in at 5:25 p.m. and Judge Hazlewood gave the chosen ones their final instruction for the day: "I would ask everybody to talk about anything other than the case, what you may have heard or read about the case. How the Packers played in the fourth quarter last night is a perfectly legitimate discussion and anything else you can think of, but not the case. Relax, come back tomorrow morning refreshed, and we'll begin the trial."

Sitting on a jury is a sacrifice. It's the most important civic duty most of us will ever be called upon to fulfill. To do it right, we must give of ourselves—our time, our effort, and our sense of fairness. After all, somebody's liberty is at stake, and in some states someone's life is on the line.

Jury selection is also where a good judge can set the right tone and provide both sides with a fair trial, and that's exactly what Judge Hazlewood did in the Avery trial. He was not only fair and impartial, but with his kind and down-to-earth demeanor, he also made jury duty as painless as possible—and, as always, he did it with good cheer.

Anticipating widespread media attention that might improperly influence the outcome of the trial, he decided early on to sequester the jury. So the jurors stayed at the Budgetel across the street from the courthouse, and in a memo to the bailiff outlining the procedure he wanted followed, the judge even covered whether the jurors could imbibe: "This is Wisconsin, so the jurors may purchase up to two alcoholic beverages during the evening hours. However, no alcohol will be allowed during any period in which the panel is deliberating on a verdict."

There's no record as to how much alcohol the jury consumed on the first night before trial, but we do know that they dined at the Colonial Inn. The "Inn" has since been restored, and it's now known as the Courthouse Pub, which is widely viewed among locals, tourists, and businessmen alike as one of east-central Wisconsin's finest restaurants.

NINE

The trial began in earnest the next morning. After breakfast at the Big Boy restaurant next door to the Budgetel, the jurors were escorted across the street and up the stairs of the courthouse. Now that the actual trial had begun, the proceedings were moved to Judge Hazlewood's regular court-room. Its close quarters were well-suited to the judge's warm personality and his commitment to connect with the troubled young men and women who appeared in front of him.

But there was nothing cozy or comforting about the courtroom on the first morning of the trial. Nerves were frayed—especially those of the attorneys. They'd been living and breathing the case for weeks and they were anxious to get started. Judge Hazlewood, too, was determined to get things moving.

Trying a case is like telling a story—you must capture the jury's atten-tion from the beginning and never let go until the case is in their hands. If you're unlucky enough to sit on a jury where a lawyer doesn't get it—if he starts with an uninteresting minor witness, hides the main witnesses in the middle, and then muddles through to the end—it's a safe bet he's either fresh out of law school or he should probably be drafting wills and pro-bating estates instead.

But Denis Vogel knew what he was doing, and he started strong. He led off with Penny Beerntsen, whose harrowing account of her assault captured the jury's attention immediately. First, he rapidly covered her bio-graphical information—married, 36 years old, a 12-year-old daughter and a 10-year-old son. And then he zeroed in on the afternoon of the assault.

Penny told the jury they arrived at Neshotah Park at 2:30 and staked out their claim in the sand, and with Vogel leading, she said it was precisely three o'clock when she said good-bye to Tom and the kids and started off on her run.

"So did you look at your watch?" Vogel asked.

"Yes, I did," Penny replied.

"And did you keep your watch on while you were running?"

"Yes."

Penny explained how she passed the strange looking man with the black leather jacket and jogged the rest of her route before turning around. Vogel had her slow down when she told them she saw the same man again on her way back, lying in wait for her near a poplar tree. She explained how she tried to avoid him by jogging into the water, but he lunged at her and grabbed her from behind.

"What happened next?" Vogel asked.

"I twisted to try and get away. I yelled out to the sailboat, 'Help, help,' hoping someone would hear me. Then he tightened his grip around my neck and cut off my windpipe, so I was no longer able to scream."

Sparing none of the gruesome details, Vogel had Penny describe how the assailant manhandled her over the sand dunes and tried to rape her at the edge of the woods.

Penny was particularly effective when she described what happened when the man found out she wouldn't give in.

"What happened next?" Vogel asked.

"I was able to kick the man in the groin," Penny replied, "but then he put both hands around my neck and began strangling me."

"Did he say anything?"

Penny quoted her assailant: "'Now, I'm gonna kill you—you're gonna fucking die.'"

Vogel continued, "Then what happened?"

"He was shaking me up and down so hard that my head and upper back were hitting the ground. Both his hands were around my neck—my windpipe, and he was kneeling over me. He was grabbing me so tight I couldn't breathe. He kept saying, 'Now are you gonna do it? Are you gonna do it?' I remember thinking he was going to kill me if I didn't cooperate, but I couldn't say anything because I couldn't get any air."

Later, Vogel asked Penny how she felt after her assailant unexpectedly left.

"I was bruised, I was bloody, I was unable to move," she replied. "It felt like my arms and legs were made of lead. I was dazed. I was humiliated."

By now, several jurors were ready to hang Steve from the courthouse rafters, but Vogel wasn't finished. It was time to re-enact the crime:

"Penny, what I'd like to do is just have you get up out of your chair," Vogel started. "Mr. Beerntsen, why don't you come up here, can you do that? What I'd like to do is go back and have you show the jury a couple things in terms of how you were grabbed. Have your husband grab onto you, have him take his arms or whatever and show how you were first grabbed as you were jogging."

With the spellbound jury looking on, Penny gave instructions to her husband: "Put your right arm there and your left arm here."

"Okay, initially his hand was on my shoulder," Penny explained. "When I twisted to holler to the sailboat, he did exactly what my husband just did. He grabbed my neck and cut off my windpipe ... you can let go now."

Vogel awkwardly chimed in: "For the record, you're demonstrating your husband has his left arm around you, his right hand would be on your right arm, is that a fair statement?"

"That's correct," Penny answered.

"Show me how you were being held when you were halfway into the woods," Vogel asked, "when the top of your swimsuit wearing a was removed."

"Okay," Penny started. "With this arm, okay, he removed his left hand and then undid, I don't know, the top or the back first. At this point I twisted. He again put his left arm around my neck and said, 'Do what I tell you, I've got a knife'."

Then, summoning up his most official sounding prosecutorial voice, Vogel pronounced that "the record should reflect a similar grasp is being shown, except there was some release of the left arm momentarily."

If the jury thought this was preposterous, they didn't voice their distaste on the record.

"When you were in the wooded area, or close to the wooded area," Vogel continued, "you told us about the conversation about touching his penis and so forth. Could you just show me in which position you were at that time?"

"Okay, we were face-to-face."

"Penny, turn the other way so we can both see. Can you see, Mr. Bolgert?"

Redirecting his attention to Penny, he said, "You indicated before that you did touch his penis—how did you do that?"

"With my right hand," Penny explained.

Vogel mercifully moved on: "You indicated he pushed you down on the ground—show me how he did that."

Penny directed her husband to grab lower on her shoulders and then she replied, "He grabbed both my shoulders like this, okay? My arms were pressed against my body, and then he pushed me down onto the ground."

"Okay, can we just slowly do that? How was he over you? That's what I want to know."

"Okay, I was lying on my back like this."

"Can everybody see okay?" Vogel asked the jury. "If you can't see, stand up."

Penny instructed her husband to move his knees back a little further, and then Vogel asked her if the assailant's pants were still open and his penis exposed.

Penny replied in the affirmative. And then, it was finished. Vogel terminated the re-enactment, and Penny returned to the stand.

So far, Vogel had placed two separate renditions—Penny's verbal testimony and the re-enactment—of the crime before the jury and now it was time for number three. A few days after the assault, Sheriff Kocourek met the Beerntsens at Neshotah Park and took dozens of photographs of the crime scene. After a few strings were pulled, a U.S. Coast Guard helicopter crew even snapped a few from the sky. Now, with Penny still on the stand, Vogel showed some of the photos to the jury.

"I'm showing you what's been marked as Exhibit 9," he started. "Do you recognize that?"

"Yes," Penny answered. "It's a photo of the area of Neshotah Beach. This is the tree where my assailant was standing. I'm looking northbound here."

"How about Exhibit 10?"

"That's a close-up of the tree, looking north."

"Exhibit 11?" Vogel asked.

"The same tree, only this time looking south."

"Exhibit 12?"

"That's the same area of the beach with the tree, looking southbound," Penny said. "I'm standing in the water approximately at that point where I began to jog into the water. My husband is standing in the shadow of the tree where Mr. Avery was standing."

"What's Exhibit 8?" Vogel continued rapidly.

"The incline of the sand dune area that Mr. Avery pushed me up."

"13?"

"Okay, this is a picture of the wooded area where I was assaulted, and I'm standing approximately on the spot where the assault occurred."

"14?"

"This is a close-up of the wooded area where I was assaulted—I'm standing on the spot where I was assaulted, where I was lying on the ground."

It was all very interesting, but it had virtually nothing to do with what the jury would have to decide, which was whether Steven Avery was the assailant. That Penny Beerntsen was brutally assaulted, and where the attack occurred was not contested. The only issue was: Who did it?

But Vogel had beaten that particular dead horse for a reason. The prosecution's case was weak, relying almost entirely on the victim's dicey identification in the face of an impressive alibi by the defense—even if the unsavory Averys were the ones claiming the alibi. If you don't have the goods as far as the evidence goes, your best shot is to play on the jury's emotions. Prosecutors aren't supposed to play this game, but that didn't stop Vogel. By placing the brutal details of the assault in front of the jury no less than three separate times, he played on the jury's emotions, and his performance went off almost flawlessly.

But after a while, even the most tough-on-crime jurors sense prosecutorial overreaching, and no matter how vicious the crime or how sympathetic the victim, at some point they start demanding proof. So it was finally time for Vogel to move beyond the viciousness of the assault to proof that the defendant was the person who committed it. Without a confession or any legitimate physical evidence tying Steven Avery to the crime, the prosecution relied almost exclusively on Penny's identification—it was the lynchpin of the state's case. The prosecution had to show that the identification was rock solid and unimpeachable.

Vogel set the scene by having Penny describe how Chief Deputy Gene Kusche came into her hospital room and worked with her to create a composite sketch of her assailant. Then he led his witness, asking, "This is important now, Penny. At any time did Deputy Kusche suggest to you any of the features that might appear on your assailant?"

"No, no, not at all," Penny answered.

"Were you the one making the suggestions to him as to what the features look like?"

"Yes."

"In other words, the changes he may have made on that drawing, how were those changes directed, by himself making those decisions, or by you telling him to make the changes?"

"No, by me telling him to make the changes," Penny replied.

In preparation for the trial, Vogel had enlarged the mug shot of Steven Avery that Penny picked out from the photo array at the hospital. Now, he directed her to get up from the witness stand and walk over to the enlargement where he resumed leading his witness.

"Is this the picture that you picked out in that photo lineup without anybody telling you what your assailant would look like, or that he might be in the lineup, that sort of thing?" he asked.

"Yes, that's the picture."

Then he asked a question that together with Penny's response would years later echo with irony. "Did you have a picture in your mind, Penny?"

"Yes, I remembered very clearly," Penny answered. "It's as if there's a *photograph* in my mind."

A convincing courtroom identification by the victim is essential in a close case like this one, so Vogel summoned up as much drama as he could and led Penny through the prosecution's standard questions for a courtroom ID.

"Would you recognize the person that attacked you if you saw that person today?" Vogel asked.

"Yes," Penny replied.

"Is that person in the courtroom right now?"

"Yes, he is," she said.

"Can you please tell me where?"

"Yes. He's seated next to Mr. Bolgert in the tan suit."

Judge Hazlewood interjected, "The record will reflect identification."

But the prosecutor wanted to get as much mileage as he could from Penny's ID, so he went on.

"Looking at Mr. Avery today, the defendant," Vogel continued, "do you understand that your ability to be positive about your assailant is important in this case?"

"Yes, I do."

"Have you thought about that from the time when this case began, when you actually became involved in the process until today's trial, have you thought about how important that is?"

"Yes, I have."

"Penny, is there any question in your mind as to whether or not the person you picked out for us today is in fact the person that attacked you?"

"There is absolutely no question in my mind."

Vogel's timing couldn't have been better. The last thing the jurors would have on their minds as they broke for lunch was Penny's dramatic courtroom identification of Steve as her assailant. He'd hit a home run.

But it was only the first morning of a trial that was expected to last a full week, so before excusing the jurors for lunch, Judge Hazlewood reminded them that they hadn't heard the whole case yet.

"It's much too early to begin discussing the evidence or to begin your deliberations," he warned. "So please don't discuss the case during your lunch break."

But with Penny Beerntsen's harrowing testimony about the assault and her surefire identification of the defendant as the assailant, some of the jurors were already convinced that Steve was the culprit. Sure, they'd officially wait until they heard all the testimony to convict him, but Jim Bolgert would need to play some extremely scrappy defense in the afternoon to avert a blowout for the prosecution. If he didn't, they might just as well serve Steven Avery's head on a platter for the jury's dinner that night.

After lunch the trial resumed with Jim Bolgert's cross-examination of the prosecution's first witness. It's Trial Practice 101. There are two things to remember for effective cross-examination: First, never ask a question if you don't know the answer; and second, don't beat around the bush—get in and out quickly. Jim Bolgert did well on both counts that afternoon.

With his bright-blue-eyed client sitting beside him at counsel table, he fired off his first question. "Ms. Beerntsen, did your attacker have brown eyes?"

"I originally said he had brown eyes," Penny admitted, "but when I picked him out of the photo lineup, I handed it to the sheriff and said, 'He's got blue eyes—I was mistaken'."

"And you also told Deputy Dvorak two days later that he had brown eyes, is that correct?"

"That's correct."

"And you were speaking from your memory when you told Deputy Dvorak that?"

"Yes."

"And you were being truthful?"

"Yes."

Then Bolgert stepped in for another jab. He'd mentioned in his opening statement that his client worked on cars for a living so his hands were always greasy, and with Penny on the stand now, he asked her if the assailant's hands were greasy. The jury's collective ears perked up as Penny responded, "No, they were clean."

Bolgert finished up with another question or two and then turned it back over to the prosecution. Vogel tried to repair the damage during redirect examination, but the point had been made and it was impossible to unring the bell.

With Penny's testimony completed, Vogel called his second witness—the emergency room physician who treated her on the night of the assault. If a picture's worth a thousand words, then showing a gruesome photograph to a jury is worth millions. So it's not surprising that the first spat between the lawyers began when Vogel tried to introduce a particularly grisly photograph taken in the emergency room that night—a photo that showed Penny's face beaten to a bloody pulp.

Arguing that the probative value of the photo was "substantially outweighed by the danger of unfair prejudice," as the evidence code puts it, Jim Bolgert objected on relevance grounds. "The issue isn't how badly the victim was beaten," he argued, "it's who committed this brutal assault. The photograph appeals to sympathy for the victim and disgust for whoever assaulted her—that's the only reason the state wants it in front of the jury, Judge."

But that's not how Denis Vogel saw it. "I don't believe there's any better way to show the nature and extent of the victim's beating than using the photographs," he argued. "The extent of the beating is critical in this case, and this photograph corroborates it, it corroborates the victim's testimony."

Noting that one of the charges was attempted murder, Judge Hazlewood agreed. "With respect to the photographs of the injuries, the court believes they're reasonable and valuable evidence to the jury," he said. "And while they're not exactly the most pleasant things to look at, I believe it's reasonably necessary for the state to use those photographs to demonstrate the nature and extent of the attack. Therefore, the objection is overruled."

The floodgates were now open.

"I'm showing you what's been marked as Exhibit 1," Vogel announced, more to the jury than the emergency room physician to whom he'd addressed the question. "Is this a photograph of the way Penny looked when you saw her at the hospital that night?"

"Yes, it is," the ER doc replied.

Vogel asked the judge if he could *publish*—legal jargon for the word, "show"—the oversized photograph to the jury. The court approved, and Vogel walked slowly along the front of the jury box, pausing before each juror just long enough to give them a good look at the photograph of Penny.

Back at counsel table, Vogel continued his questioning of the ER doctor. "Do you have an opinion to a reasonable degree of scientific certainty, Doctor, as to whether or not the bruise at the base of Penny's neck would be consistent with someone choking her?"

"It very well could have been."

"The degree of force required, Doctor, to cause that sort of bruising, do you have an opinion to a reasonable degree of scientific certainty as to the amount of force required to cause that?"

"It's relatively hard to cause the breaking of the blood vessels there to cause that kind of bruising," the doctor stated.

"Do you have an opinion to a reasonable degree of scientific certainty as to how much force would be required to cause bruising to her back the way you saw it, to a reasonable scientific certainty, that it would be consistent with Penny being shaken or pushed on the ground up and down several times?"

"Could very well have been, yes," the ER doctor mildly replied.

As his next witness, Vogel called Sherry Culhane from the State Crime Lab in Madison. Among other things, Culhane and the other analysts at the Crime Lab examine biological evidence—hair, blood, semen, saliva, for example—in an attempt to identify their source, which is often a key piece of evidence in solving a crime. But back in 1985, the science of hair examination—if it could even be called a science—was extremely limited. It was ten years before the advent of forensic DNA testing, and with the tools available at the time, hair examiners couldn't even come close to making a positive identification—the best they could do was to say that two hairs were "consistent."

The police had confiscated Steve's T-shirt on the night of the assault, and Culhane had collected various hairs from it. One of the hairs was a possible match with the standard hair sample provided by Penny Beerntsen, but all Culhane could say was that the two hairs were similar. But as dutifully elicited by Vogel, at least her opinion was "to a reasonable degree of scientific certainty."

Jim Bolgert destroyed the "science" of hair examination during cross-examination, and to her credit, Sherry Culhane didn't try to make hair examination sound more useful than it was.

"Is it possible to prove identification by hair analysis?" Bolgert began.

"No."

"Is the hair of many people consistent with each other?"

"Yes."

"Is it unusual for hair from different people to be consistent with each other?"

"No, it's not."

"For example, is it unusual for the hair of white Caucasians to be consistent with each other?"

"No."

"If you take a hair from ten different people, would it be unusual to find the hair from those different people to be consistent?"

"No."

"Did you have any standards from hospital or ambulance personnel?"

"No, sir."

"Did you have any standards from the husband of the victim?"

"No, sir."

"Any standards from any of Mr. Avery's children?"

"No, sir."

The sheriff's deputies came next. Vogel called four in a row to establish that it was none other than the defendant himself who the sheriff's deputies arrested that night for this despicable crime. Sergeant Petersen explained that with the assistance of the defendant's uncle, Deputy Arland Avery, they were able to take the "subject" into custody without incident.

Then, out came the smoking gun. Two officers testified that the defendant knew the victim was a woman even though nobody told him. Sergeant Petersen was the first to drop the bomb.

"What happened next?" Vogel asked.

"The defendant's wife came downstairs and asked him what was going on, and he said, 'They say I murdered a woman.'"

"Did he use the word 'woman'?" Vogel asked, to make sure the jury appreciated the weight of the moment.

"Yes," Petersen replied.

"Prior to that time, you hadn't mentioned the word 'woman' when you arrested him, had you?"

"No, not at all."

"Had anyone else mentioned that it was a woman?"

"Not in my presence."

Then it was Deputy Froelich's turn. First, he explained how he hid in a closet until the defendant came downstairs and then followed him into the kitchen where he and Sergeant Petersen arrested him.

Vogel took it from there, asking, "When the defendant's wife came downstairs, did she ask him anything?"

"His wife asked, 'Would somebody please tell me what's going on?' And then Sergeant Petersen and myself, we just looked at each other, and Steve—Steve looked at his wife and said, 'They said I murdered a girl.'"

"When he said that, did you specifically make note of that, a mental note that he said it?"

"Yes."

Then Vogel went in for the kill. "Why?"

"Because at that point, no one had said it was a male or female."

Penny Beerntsen told the police several times that the assailant was wearing a worn-out, waist-length, black leather jacket. But since black leather jackets aren't uncommon, neither party made much of it until just three days before trial, when Vogel sent word to the defense. He disclosed that over the years, Deputies Froelich and Dvorak had both seen the defendant wearing a black leather jacket. As a matter of fact, it was just like the one Penny described.

Now, with Froelich still on the stand, Vogel asked him about the jacket. "Prior to July 29, 1985, had you ever seen Mr. Avery wearing any sort of a leather jacket?"

"Yes," Froelich replied.

"More than one time?"

"Yes, it's a black, waist-length, motorcycle type leather jacket."

"Is that an old-looking jacket to your knowledge?" Vogel asked, leading his witness.

"Yes, old-looking," Froelich parroted.

"Are there any specific dates or times you remember specifically seeing him having that jacket?"

"Yes," Froelich said, pulling out a copy of a child safety-seat warning that he'd issued to Steven Avery on April 6, 1984, and handing it to Vogel.

"For example," Vogel continued, holding up the warning, "on this particular date and time, do you remember what Steve was wearing?"

"He was wearing the black, faded black, motorcycle jacket. And I've seen him wearing the jacket more recently, but I just don't remember any specific dates."

But only one other officer, Deputy Judy Dvorak, testified to having seen Steve with a black leather jacket like Penny's assailant had on. And when they executed the search warrant at Steve and Lori's house the morning after the attack, the police found a leather jacket, but it didn't look anything like the one Penny described. Also, despite seeing him every week for as long as he could remember, Deputy Arland Avery, Steve's uncle, never saw him wearing any leather jacket—not once. Vogel later called Arland to the stand, but conveniently, Vogel didn't ask him if he ever saw his nephew wearing a leather jacket.

Vogel called Deputy Dvorak next. The lawyers now had their second spat—and it was a good one. The fireworks started halfway through direct examination, when Vogel asked Deputy Dvorak to read out loud Penny's entire six-page statement. A few days had passed since Penny's dramatic testimony, and its effect on the jury was probably wearing off. It would help immensely, Vogel thought, if he could get the brutal assault back in the forefront of their minds.

Bolgert objected before Dvorak could start reading Penny's statement, and then all hell broke loose. Spewing out legal concepts like hearsay, prior consistent statements, and implied allegations of recent fabrication, the attorneys made their respective positions known to the court, snarling at each other the whole time. Then the judge stepped in to clear the air.

"How much more are we going to hear about this statement?" Judge Hazlewood asked. "How many times should we be rereading these statements is almost a battle of who gets the last kick at the cat; this [is the] kind of an argument I'm hearing. I'm beginning to think this is just wasting a lot of time."

Vogel unwisely interrupted, saying, "Judge, I agree with what you're saying—at some point in time you might hear too much, and we want to get on with other witnesses."

Judge Hazlewood dryly cut him off, "We sure would." But the judge eventually gave in and Vogel got what he wanted. He had Deputy Dvorak read Penny's riveting six-page statement—reminding the jurors once again of the viciousness of the assault, lest they start to think the state's case was less than convincing.

Vogel was delighted, but during his cross-examination, Jim Bolgert came back strong. "You stated after that statement was signed, that Penny changed her description of the eyes from brown eyes to blue, isn't that right?"

"Yes," Dvorak admitted, "it was not noted on the statement."

"Did that happen the same day or is that on your interview of August 1?"

"I believe this is what she told the sheriff, possibly that first evening."

"Did she ever tell you the attacker had blue eyes?"

"Yes, after I had taken the second statement."

"On August 1?"

"Yes."

Bolgert continued, "So the first time she told you about the blue eyes was on August 1—three days after the assault?"

"Yes."

Then he shifted gears and scored a few more points. "Deputy Dvorak, did you specifically ask Ms. Beerntsen whether the attacker's hands were dirty or greasy?"

"Yes, I did," Dvorak answered softly, "and she did not include any mention of them being greasy or dirty."

He let her response sink in before he moved on. "You don't know if Steven Avery owns a leather jacket like the assailant was wearing, do you?" he asked.

"No, but I have seen him with an older looking dark leather jacket."

Noting vagueness, and suspecting disingenuousness, Bolgert honed in.

"When is the most recent time?"

"I couldn't be sure," Dvorak backtracked, "but I remember last fall I had seen him wearing it several times, and during the winter."

"Where did you see him?"

"Steve lives across Old County Highway Y from where I live. Our residence is just to the east on the opposite side of the road."

"So you would see him when you drove by occasionally, is that when you'd see him?"

"I would see him in the yard as I walked by, or I jog frequently, or when I do walk, when I drive by, yes," Dvorak babbled.

"Was there any reason for you to take note of what he was wearing?"

"Not really. I also have the project child safe car, the safe car-seat project, and I had to pick up a car-seat from Steve once in his home also."

"He was wearing that coat?"

"I can't be sure on that, but I believe he may have."

"But you had no particular reason to remember what he was wearing, did you?"

"No, I did not."

"Did you make notes when you saw him wearing different items of clothing?"

"No, I did not," Dvorak said defensively. "This is not a thing you generally do about your neighbors."

Bolgert deadpanned, "I agree," and then he wrapped it up.

"Were you specifically asked whether you had ever seen Steve wearing a short leather coat for the purpose of this case?"

"Yes," Dvorak said vaguely. "It has come out in a conversation."

Vogel's next witness was Chief Deputy Gene Kusche, pronounced, *Kushay*, with the emphasis on the second syllable. He began with the prosecutor's standard "would-you-please-state-your-name-and-occupation" question, and Kusche, as he did with everything in life, replied with a flourish, saying, "I am Eugene Kusche, Chief Deputy Sheriff for Manitowoc County."

Kusche had attended a course at the FBI Academy just a month before Penny was assaulted, and Vogel asked him if the training included eyewitness identification procedure and police artist reconstruction.

"Yes," the Chief Deputy responded. "I attended a course in what's called rapid visual perception. It's on how to train individuals, such as bank clerks or what-have-you, on what to look for in facial characteristics. Part of the course was also on how to prepare the drawing, the composite comparisons."

Then, sounding uncharacteristically defensive, Vogel set the stage for Kusche's drawing of the composite sketch.

"In this particular case, did you have any suspects in mind before you made the drawing for Penny Beerntsen?"

"Did I have in *my* mind?" Kusche responded with a question of his own.

"Yes," Vogel answered.

"Visually?" Kusche asked.

"Yes, visually or any other way," the prosecutor replied.

"I was told a name earlier, but I did not know the person," Kusche finally answered.

Then Vogel led with a mouthful, asking, "So you had no preconceived ideas of your own of any particular features or any drawings or any descriptions of anybody prior to talking to Penny Beerntsen?" And just in case the jury didn't get the picture, he continued, "So you're saying you didn't see any photographs and neither did the victim, is that correct?"

"I did not, and to my knowledge the victim did not," Kusche answered, catching on, with more certainty this time.

"At any time during your interview of Penny," Vogel continued, "did anyone come in and suggest to you a name or a description?"

"Not a description, I know a name was stated to me," Kusche answered. "But I don't know if she was within earshot at the time it was stated to me."

Vogel moved on. "Now, once you had the victim at ease and began the interview, did you suggest any features of a face to the victim?"

"No, sir. You ask them to tell you, then you draw what you think they mean and if it is not, like I said, they will correct it, and one of the important portions of the training is not to be suggestive, like you don't say, 'Did the person have a round face?' Instead, you ask 'What was the shape of the face?' So that way," Kusche said, "you're not putting anything in their mind.

Then it was time to present the artist with his masterpiece. "I show you what's been marked as Exhibit Number 26," Vogel confidently declared, "and I ask if you recognize it?"

"This is my original drawing—the charcoal drawing."

"Is Exhibit Number 26 the final product?"

"It is," Kusche said, "this was the original and final drawing."

Sensing that the prosecution had scored a few points for the defense, or at least that they'd turned the ball over a few times, Jim Bolgert kept his cross-examination short and sweet.

"You mentioned that the mug shots for the photo lineup had been pulled before the composite was done. Is that standard practice?" he began.

"Apparently from the description prior to me arriving at the scene or at the hospital, the officers had some idea of who it might be. Therefore, it would not be unusual that photographs would be pulled," Kusche replied.

"Did she give you a description of eye color?"

"I can't say that I asked," Kusche demurred, "so I don't remember that."

"That wouldn't be part of your standard procedure, to ask eye color?"

"It would probably be, but in this case I can't recollect having asked her. I may have, but as I did not do this in color I didn't make any representation in color."

By being so adamantly defensive about whether their immediate suspicion of Steven Avery affected the integrity of the composite drawing and the identification process itself, the prosecution invited speculation that it had done just that. Indeed, both the composite drawing and Steve's mug shot taken seven months earlier, marked as Exhibits 26 and 22, respectively, figured prominently in the trial. And over the years, more than a few persons who've seen them have commented that the two depictions look *exactly* like one another. Indeed, Judge Hazlewood also referred to the two depictions as bearing an "uncanny resemblance" to each other.

* * *

Next came the time frame. Both lawyers knew it was tight. If Steven Avery had attacked Penny Beerntsen on the beach that afternoon, he had to have moved fast. Penny was as precise about the time of the assault as she was sketchy about the assailant's appearance—she checked her watch when she first saw the man hiding in the poplar trees, and it had been ten minutes to four.

But Steve and his family were adamant that he came into the house right after *Divorce Court* ended at three-thirty. That would have left him with just twenty minutes to drive to Neshotah Beach and position himself under the poplar tree ready to pounce on his prey. It's a fifteen-minute drive from the Avery Salvage Yard to Neshotah Park, so he would have had just five minutes to park and shuffle the half mile up the sand to the poplar trees— it was close to impossible.

Vogel's ace in the hole was the cement truck driver, Donald Cigler. Steve's wife, his mother, and various other members of the Avery clan all told police the cement truck was still there when Steve came in after *Divorce Court* ended at three–thirty. But that's not how Cigler remembered it. He testified he arrived at one o'clock that afternoon with ten yards of concrete. Then Vogel asked him what time he left, and Cigler took it from there.

"Well, they poured a slab for a sheep barn, and then they had some small odd pours around the building. I must have left around two–thirty I'd say—somewheres in there. Then I went back to the pit. It's about five or six miles back to the pit. When I got back to the pit, I washed up the truck with some water in there and then dumped that, parked it, and shut it off. It takes about ten minutes or so to wash the truck, so I estimate it was half an hour after I left the Averys' that I checked out and went home. We have timecards that we fill out ourselves, and on that date I entered seven and a half hours, so since I began work at seven-thirty and worked right through noon without a lunch hour, that means I checked out at three. So I'd say it was around two-thirty when I left the Avery place."

If the cement truck left at two–thirty like Donald Cigler said it did, then either the defense witnesses were mistaken or they were lying. It also meant that Steve finished helping with the cement project much earlier than he claimed and he would have had plenty of time to drive to Neshotah Park and be in position to attack Penny at ten minutes to four.

During cross-examination, Bolgert established that Cigler worked different hours each day and that he didn't punch out on a time clock—he kept track of his hours in a notebook he kept at home instead. And no, he didn't tell his boss how many hours he worked that day.

Nevertheless, Donald Cigler probably saved the prosecution. In his round-about way, he laid out a time frame that made it possible for Steven Avery to be at the scene of the crime at the time Penny was attacked. Never mind that years later, a private investigator would discover that Cigler was overheard saying as he left the courtroom that day, "I think I'd gypped myself out of an hour."

The prosecution also had to come up with a credible time-line for what Steve did after the assault, and the window of opportunity wasn't open much wider on that side of the equation. Penny said the assailant ran into the woods at five after four, but Steve and his family were in the checkout lane at Shopko in Green Bay at five–thirteen. To make it on time, he would've had to run from the crime scene back to where he parked his Blazer, hustle back to his parents' place to pick up his wife and five children, and then drive thirty miles up the Interstate to Green Bay—all in sixty-eight minutes! It was nearly impossible.

So Vogel called Detective Fred Nicholson, who had previously conducted a dry run at the sheriff's request. Nicholson told the jury that by "averaging fifteen miles per hour over the limit, but never more than fifteen over," he was able to make the time-frame work with eleven minutes to spare!

Detective Nicholson's math was fine, but he left a few numbers out of the equation. He didn't count the time it would have taken Steve to pick up Lori and the kids, including two infants, and the time he would have spent strapping four of them into their car seats, nor the time they spent at the Burger King drive-thru and the car wash across the street.

Hoping to finish strong, Vogel called Sheriff Kocourek as his final witness. "Could you please tell everyone what your occupation is?" he began.

"Sheriff of Manitowoc County," Kocourek replied.

"And were you involved in coordinating the investigation of the incident regarding Penny Beerntsen?"

"Yes."

"When you presented the photo array to her, did you lay them out for her, or just give her a stack to finger through?"

"I just spread them out on a table and she looked at all of them at the same time."

"And did Penny Beerntsen pick out any one of those photographs for you?"

"Yes, she did."

"Which one did she pick?"

"She picked out photograph number 3746, which is of Steven Avery," the sheriff answered.

"Was there any hesitancy that you could observe about her when she was asked to pick out a photograph and when she did in fact pick out that photograph?" Vogel asked.

Kocourek replied in his measured, convincing voice that he didn't detect any hesitancy. "As a matter of fact," he said, "I noted that she was kind of drawn to that one, and then she sort of held her hand on this one and looked at the others—but then she came right back to this one and said, 'This is the man.'"

Then Vogel turned his witness over to the defense. Though not without his flaws, Tom Kocourek is a man of high ideals and solid integrity, and his testimony during Jim Bolgert's cross-examination bears that out. There's no doubt about it—the sheriff took his oath to tell the whole truth and nothing but the truth seriously.

"Before July 29, did you know Steve?" Bolgert began.

"Yes, I did," Sheriff Kocourek answered.

"And that was through professional contacts?"

"That's correct."

"When you heard [Penny's] description, you suspected Steve?"

"Yes."

"And did you tell the victim that you had a suspect in mind?"

"Yes."

"And did you direct some deputies to pull some photographs?"

"Yes."

"And did you instruct them to include a few mug shots of Steven Avery?"

"Yes."

"When did you do that?"

"It would have been during the evening of July 29," Kocourek said.

"Before the composite was drawn?"

"Yes."

"Did you have those photos before you," Bolgert continued, "before the composite was drawn?"

"They were delivered to me at the hospital," the sheriff replied.

"Before the composite was drawn, did you indicate to the artist that you had a suspect in mind?"

"Yes."

"When the composite was done, did you immediately present the photographs to [Penny Beerntsen]?"

"After the composite was complete and she was sure in her mind that there wasn't much more that she could offer to, you know, change the composite, the composite was set aside and the photographs were presented to her."

"Do you think she realized that those photos had been pulled before the composite was drawn?"

"I'm sure she probably did, yes," the sheriff replied.

Then Bolgert switched gears and finished up crisply, asking, "The other times you've seen Steven Avery, did you ever see him wearing a waist-length leather jacket?"

"No."

"That's all I have, thank you."

"Any redirect, Mr. Vogel?" Judge Hazlewood invited. Vogel's barely audible reply was a curt, "No."

"Mr. Vogel, anything else?" the court repeated.

"No, Your Honor; the state rests."

Jim Bolgert had come back strong and, for once, Denis Vogel had nothing to say.

The prosecution had called twenty-one witnesses and offered forty-nine exhibits into evidence, and now it was finally time for the case to pass to the defense. Even though there was time for a witness or two, Judge Hazlewood decided to call it a day. The defense could start fresh in the morning that way—and besides, the weather had turned ugly outside. The first cold snap of the year had descended upon Wisconsin, and with a few of the older jurors getting nervous, the judge tried to put them at ease.

"Some of you expressed concerns about your automobiles. If you're concerned about the cars not starting, or if you'd like someone to start up your car or something like that, perhaps we could collect the keys tomorrow morning, and we could have people out starting the cars and turning them over," he said. "It hasn't been real cold in the evening, so if the car's in good winter condition, it probably should start, but we'll check."

With the state's case in, and the defense ready to take over the following morning, the judge finished the day by reminding the jury not to begin deliberating until they heard all the evidence.

"I know the temptation is tremendous to sit down and start trying to decide the case, but there's still more evidence to come, so don't begin your deliberations at this time," he warned. "Hopefully we can provide you with a good dinner—I haven't heard any complaints yet—that's always a good sign. I thank you for the attention that you've given to me and to counsel today. At this point we're adjourning. Thank you, ladies and gentlemen."

TEN

It's customary, and almost universally a waste of time, for the defense to ask the court to dismiss the charges after the state rests its case. Not to do so is to risk a claim of ineffective assistance of counsel. So with both counsel and the defendant present in chambers, Judge Hazlewood asked if the defense had a motion, and Jim Bolgert dutifully, if unenthusiastically, replied, "I move to dismiss on the grounds the state hasn't met its burden of proof, Your Honor."

Still following the script, Judge Hazlewood invoked the equally meaningless legal standard for such matters and efficiently dispatched the motion. "Based upon the testimony in the record at this time, the court is satisfied that a reasonable jury could find beyond a reasonable doubt that the defendant is guilty," he said. "The court therefore respectfully denies the motion."

The term "reasonable" shows up often in the law. It allows for plenty of wiggle room since to some extent, whether something is reasonable is in the eye of the beholder.

Now came the moment the Averys had been waiting for. In the five-and-a-half months since Steve's arrest, they had lost what little faith they had previously held in the criminal justice system. But once the facts were placed before a jury of their peers, they thought, justice would surely prevail. How couldn't it? Steve was innocent; he had been with them all day.

As his first witness, Jim Bolgert planned to call Dr. Steven Penrod, a highly regarded expert in human memory and eyewitness identification procedures from the University of Wisconsin in Madison. Given how the police extracted his client's identification from the victim in this case, Bolgert knew that Penrod would make an excellent witness, and somehow he managed to convince the State Public Defender's Office to approve the expert's fee.

But Denis Vogel tried to head him off at the pass. He moved to exclude much of Dr. Penrod's proffered testimony on the grounds that it would invade the province of the jury. On its surface, at least, the law seems fairly simple: Unless there's a question of fact that is "beyond the scope of ordinary laypersons' knowledge and experience," testimony from expert witnesses is inadmissible at trial. The jurors are the finders of fact—not some expert witness retained by one side or the other at some exorbitant fee.

But applying the law is rarely straightforward, and after Vogel objected, Judge Hazlewood launched a lengthy discussion with the attorneys about whether Dr. Penrod should be allowed to testify.

"I've indicated to counsel that the court would permit testimony of a properly qualified expert—and I do not at this time mean to imply that I have a feeling one way or the other with regard to Mr. Penrod's qualifications—I presume we'll hear more about that on the record," Judge Hazlewood said. "But perhaps I better hear the state's objection to the proffered testimony. And perhaps before we even hear the state's objection, we'd better hear what the defense expects to do with the testimony."

"Your Honor, the expert's name is Steven Penrod, and there's no doubt in my mind he's qualified," Bolgert replied. "After his qualifications, I'm going to ask him to speak about the area of human memory and eyewitness identification. He speaks of memory as having four stages: perception, encoding, storage, and retrieval. I'll ask him to explain each. As you know from my questions on cross, there are specific elements of the identification I'd like to ask him about—specifically, the effect upon the victim of assuming the sheriff had a suspect and that he was in the [photo] array; the effect of confirmation of her choice and the subsequent arrest; the effect of her knowledge of the person who was arrested and in custody before the live lineup; the confirmation that she picked the suspect after the live lineup; and later information that this person had some prior contact with law enforcement. With the court's permission, I'd also show him the photo lineup, and not ask for his opinion, but to critique it as a functional array."

That's when Vogel jumped in, saying, "What Mr. Bolgert wants to do has been accepted, Judge, but not to the extent he wants to have it applied in this case. What he wants to do is apply the general theory that Penrod apparently has of perception, encoding, the retention—or in his words, storage and retrieval—and then take that general theory and apply it specifically to the facts in this case and have him comment on the facts in this case but not get to the ultimate conclusion, that being, 'Do you think it's a good or bad identification?' It's invading the province of the jury, Your Honor, and really, although he's not asking him the ultimate question, he is asking him to draw an opinion, and by going that far, the jury would draw the inference as to what his opinion is. I don't think it's admissible to go as far as Mr. Bolgert wants him to. I believe it would be an abuse of the court's discretion to allow Penrod to do that, and that's the standard under the *Hampton* case—abuse of discretion."

Under what circumstances courts should permit expert testimony about eyewitness identifications is the sort of thorny legal issue Judge Hazlewood savored, and now that the lawyers had their say, it was time for the court to decide.

"This is an area of law that is causing us a great deal of trouble in the law," the judge began. "And in recent years, it's become a difficult matter to control, most critically in civil cases. But now it's become more a factor in criminal cases; that is, the place of the expert in the courtroom and whether or not the expert will, in effect, supersede the jury in reaching these determinations. Fundamentally, it's a question of where we place our confidence. Do we place our confidence in twelve persons from the community, or do we place it in listening to two experts? The thing I'm stricken with in many cases with regard to experts is how two persons with impeccable credentials, incredible academic efforts attested to by their many publications, and a great deal of practical experience in the field in which they testify, can come to diametrically opposed conclusions. I'm conservative, and I retain a considerable amount of faith in the jury system. I tend to believe that expert testimony is admissible only when it assists laypersons in reaching conclusions, and when the expert can provide, because of his expertise and experience, insights into matters that are relevant and that are beyond the pale of the average person to understand or appreciate fully."

Clearly enjoying the argument, which by now had turned one-sided, Judge Hazlewood continued, adding, "The factors which affect memory and perception—I'm sure all of us have opinions on. I'm also certain that with respect to whatever opinions we may hold, and whatever beliefs we may hold, it is not necessarily going to adversely—and it could very well properly assist us—in applying not only our opinions but in considering them in light of the studied opinion of an expert in the area to a specific set of facts.

"I am unwilling, however, to allow experts in the field of identification to comment or to testify on the deficiencies of a particular identification in particular situations, or give an opinion on the reliability of that particular identification. I do not have any basis to believe that the fields of psychology and psychiatry have reached such a point where one can reliably put in the hands of psychiatrists and psychologists or other persons specifically trained in these areas the task of reaching the conclusion that the jury will be reaching.

"Now, when we say ultimate issue, the ultimate issue is the guilt or innocence of the defendant," the judge continued. "But in getting to that stage, there are many other decisions that, absent some considerable proof that this area of science has arrived at a consistent opinion that would remove the matter from the area of the layperson's application of wisdom and logic, are properly left to the jury. Therefore, I believe the expert should be permitted to testify in this instance. However, I do not believe it is proper to ask him questions that go to the quality or the deficiencies of the identification process in this particular case, or to offer a critique, if you will, of the photo lineup or the live lineup."

It sounded like the court was finished, but Judge Hazlewood had one last point. "I would add, by way of editorial comment, that certainly psychiatric testimony and psychological testimony is one area where people with incredible credentials come into court with diametrically opposed opinions on the critical facts. And again, I would pose the same question of whether these two people—and whatever can be gleaned from that academic debate in the courtroom—is ultimately the better one, or whether that should be left to twelve people. I don't know."

With the issue finally resolved Judge Hazlewood asked the bailiff to bring in the jury. The legal wrangling over the admission of expert testimony took nearly an hour, but the judge greeted the jurors with his usual good cheer. He also had a comment about the weather outside, as the temperature had dropped to well below zero.

"In light of the control over the news broadcasts, some of you may have missed the weather report. It's getting much colder, so if any of you want your cars started or turned over, why don't you make arrangements to leave your keys with the bailiff with a license number, and we'll try to accomplish that for you today. And if the car won't start, we'll make arrangements to have the appropriate starter devices here and people to assist you in getting your car started. It's gotten quite cold."

Then he addressed the delay, saying, "Also, I don't want you to get the idea that because we're starting after nine o'clock that we're all drifting in here late in the morning and having long breakfasts while you're ready to go. There are numerous details that have to be dealt with in any jury trial, and it's difficult to predict how long these will take when the judge—who is supposed to know everything—has to nonetheless open a book and look at some law, as happens from time to time. I can assure you, counsel have been arriving promptly at eight-thirty. I can't assure you the court got here quite at eight-thirty today; I was about three minutes late. But we're trying not to waste your time."

It was finally time for Dr. Penrod to take the stand.

"How are you employed?" Bolgert began.

"I'm a professor of psychology at the University of Wisconsin in Madison."

"What's your educational background?"

"I have a bachelor's degree from Yale in 1969," Penrod replied. "And I have a law degree from Harvard Law School in 1974, and a Ph.D. in psychology from Harvard University in 1979."

"Where were you employed prior to the University of Wisconsin, Dr. Penrod?"

"I was a graduate student at Harvard University where I was employed as a teaching and research assistant. Prior to that time, I was in the Navy—I worked as a legal officer in the Navy, and I had various other and sundry jobs before that."

"What are your duties at the University of Wisconsin?"

"First would be teaching, second would be research, and third would be administrative responsibilities. Most of my research is conducted in areas where psychology and law intersect. I draw upon both of my sources of training for that research. At the moment, my primary research activities are focused on issues concerning eyewitness reliability, problems of eyewitness identification, and methods that might be used to assess the reliability of eyewitness identification. A couple years ago, I conducted a series of seminars for the Madison Police Department on methods of investigation, interrogation of witnesses, and construction of lineups, problems of eye-witness identification."

Then Bolgert offered Dr. Penrod as an expert in the study of human memory and eyewitness identification, and the court asked Vogel if he had any objection.

Vogel unwisely replied, "I believe he's stated his qualifications in terms of his background, but I'm not sure if he specifically qualified himself as an expert on...."

"Well, I can do with a yes or no," Judge Hazlewood cut him off, clearly impressed with Penrod's credentials.

"Yes," Vogel curtly replied.

"Thank you. The court will receive further testimony from Mr. Penrod."

Trial attorneys love calling expert witnesses. It's a rare opportunity to ask open-ended questions and sit back while your witness does the heavy lifting. It's even more enjoyable if your expert not only knows his stuff, but also knows how to speak to the jury in terms they can understand. Steven Penrod excelled at both.

"Would you please tell the jury how human memory operates, Dr. Penrod?" Bolgert began.

"Most psychologists break human memory down into four stages," Penrod answered. "The first stage is perception, which just refers to the stage at which whatever sensory system we're using—I'll concentrate on our visual system—actually receives stimulation. In the case of the eye, it receives light. Stimulated by light, we pick up visual images. That's the perception stage. A second stage commonly discussed is the encoding stage. It really refers to the active processing in terms of thinking about the information that's perceived. The third stage is commonly referred to as the storage stage, or sometimes, the retention interval. It refers to the period of time between the perception and encoding of information and then the later effort to pull that information out of memory. And finally, the retrieval stage, which is that stage of trying to retrieve information out of memory. Now, the reason that we break them down into those stages is because in fact, different things are happening at those stages in terms of forming the memory, and the eyewitness is prone to a variety of errors or problems at each of those different stages.

"We also know that things can happen even while information is being stored," Penrod said, zeroing in on what might have occurred in this case. "So even if the person starts out with a good, rich, solid memory for an event, that doesn't mean that at some later point in time they're going to be able to retrieve that information from memory in its original and pure, pristine form. The reason is that events that take place after, let's say a crime, events that take place after viewing a crime can change or distort the original memory, and what happens is that if people pick up information after the crime, that information can literally become part of their original memory. While information is sitting in the storage stage, it can undergo changes, or transformations, that in essence can destroy the original memory. We know, for example, there have been several studies on the effects of overhearing another person talk about the characteristics of the perpetrator. Let's say witnesses had seen a staged crime or a videotape of a crime, and later they hear somebody say, 'I think he has a mustache,' or, 'I think he has curly hair,' those characteristics, those pieces of information—and they're false information and they've been sort of set up by the researcher to see what effect it will have on the witnesses' memories—those pieces of false information can find their way into an individual witness' memories, and at a later point in time they are significantly more likely to misidentify an individual who has the mustache as the perpetrator when the original perpetrator didn't, or an individual who has curly hair when the original perpetrator didn't have curly hair. These effects can be produced in very subtle ways."

Bolgert looked up from his notes and briefly interjected, "I was going to ask—is that a conscious process?"

"Absolutely not," Dr. Penrod replied. "This is not something where people sort of intentionally take that information and now put it into their memory. It's something that happens unintentionally, and indeed the witnesses who display these kinds of effects are trying the best they can to make a totally accurate report, but these influences are very, very subtle, but can nonetheless have a very profound effect on the witness' memory, and in some sense, the most disturbing aspect of this is that it proves to be virtually impossible for a witness to somehow go back and restore or retrieve their original memory."

"You said the viewing of a photo lineup could change the original memory," Bolgert chimed in. "How is that?"

"Well," Dr. Penrod explained as he turned to face the jury, "because the information that is picked up after an event—but it's relevant to the event—in a sense now becomes intermingled with the original information. We don't know exactly what goes on in the brain that produces this effect, but what we do know is that post-event information seems to become mingled, intermingled with the information from the original event. It can in some instances literally displace it so that it's impossible to retrieve memory about the face of the original perpetrator because it's been supplanted, replaced by, pushed out by, or intermingled with information that's picked up from these photographs."

Bolgert interjected again, saying, "This change in original memory, is that a conscious process?"

"No," Penrod replied. "Again, it's not a conscious process, and it's something that proves to be fairly difficult to prevent. Indeed, it's a common problem."

Bolgert moved on. "We're specifically interested, Dr. Penrod, in what effect expectation might have on a photo-identification."

"If a person has an expectation that the perpetrator is going to be there," Penrod explained, "it seems to change the identification task for them. Instead of having the sole responsibility for saying, well, out of these six possible suspects this is the person, and then the case proceeds solely on the basis of that identification, the task now seems to be one of confirming or disconfirming police suspicions and the thought is that if a misidentification occurs—if the wrong person is picked—there won't be any harm done. On the other hand, if I pick the same person that the police have picked, we'll have some corroborating identifications, if you will, so it seems to change the task and simply make people more willing to make identifications. They're just not as conservative about making their identifications."

Penny Beerntsen had testified confidently—she was absolutely certain the photo she picked out was her assailant, so Bolgert wrapped up his direct examination by asking Dr. Penrod whether there was a relationship between the accuracy of the identification and the confidence in the person that they've made a proper identification.

"Unfortunately not," Penrod answered. "And despite the fact that it defies common sense, there have been a large number of studies which show that if there is a relationship between confidence and accuracy, it's only a weak relationship. We just are not very good at sort of crawling inside our memory and trying to determine whether it's a good, solid memory or not so good a memory."

With that, Bolgert was finished and he passed his witness to the prosecution. Dr. Penrod's testimony was fascinating, but after nearly two hours of sitting and listening attentively, the jurors were getting restless, and no one objected when the court adjourned for the morning break. Besides, having strained for most of the morning to keep up with the articulate but wordy academic's scientific testimony, the court reporter's fingers were probably smoking.

It wasn't going to be easy for Vogel to discredit Dr. Penrod. His testimony about the stages of human memory and how they may have affected Penny Beerntsen's identification of the defendant had been convincing. So rather than attacking the message, the prosecutor attacked the messenger instead.

This is the Midwest, and like every other region of the country, it has its own peculiar set of biases and prejudices. And Denis Vogel wasn't above taking advantage of them at trial. He made sure the jury understood exactly what kind of person Dr. Penrod was. Not only was he a high-powered expert witness for the defense, but he was also an attorney, a psychologist, and a Ph.D. from Harvard! What could he possibly know about the real world?

Vogel wasn't above bending a little psychology his way if it assisted the prosecution's theory of the case.

"Is there a term called 'feedback factor,' Mr. Penrod. Do you know what that means?" Vogel asked confidently.

"I'm not sure what you're referring to," Penrod replied.

"Alright, when witnesses have a chance to get together and talk to each other about what they've seen, is there a psychological term for that?" Vogel asked.

"Well, people may have coined a psychological term, but it's not one that's in widespread use."

"Have you done research in that area?"

"No, sir."

Vogel had reached a dead end, but it didn't matter—he had made his point just by asking the question. He knew that Jim Bolgert would be calling close to a dozen witnesses to back up Steve's alibi, and by asking Dr. Penrod about "feedback factor," he laid a foundation that he could use later to suggest that Steve's witnesses were all lying—that they had gotten together and matched up their stories. And he did it through the defense expert, no less.

But Jim Bolgert was confident that Dr. Penrod had diminished the reliability of Penny's identification of his client, at least to some extent, and it was time to move on to his next witness.

* * *

To testify or not to testify, that is the question. Not quite as existentially weighty as the question posed by Shakespeare in *Hamlet*, but it's the most agonizing decision an accused and his attorney face during trial.

A defendant has an absolute constitutional right not to testify, and the judge instructs the jury not to hold it against him if he decides not to. That's the theory. But in practice, the jury wants to hear from the defendant. "If he's innocent," they figure, "what's he got to hide?"

Constitutional niceties aside, Steven Avery really didn't have a choice. He'd been identified as the perpetrator of a despicable crime committed against an incredibly sympathetic victim, and no matter how much the judge instructed the jury about the presumption of innocence, the burden of proof, and the right not to testify, he simply had to take the stand.

So Steve took the stand and gave the jury a full accounting of his day, beginning with the errands he ran with Lori that morning and ending with their return from Green Bay later that night. He told them about pouring concrete at the salvage yard and about taking a ride on his four-wheeler with his sister in the quarry. And then he finished by credibly professing his innocence.

Denis Vogel tried to rattle him on cross, but for the most part, Steve held firm and improved his chances for an acquittal.

Next, Jim Bolgert called his client's wife to firm up the alibi. Lori Avery told the jury about their entire day—running errands in town that morning, visiting relatives at Steve's parents' in the afternoon, driving to Green Bay in the evening, and then coming back home later that night. She was a convincing, credible witness, who gave specific times and didn't try to dress things up. She gave the jury the same timeline that she gave to the police in her written statement the day after Steve was arrested, and the jury's ears especially perked up when she identified the receipt from Shopko that proved they were in Green Bay at 5:13 p.m.

Anticipating Vogel's cross-examination, Bolgert asked her if she spoke with her husband before she wrote the statement.

"No," Lori answered. "I didn't hear from Steve until a week later, on August 7, when he was allowed to make his first phone call."

"Did Steven ever tell you what to put in your statements?" Bolgert asked.

"No, he didn't even know I wrote them up."

"Did anybody tell you what to put in your statements, Lori?" Bolgert pressed.

"No, they didn't. I was there by myself when I wrote them."

Then, he asked her about one of her husband's more unusual habits. Penny Beerntsen had noticed that the assailant was wearing white underwear, an observation that wouldn't be very important in most cases since most men wear white underwear—at least they did back then. But it was highly significant in this case.

"Does Steve wear clothes when he sleeps?" Bolgert began.

"No, he doesn't," Lori replied. "Just socks sometimes, if his feet are cold."

"Was he wearing underwear when he was arrested?"

"No, he wasn't; he doesn't wear underwear."

"Does he own any underwear?"

"No, he doesn't."

After Lori Avery was finished testifying, Jim Bolgert called one witness after another to hammer home the alibi. They each repeated the same refrain: "Steve couldn't have assaulted Penny Beerntsen—he was with us at the salvage yard that day."

Marvin Mott was only there between one-thirty and two, but he saw Steve. Rose Scherer was there, too. She looked out the window when *Divorce Court* was almost over, and Steve was still outside—and so was the cement truck. Chuck Avery saw Steve take his sister Barb to the gravel pit "at three or three-thirty or so." Steve's brother-in-law saw Steve and Barb go into the gravel pit, too, though he couldn't recall what time. Lloyd Scherer helped Steve and the other guys pour concrete that day, and he remembered seeing Steve and his family leave at about ten minutes to four.

Judy Blanke was an especially effective witness for the defense. She and her husband were close friends of the Averys, and that afternoon they went to the salvage yard to cash in some aluminum cans. They arrived at about a quarter to three, Mrs. Blanke testified, and while she was helping her husband unload the aluminum cans from the trunk, she saw Steve and a couple of other guys smoothing out the cement. She even stopped to talk with them for a while before going into the house to join the ladies. She said Steve came in at the end of *Divorce Court*, and now that she thought about it, she remembered him playfully turning off the TV to get a rise out of them.

The jury seemed especially interested when Mrs. Blanke described what happened when she and her husband Bill got ready to leave. She and Bill were getting into their car when she looked over and saw Steve loading the kids into his Blazer. Bill had recently washed the car and he didn't want any dirt on it, so he let Steve pull out of the gravel driveway ahead of them and they waited for the dust to settle before pulling out.

That kind of detail is hard to make up, and Mrs. Blanke came off as an honest and credible witness for the defense.

Denis Vogel knew he was in trouble if the jury believed that Steve was still at the salvage yard when *Divorce Court* ended at three-thirty. So he had to convince the jurors that the Averys were lying and that the cement truck driver, Don Cigler, was the accurate reporter of time. His method of operation was to ask each member of the Avery clan on cross-examination if they had discussed the case amongst themselves.

Most people could handle that question by confidently responding that of course they had, "Wouldn't you?" they'd say. "He's part of our family." But the Averys aren't most people, and Vogel knew that no matter how they answered he couldn't lose. If they admitted they discussed the case, he could act like that was unusual and imply that they did so to get their stories straight. Or if they claimed they'd never discussed the case, the jury wouldn't believe them and they'd suspect they were lying about everything else, too. Either way, their credibility would be shot.

Vogel's cross-examination of Steve's mother, Delores Avery, was particularly aggressive. He took off the gloves after she foolishly denied discussing the case with her husband or with other family members.

"You mean you didn't talk to your husband about the time when all the women got together, you didn't discuss that with anybody?" Vogel asked.

"No," Mrs. Avery replied.

"You didn't get together and try to remember what time it was you got together at your house?" Vogel pressed.

"No, uh-uh, because I know we watched *Divorce Court*, us women and all, so...."

Vogel interrupted, asking, "You didn't sit down and discuss what time it was when he may have left the house that day?"

"No."

"So you and Allan haven't talked about this case at all?"

"Uh-uh, no," Mrs. Avery said unconvincingly.

"You talked about what happened on the day of the twenty-ninth amongst yourselves to try to figure out where everybody was and what everybody did, right?" Vogel insisted.

"I told you exactly what I remember."

"I know that. I'm just asking you, you have talked about it with the other people, trying to figure out what happened that day?"

Mrs. Avery stammered, "No, not about, no, I haven't."

"You haven't stood around," Vogel said, "and I'm not talking about the last couple of days, I'm talking about before the last couple of days when you've been to court—you stood around talking with the other people that have been here to just try to figure out what happened on the twenty-ninth?"

"I don't have to figure out what happened on the twenty-ninth," Mrs. Avery rallied. "I know what happened on the twenty-ninth."

"Right, but you've asked other people if they remember what happened on the twenty-ninth," Vogel persisted.

"No, I haven't."

But Vogel wasn't done.

"I'm not accusing you that because of talking to people there was any harm—I don't want you to get that impression," he lied. "I'm just asking if you talked amongst your family members about what happened on the twenty-ninth, and you said before that there were some statements that you heard, and I'm just trying to find out from you what those statements might have been, or who might have made those statements. Do you understand?"

But Mrs. Avery held firm, saying, "Oh, I don't remember nothin' like that."

"That's all," Vogel said, finally leaving the defendant's mother alone.

Delores Avery had gone toe to toe with the district attorney without flinching, so Jim Bolgert kept his redirect examination short.

"Has all your testimony today been the truth?" he asked.

"Yes, it has," Mrs. Avery answered.

"That's all I have."

Steve's sister Barb was next. Vogel tried pinning her down along the same lines he used with Delores Avery, but this time he even suggested that her brother's attorney had coached her about what to say. Barb sounded defensive in a few of her responses, but for the most part she handled herself well—especially about being coached by Bolgert.

Vogel's accusation that he coached his witness was hard to stomach for someone with Jim Bolgert's integrity, so in his redirect examination, Bolgert put that one to rest immediately.

"Did anyone tell you what to say Barb?" he asked.

"No."

"Did I?"

"You just told me to be honest and tell the truth."

"Ms. Avery, did you sit down and discuss where Steve was that day and where he might have been—what he was doing?"

"No—'cause I already knew."

"Did someone tell you to say you went down in the pit with Steve and his jeep?"

"No."

While Steve's wife, sister, and mother held their own on the stand, many of the other defense witnesses didn't fare so well. Denis Vogel's insinuation that they were lying about not discussing the case ahead of time tripped them up. Of course they discussed Steve's case. What family wouldn't talk about criminal charges filed against one of their own—especially if the charges could land the person in prison, like the charges in this case could?

But why did they lie if they didn't have to? Maybe they thought it would look bad if they admitted they talked to each other, maybe they couldn't distinguish between discussing Steve's case and hatching a plan to get him off, or maybe they were just not very sophisticated people. But whatever the reason, when the Averys tried putting the best face on the defense, they smothered it instead.

But all things considered, when Jim Bolgert rested his case, he felt pretty good about the prospects for an acquittal. He believed firmly in his client's innocence, and left nothing on the table in presenting his defense. He had treated Steve and his family with dignity and respect since the day he was appointed, which, given the severity of the charges and, to put it mildly, their colorful personalities, not every defense attorney would be capable of or inclined to do.

He had cautioned each of his witnesses to be impeccably honest when they testified. For one thing, they could be charged with perjury if they weren't. But also, no matter how inconsequential the question, if the jury sniffed even the hint of a lie in the answer, they would discard the entire defense and promptly convict.

ELEVEN

The evidence was in. The lawyers had called a total of forty-three witnesses and introduced sixty-two exhibits. Soon, Steven Avery's fate would rest where it belonged—in the hands of twelve of his peers.

Judge Hazlewood read the standard instructions before the jury retired for deliberations. Packed full of legal concepts, jury instructions have a reputation for being boring and burdensome, but my sense is that most jurors listen to them attentively and a few even find them enlightening. He emphasized the instructions that listed the "elements" of each charge that the prosecution must prove, and after covering various other legal principles, he finished with the instruction concerning the burden of proof:

Ladies and gentlemen, the defendant is not required to prove his innocence. The burden of establishing every fact necessary to constitute guilt is upon the state. Before you can return a verdict of guilty, the evidence must satisfy you beyond a reasonable doubt that the defendant is guilty. If you can reconcile the evidence upon any reasonable hypothesis consistent with the defendant's innocence, you should do so and find him not guilty.

Now, in reaching your verdict, examine the evidence with care and caution. Act with judgment, reason, and prudence.

The term "reasonable doubt" means a doubt based upon reason and common sense. It is a doubt for which a reason can be given, arising from a fair and rational consideration of the evidence or lack of evidence. It means such a doubt as would cause a person of ordinary prudence to pause or hesitate when called upon to act in the most important affairs of life.

A reasonable doubt is not a doubt which is based upon mere guesswork or speculation. A doubt which arises merely from sympathy or from fear to return a verdict of guilty is not a reasonable doubt. A reasonable doubt is not a doubt such as may be used to escape the responsibility of a decision. Now, while it is your duty to give the defendant the benefit of every reasonable doubt, you are not to search for doubt. Rather, you are to search for the truth.

The duties of counsel have been performed, and the great weight of reaching a verdict is to be thrown wholly upon you, the jurors, called to exercise this important duty. You are not to be swayed by fear, sympathy, passion, or prejudice. You are to act with judgment, reason, and prudence. I charge you now to exercise your duty faithfully.

There were other instructions, too, and perhaps a few of the jurors lost their concentration, but most of them paid close attention since a man's fate rested in their hands.

I once heard from a speaker at a prosecutors' conference that jurors are in a constant state of tension—they don't want to send an innocent man to prison, but they don't want to set a guilty one free. The prosecutor's job, said the speaker, is to "ease their pain" by presenting the case so clearly and forcefully that the defendant's guilt is unmistakable.

It's great advice for clear-cut cases, but what if it's a case like this one, where the evidence is not so overwhelming? The law doesn't say the jury *can* find the defendant not guilty if they have a reasonable doubt—it says they *must*. But do jurors really give defendants the benefit of the doubt—especially when the crime is as vicious as this one and the victim as sympathetic as Penny Beerntsen? Steven Avery was about to find out.

* * *

The jury started deliberations right after dinner, but a few hours later they asked to see one of the exhibits. The sheriff's deputies had confiscated Avery's shoes when they arrested him, and now the jury wanted to check them—probably for dried cement or particles of sand. After consulting with the lawyers, Judge Hazlewood sent Steve's not-so-sweet smelling shoes to the jury room.

The shoes contained neither cement nor sand, so the inspection didn't take long, and five minutes later—it was after midnight now—the jury made another request. This time, they wanted to see Exhibit No. 41.

Vogel and Bolgert exchanged glances as they watched the clerk check the exhibit list and wondered what the hell Exhibit No. 41 was. The clerk turned the page, and there it was. It was the note that Donald Cigler, the cement truck driver, had kept at home to keep track of his hours. Vogel had moved it into evidence on the second day of trial.

The lawyers knew it all along, and now the jurors' request for Cigler's notes confirmed it. When all the testimony was in and the exhibits admitted, when all the objections and arguments were over and the jury finally had the case, the rubber would meet the road on the timeline. Did the defendant have enough time to be in position to commit the crime. If Donald Cigler's time line was correct, he did; if not, it was impossible—or at least close enough to impossible to constitute reasonable doubt.

Close your eyes and you can almost hear Johnny Cochran making the argument: "Ladies and gentlemen," he'd practically shout to the jury, "ask yourselves this one very simple question: 'Did the defendant have the TIME to commit the CRIME?' Because if the timeline doesn't FIT, you must ACQUIT!"

Jim Bolgert anxiously awaited the jury's decision in the dimly lit, empty halls of the Manitowoc County Courthouse that night. Not only did he believe his client was innocent, but he also believed the jury would find him not guilty—the alibi was that strong. But they were taking an awfully long time, and he was becoming increasingly worried.

Was subconscious, or maybe not-so-subconscious, class bias playing a role in the deliberations? Bolgert hoped not, but when you put the Averys next to the Beerntsens ... well, you get the point. What if some of the jurors didn't really care if the prosecution met its burden of proof? "He's probably assaulted other women," they might be thinking, "and he probably assaulted Ms. Beerntsen, too. Besides, why would the police arrest him if he wasn't the assailant, and why would the prosecutor be so certain he was guilty?"

The jury retired at 1:45 a.m. without reaching a verdict, and deliberations resumed at nine the next morning. Six hours later, they finally reached a verdict.

The winter sun was already low in the sky when the jailers walked Steven Avery across the courtyard to receive his verdict. The lawyers feigned calm and put their game faces on as the jurors solemnly filed into the courtroom with their heads bowed down. Steve had been sweating it out over at the jail since ten o'clock the night before, and now he was about to learn his fate from twelve strangers that barely knew his name.

Judge Hazlewood addressed the foreman, "I see you're holding some documents in your hands," he said calmly. "Has the jury reached a verdict?"

"Yes, Your Honor."

The courtroom was silent as Judge Hazlewood leafed through the verdict forms. Then he finally announced the verdict.

"Let the record reflect—I'm not going to drag this out—the verdict of the jury with regard to the charge of first degree sexual assault: guilty. With regard to the charge of false imprisonment: guilty. With regard to the charge of attempted murder in the first degree: guilty."

It was a clean sweep for the prosecution.

✳ ✳ ✳

It's not unusual for a recently convicted offender to send a letter to the judge who presided over his trial. Maybe they're asking for a shorter sentence, maybe they're complaining about their lawyer, or maybe about the food in the jail. But rarely are they actually protesting their innocence. Steven Avery was one of the exceptions. On January 29, 1986, a month and a half after the jury had reached its verdict, he sent the following letter to Judge Hazlewood:

Dear Judge Hazlewood,

I am writing in regards to my case. I truly believe I did not get a fair trial. Why on god's green earth would I go out and hurt a woman I don't even know and when I am Happily married and my wife just got out of the Hospital with our twins the day before. Why should My Wife have to raise our children alone, and Why should my kids have to grow up with out a father, especially When I did not do this and I am an innocent man.

I pray every night to god that the guy who did this Would turn himself in as I don't have a life setting up here and I have to worry about my Wife and 5 kids out there alone With that guy Still running around out there.

I really feel sorry of Mrs. Beerntsen as I Would not want anyone to have to go through something like that. I know I have done some bad things in my past, but I started to realize it after I pulled an empty gun on Sandy Murphy that I Went about it in the Wrong Way and I started to turn my life around. I had heard that Sandy Murphy wanted to drop the charges against me but Mr. Vogel won't. Why is everybody against me, am I really that bad?

I was Wondering if you could please help me and my family as our future is in your hands. I am scared shitless as to the outcome of my case and I am also scared for my family. I am not lieing with god as my Wittness. Please help me in any way you can I would Really appreciate it.

Thank you for your time. please help me thank you Judge.

sincerely,

Steven Avery

But Judge Hazlewood was hardly in a position to reverse the jury's verdict, and on March 10, 1986, he sentenced Steven Avery to thirty-two years in the Wisconsin State Prison System—fifteen years for attempted first degree murder, fifteen years for first degree sexual assault, and two years for false imprisonment. The state owned Steve now. And since he was in the legal custody of the Wisconsin Department of Corrections they even changed his name—from now on, he was Inmate No. 018375.

Allan Avery called Judge Hazlewood on the morning after his son was sentenced. With a liberal sprinkling of garden-variety vulgarities along with a few more creative strings of expletives and repeated insertions of the f-word, Mr. Avery insisted that Steve was innocent and his conviction was a travesty of justice. In a not-so-veiled threat, he asked Judge Hazlewood to release his .30–06 rifle because, in his words, he wanted "to start making his own probable cause determinations." Here is the Judge's admirably patient and reasoned reply:

Dear Mr. Avery,

Your phone call to me on Tuesday, the 11th of March, 1986, requesting that I authorize the release of a 30–06 rifle to you is denied. My reasons are as follows:

1) The rifle is evidence in a pending case;

2) Your request—a phone call to my house at 7:30 a.m. in the morning, is not in proper form;

3) Your stated reason for requesting the gun back; that is, that you wanted to start making your own probable cause determinations, is hardly a reason to give anybody a gun, and;

4) I don't even know whether you own the gun or have any rightful claim to own it.

For the above reasons, your request for the return of the firearm is respectfully denied.

Very truly yours,

Fred H. Hazlewood

Circuit Judge

Dodge Correctional Institution is located seventy miles southwest of Manitowoc in Waupun. Its security level is one step below the state's "super-max" prison in Boscobel, but, as they say, it's impossible to get out of Dodge. Steven Avery was escorted through three sets of steel gates; each door clanged shut with a bang. It would be eighteen years before he'd walk out.

But, unlike his anonymous arrival, his departure would be anything but tame.

TWELVE

Three months after Steven Avery was sentenced, the Wisconsin State Public Defender's Office in Madison appointed attorney Jack Schairer to represent him on appeal. Schairer reviewed the entire file, and then he interviewed his client in prison. The more time he spent on the case, the more convinced he became that Steve was innocent. It was an easy call to file an appeal.

But prior to seeking relief from a higher court, Wisconsin law requires a convicted defendant to exhaust his remedies at the trial court level by filing a "motion for post-conviction relief." So on July 25, 1986, Schairer filed his motion and petitioned Judge Hazlewood to grant his client a new trial.

Schairer claimed he'd uncovered specific and material "exculpatory" evidence—evidence that tends to negate the guilt of the accused—that was not turned over to the defense. The state's failure to turn over such evidence is grounds for a new trial, and if intentional, is considered serious prosecutorial misconduct. Schairer claimed Vogel knew about the evidence and that his failure to disclose it robbed his client of a fair trial and violated his constitutional rights to due process under the law. In the interest of justice, Schairer pleaded, Steven Avery deserved a new trial.

He also filed two other motions. The first was a motion for bail pending appeal, which didn't stand a chance, and the other was for an *in camera* inspection of the prosecutor's file. He wanted Judge Hazlewood to privately review the prosecutor's entire file in chambers to determine whether any additional exculpatory evidence had been withheld.

Denis Vogel fired back with a sworn affidavit, attesting that he'd faithfully complied with the discovery statute and had turned over a complete set of the police reports and everything else the defendant was entitled to. Then suddenly, with another high-profile conviction under his belt and a promising career ahead of him, maybe even a seat on the bench, Vogel inexplicably resigned. He'd apparently landed a more lucrative position in a private law firm in Madison, so he and his wife shook the dust off their feet and promptly left town.

Governor Tony Earl tapped Assistant District Attorney Elma Anderson to fill the vacancy. Citing insufficient staff, Anderson appointed local attorney Ron Kaminski as a special prosecutor to handle the post-conviction motions in the Avery case.

Kaminski would describe years later how Tom Beerntsen appeared in his office almost daily to make sure he was up to speed. The last thing Tom wanted was for Penny to go through a second trial and have to relive the assault all over again. But Tom Beerntsen need not have worried. Although Kaminski later conceded the evidence against the defendant was awfully thin, as an advocate for the state and unaware of certain facts not yet revealed, he did an excellent job fighting Schairer's motions and the state prevailed.

"None of the evidence characterized by the defense as exculpatory, neither individually nor collectively," Judge Hazlewood wrote in his decision denying the motion, "materially affected the question of whether the defendant committed the assault." The judge also declined Jack Schairer's invitation to go fishing in the DA's file for additional exculpatory evidence, and he didn't even see the need for a formal hearing to consider the invitation. "At this point, there is no reason to believe that testimony will produce anything other than what has already been demonstrated by way of the affidavits on file," the judge wrote. "The only interest of the defense that might be served by taking additional testimony would be to have an additional crack at the prosecution witnesses."

If Steven Avery was to be granted a new trial, it wouldn't be ordered by Judge Hazlewood, at least not on the basis of what had been presented to him so far.

Having exhausted his remedies in the trial court, Jack Schairer filed a notice of appeal with the court of appeals. Once again, he argued for a retrial on the grounds the DA had failed to disclose exculpatory evidence. This time, he relied on his writing skills because oral argument is rare in the state court of appeals. To make an oral argument, you must make it to the state's supreme court. Schairer's brief was forty-nine pages long, and that didn't include the appendix.

What was this exculpatory evidence that Vogel supposedly withheld?

With the assistance of an investigator in the Wisconsin State Public

Defender's Office, Schairer had conducted a bit of his own investigation into what happened the day Penny Beerntsen was attacked over the dunes. One of the witnesses he interviewed was Kathy Sang. She and her boyfriend spent that afternoon in a small sailboat a few miles north of Neshotah Park, not far from where Penny was assaulted. They had stayed close to the shoreline, never more than a couple hundred yards away from the beach. Occasionally they even swam back to shore.

At about three-thirty that afternoon, Kathy explained, they saw a woman jogging north along the beach wearing a swimsuit. The woman turned around near a small creek that flowed into the lake and then headed back in the direction she came from, which is exactly what Penny said she did that day at exactly that time. Less than a half hour earlier, Kathy said they saw a man dressed in long pants and a black shirt walking north toward the area. He'd had a "beer belly" and his shirt was open in front with the shirttails exposed.

The private investigator showed Kathy a photograph of Steven Avery. After taking a very careful look, Kathy told him she was positive that the man in the photograph was not the man she saw on the beach that day.

Kathy also told the investigator that a sheriff's deputy had interviewed her on the day of the assault and she gave him a description of the man she saw on the beach. But Schairer had carefully reviewed everything in the file, and Kathy's statement wasn't there. In fact, the reports mentioned nothing at all about a Kathy Sang.

Schairer practically begged the court of appeals to grant his client a new trial. Kathy Sang's description of the man she saw on the beach that afternoon was evidence the defendant was entitled to know, he pleaded. It pointed to the defendant's innocence and someone else's guilt, and justice demanded that Steven Avery be granted a new trial.

Schairer bolstered his argument by noting that the state's case hinged almost entirely upon the victim's identification of the defendant. Under these circumstances, he argued, evidence that shortly before the assault, a witness saw a suspicious man who didn't match the defendant's description might very well have led to an acquittal, especially because the defense had presented powerful evidence that Avery was somewhere else at the time of the assault.

It was unbelievable! An eyewitness tells a sheriff's deputy on the first day of the investigation that she saw a man walking along the same stretch of isolated beach where Penny Beerntsen first saw her assailant. The man was wearing a black shirt and long pants—unusual attire for a walk along the beach on hot sunny day—just like Penny said he was. The description, timing, and location matched perfectly with Penny's observations, and the witness was positive it wasn't Steven Avery. Yet, the state doesn't tell the defense about the eyewitness.

Schairer's next line of attack concerned what police call a neighborhood canvass. In the days immediately following the assault, deputies from the sheriff's department conducted an extensive canvass in the neighborhood adjacent to Neshotah Park where Penny was assaulted. They went door to door with one photograph of Steven Avery and another of his Chevy Blazer and asked if anyone saw the man or the vehicle depicted in the photos on the day of the assault. Nobody had.

But the results of the neighborhood canvass, or even the fact that one was conducted, were not shared with the defense.

Given how close this case was, Schairer argued, if the jury had known about the eyewitness and neighborhood canvass they very well might have voted to acquit. In the interest of justice, he again demanded, the defendant should be granted a new trial.

Jack Schairer's final argument concerned the observations of Steve's uncle, Deputy Arland Avery, on the night his nephew was arrested. Arland had noticed cement powder on the shirt Steve had worn that day, but that fact wasn't disclosed to the defense either. The presence of cement on the defendant's shirt would have significantly bolstered his alibi, Schairer argued, and had the jury known about it, the defendant may have been acquitted.

At the end of his brief, Schairer summed up his case for a new trial:

> While the state's evidence consisted primarily of the complaining witness' identification of the defendant as her assailant, the defendant called sixteen alibi witnesses and testified categorically denying any involvement in the crime. His alibi is consistent with the story he told the sheriff at the station house right after he was arrested. However, the jurors were not told that Kathy Sang, the last person to have seen

Penny Beernsten jogging before the assault, had seen another man on the beach near the time of the assault. Nor were the jurors told the police had conducted a canvass near the crime scene showing pictures of [Steven Avery's] vehicle to people in the area, and none of them identified him. Also, they did not know that Officer Avery had seen cement on Steve's clothing at the time of his arrest.

All of this evidence is exculpatory. And regardless of whether it's characterized as evidence improperly withheld by the state, newly discovered evidence, or evidence not presented due to the failure of defense counsel's investigation, this evidence warrants the granting of a new trial.

Assistant Attorney General Tom Becker was assigned to handle the appeal on behalf of the state, and on January 6, 1987, he wrote to Jim Fitzgerald, the newly elected Manitowoc County District Attorney. Becker asked Fitzgerald to send him copies of any briefs or memorandums that his predecessor prepared in the trial court relating to the issues raised on appeal. He also sent him a copy of Jack Schairer's brief and asked him to respond. Jim Fitzgerald sent Becker a letter in reply indicating that he contacted former District Attorney Vogel, and Vogel told him that while he addressed some of the issues in the trial court, he hadn't prepared any formal briefs or memorandum.

So Becker filed a rather generic brief without any input from Vogel. Essentially, he argued that the defense hadn't proved that the state withheld exculpatory evidence so the defendant's conviction should stand.

Appellate courts rarely reverse a jury's verdict, or even negate it and grant a new trial. Otherwise, what's the point of having a jury decide? So it's not surprising that most appellate court decisions are the same as those made by NFL referees: "After further review, the play stands!" And that's what the Wisconsin Court of Appeals did with the Avery case. On August 5, 1987, they denied Steven Avery's request for a new trial.

Jack Schairer then petitioned the Wisconsin Supreme Court to review the decision, but he knew his chances were slim. The high court's jurisdiction is limited to cases that meet one or more of three statutorily defined criteria. The court can—not must, but *can*—review a lower court's decision if (1) the issue at hand is of statewide importance; (2) a decision is needed to clarify conflicting decisions among the lower courts; or (3) the interest of justice demands a review.

One and two were nonstarters in the Avery case, leaving number three. But every litigant believes his case cries out for justice and there was nothing unusually attractive about Steve's to attract the court's attention. Besides, like beauty, whether "the interest of justice demands a review," resides squarely in the eyes of the beholder, and the Justices on the Wisconsin Supreme Court are rarely attracted to an ordinary suitor.

So Jack Schairer wasn't surprised when the court promptly denied his petition. Steven Avery had come to the end of the line.

* * *

At the same time his attorney was seeking a new trial from the court of appeals, Steve and his dad were seeking a pardon from the governor. But in a heartfelt, three-page letter to Governor Tommy Thompson, Sandy Murphy, the reserve deputy's wife who Steve had accosted at gunpoint back in January 1985, strenuously objected to the request. Murphy had read an article about Avery's pardon application in the local paper, and she wanted to weigh in with her opinion. If you're familiar with the politics of Tommy Thompson—nobody's ever criticized the governor for being soft on crime—then you know that Sandy Murphy had nothing to fear. But she was understandably concerned for her own safety and for that of the public in general if Avery was released, and she wanted to register her concerns.

She recounted the terror she felt when Steve pointed the rifle at her and told her to get into his car. "Avery never said what he planned to do to me," she wrote, "but after what he did to that woman on the beach that day, I can only guess. I hope in your wisdom you can see Mr. Avery for the kind of person he is, and don't give him the chance to hurt anyone else. A person can only guess what Mr. Avery would be capable of doing if he's released."

* * *

On May 18, 1987, fourteen months into Steve's thirty-two year prison sentence, Lori Avery filed for divorce. Considering what Steve had put her through during their marriage, it's amazing she stayed with him as long as she did.

With his wife filing for divorce, and his plea for a new trial from the court of appeals and his petition for a pardon from the governor both ending in failure, Steve channeled his energy into anger.

The letters started arriving soon after the divorce papers were filed. Lori wasn't overly concerned at first—Steve was bitter about the divorce, she figured, and pretty soon he'd get over it and move on. But the letters didn't stop. In fact, they continued for the entire time he was in prison, and they got worse as time went on.

In early 1994, Steve started sending Lori sympathy cards. "May these words bring to you our most heartfelt sympathy," was the message on one of them, to which Steve added in his own scratchy handwriting. "To my Love, Forever Lori—From Your Ex-husband Forever. Do You Love me? Tell me, then I will be good! And you can be my wife," he wrote.

A few weeks later he sent the same generic sympathy card, but this time he scribbled an additional message on it that read, "I'm Sorry about your Daughter! Love forever!" The only problem was that nothing had happened to Lori's daughter.

It was after Steve's next communication that Lori started getting scared. He'd sent an open records request to the Two Rivers Police Department a few months earlier seeking any current information he could get about Lori, including her address and any vehicles she owned. At first, the police department wisely denied the request, advising him that the open records law required specificity and pointing out that his request was too broad. But then Steve limited his request, and under the erroneous impression that Wisconsin's open records law required them to honor his request, the police department sent him the records. At least they made him pay the $1.57 copying fee up front.

A few weeks later, Lori received a diagram of her home with a note in Steve's handwriting indicating, "Home $19,000." There was also a picture of a minivan of the same make and model as hers with a notation that it was tan and it was "a piece of junk." He'd received the records concerning Lori's new address and her minivan from the police department, and he must have accessed the real estate and vehicle information from the computers in the prison that were provided for the inmates.

Lori scanned the torn notebook page and came across more of her ex-husband's chicken-scratch. He'd written, "See yours Lori. Ha-Ha—You don't knew what I'm going to do when I'm out, Do you? I do knew whats going to happen. It ant good at all? I Don't care if you hurt me. I Don't care!!!"

"I hate you, you got your divorce now you will pay for it," he wrote in an undated letter mailed to Lori from prison. In another letter, he wrote, "If you don't brang up my kids I will kill you. I promis. Ha. Ha."

Later, the letters got even worse. "Hi Lori ass," began one of them. "I hate you and your family!!! I hate you motherfuckers!! Hate, hate, You made me hate. I hate this Place!! You did this to me. I will be in trouble one more time when I get out and then I will die!!!! Now I'm going to die when I get out so I don't care!"

Lori applied for a restraining order. It didn't matter that Steve was locked up. Who's to say he couldn't contact someone on the outside to rough her up, or even worse—take one of the kids? Lori occasionally felt bad about what she still considered to be her husband's wrongful conviction, but it didn't matter anymore. Prison had turned him into a monster, and she was scared out of her mind.

THIRTEEN

It's true—blood really is thicker than water. So while Lori Avery under-standably moved on with her life, Allan Avery continued to fight for his son's release. He would never give up on Steve. He was certain Steve was innocent and was determined to convince the justice system to set him free.

But Allan Avery knew the burden of proof had shifted, that no court would buy his son's claim of innocence unless, this time, the defendant proved it beyond a reasonable doubt. So in late 1992, he hired a private investigator by the name of James Stefanic to see what he could dig up. Stefanic got hold of the police reports from Jack Schairer and spent the better part of a week reviewing the file. Then he started snooping around.

First he interviewed Frank Butler, the local private investigator who worked with Schairer on Avery's first appeal. Butler told Stefanic that he'd always felt there was something that just wasn't right with the Avery case. One of the deputies saw cement dust on Steve's clothes when he was arrested, for example, but the deputy was told he'd lose his job if he signed an affidavit saying so. Also, since Steve was denied visitors and phone privileges until eight days after he was arrested, it would have been impossible for the defense witnesses to make up the alibi. Butler said he didn't know whether it had anything to do with how the case was handled, but the victim and her husband were prominent members of the community, and the sheriff knew them. Also, during the five years he worked in Manitowoc, Butler said he never saw Sheriff Kocourek personally inves-tigate another case—not once.

"There's something people know [that] they aren't saying," Butler explained. He was all set to interview Don Belz, the captain at the sheriff's department who Allan Avery called the morning after his son's arrest, but then the door slammed shut and Belz wouldn't talk.

So Stefanic called Captain Belz himself. Belz said he told Allan Avery he knew his son was innocent, but he couldn't do anything about it because the sheriff told him not to talk about the case. "Between you and I," Belz told Stefanic, "there's a damn good possibility he's innocent."

Then Stefanic interviewed Arland Avery, Steve's uncle. Arland said Steve got "a railroad job." He told Stefanic the reason he helped arrest Steve that night was because he didn't want the SWAT team storming the house. He also said he saw cement powder on Steve's shirt and told Denis Vogel about it, but Vogel never asked him about it while he was on the witness stand. Stefanic noted in his report that "the cop who saw cement dust on Steve at the time of his arrest was told that if he signed an affidavit saying so, he'd lose his job."

Arland didn't have much good to say about the officers who interviewed Penny at the hospital that night either. He said Judy Dvorak was a reserve officer at the time and she would have done anything to get on the department full time. As for Gene Kusche's composite drawing, Arland said he thought Judy Dvorak described Steve to Kusche before he even started the drawing.

Stefanic also spoke with retired Detective Leo Jadowski. Leo said he never thought Avery was guilty. He wanted to reopen the case, but the sheriff stood in the way.

He also interviewed Lori Avery. Lori told him that the sheriff's department never liked Steve because he was always in trouble. "It was a vendetta," she said. "Steve fit the description, and they hung him; he was convicted before he went to court." Lori said there was no way Steve could have committed the assault because he was with her the entire day.

Like every other investigator and attorney who worked on the case, Stefanic quickly became convinced that Steven Avery was innocent. But that wasn't enough to free him. For that, Stefanic would have to find the guy who did it, which meant some more digging.

He came up with three suspects, two from Sheboygan and one from Manitowoc. Then he called a detective friend at the Sheboygan County Sheriff's Department and asked him to check if any of them were on file, and if they were, could he run a check on the suspects to see if any of them matched the victim's description of her assailant. He explained that Avery wasn't even close to matching Penny Beerntsen's initial description of the assailant. Penny said he was five six or seven, with long sandy hair, a brown scraggly beard, and brown eyes. But Avery's only five feet tall—five foot one at most, and he has blue eyes, not brown. She'd also said the assailant was in his early thirties, but Avery was only twenty-three at the time.

The detective from Sheboygan came up empty; none of the three names fit the description. But Stefanic didn't give up. On May 22, 1993, he sent a letter to WBAY TV in Green Bay outlining the case for Steve's innocence. He included the relevant documents that proved it and concluded with, "I believe that an innocent man is in prison for a crime he did not commit."

WBAY never followed up.

FOURTEEN

The science of deoxyribonucleic acid (DNA) was just beginning to seep into the practice of law in the early 1990s. The nation's top-notch criminal defense attorneys immediately grasped its potential. They saw in DNA a great new hope for wrongfully convicted defendants who have exhausted their remedies for relief in the courts of appeal. With increasingly sophisticated methods of analysis to identify its genetic footprints, DNA gave them one more shot to prove their clients' innocence.

Attorney Steven Glynn of Milwaukee was one of those top-notch attorneys. He is widely regarded as one of the best, if not the best, criminal defense attorneys in the state of Wisconsin. As a lawyer friend of mine once put it, Steve Glynn has the whole package—he's an expert in the law, but he's also great with a jury. His intelligent appearance and gentleman's demeanor make you like him immediately, and his full mane of prematurely gray hair reassures the jury of his wisdom and professional sincerity.

Sales of junk cars must have been brisk in the mid-1990s because in October 1994, seven years after the court of appeals rejected the defendant's first appeal, Allan Avery retained Steve Glynn to represent his son. Like the attorneys before him, Glynn and his associate, Robert Henak, reviewed the entire file—the police reports, the crime lab reports, transcripts from the motion hearings and from the trial, and other miscellaneous papers common to a case file. They had their work cut out for them—the trial transcript alone was 1,029 pages long.

The lawyers were on the lookout for evidence that might contain DNA. The police had retrieved a good deal of physical evidence—hair, blood, clothing, fingernail scrapings—from both the defendant and the victim and Glynn hoped it was still around. He sent a letter to the current district attorney, Jim Fitzgerald, advising him that he'd been retained to investigate and pursue post-conviction relief on behalf of Steven Avery. He asked

Fitzgerald if the physical evidence still existed, and if it did, to make sure it wasn't destroyed.

Jim Fitzgerald had defeated Elma Anderson in a hotly contested race for district attorney in 1986. Both he and Elma had been assistant district attorneys under Denis Vogel, and although Elma was appointed by the governor after Vogel unexpectedly left town, the regular election took place six months later. Fitzgerald threw his hat in the ring, and after the recently departed but still well-connected Denis Vogel put his political weight behind him, he defeated Anderson and became the new DA.

Now it was eight years later and Fitzgerald had inherited the Avery file. He called the sheriff's department after he received Glynn's letter, and asked if they still had the physical evidence from the Avery file. None other than Chief Inspector Gene Kusche replied a few days later by memo. Gene said he checked the evidence room and there was no physical evidence from the Avery case on file.

Fitzgerald thought he better check with the clerk of courts' office—maybe the court file would at least have the physical evidence that was introduced during the trial. A week or so later, the chief deputy clerk—there's never a shortage of chief deputies in government—advised Fitzgerald by memo that she finally found the exhibits in a box in the communal vault in the courthouse basement. She explained that she hadn't taken the exhibits out of the box, but it looked like they were all there. She also noted in her memo that Gene Kusche had stopped in a few weeks earlier looking for the evidence.

Fitzgerald called Steve Glynn to tell him the evidence had been preserved in the court file, and they arranged a time for Glynn to come up to Manitowoc to view the exhibits. Glynn drove up a few days later and pored over the contents of the box. Two of the exhibits immediately caught his eye. The first was a pubic hair, possibly the assailant's, that was collected from the victim on the night of the assault. The second was biological material retrieved from underneath the victim's fingernails. Either one could contain the biological blueprint of the true assailant and prove Steven Avery's innocence once and for all.

One more thing about that box. It would be retrieved from the basement vault again ten years later, this time in connection with one of the highest profile criminal cases in Wisconsin history. Two attorneys in that case would raise Cain about lax security procedures for storing evidence in the clerk of courts office.

A few weeks later, Steve Glynn filed a post-conviction motion in the trial court seeking release of the pubic hair and the fingernail scrapings for DNA analysis. Still on the bench, Judge Hazlewood conducted the hearing a few months after that. Glynn asked the court to release the evidence so it could be tested for DNA and run through the state's new sex offender DNA data bank. The case was an extremely close one, Glynn argued, and since the day he was arrested, Steven Avery had consistently professed his innocence.

Under the law, newly discovered evidence is not a sufficient basis for granting a defendant a new trial unless the evidence creates a reasonable probability that there would be a different result on retrial. At first blush, the pubic hair and the fingernail scrapings from the court file weren't "new evidence" since they existed at the time of the original trial. But Glynn argued that they should be treated as such because the current DNA analysis employed science that did not exist in 1985, so depending upon the results of the testing, his client should be granted a new trial. All he was asking, he pressed convincingly, was to have it retested. And besides, wouldn't the public itself benefit if the test results proved his client was innocent—especially if there was a hit in the data bank and the real assailant was brought to justice?

Jim Fitzgerald argued that Glynn hadn't laid a sufficient foundation to justify retesting the evidence. But Judge Hazlewood sided with the defense and granted the motion. "It's arguably probable that the result of the testing may be beneficial and consistent with justice," he ruled, "and justice is best served by allowing a test under controlled conditions by agencies, persons, or entities with appropriate skills in this area."

The attorneys settled on a private firm in Virginia—Laboratory Corporation of America—to conduct the DNA analysis. It took a long time, but nine months later, the results were in.

The scientist who performed the analysis, Anita Lynn Matthews, compared the DNA in the pubic hair and the fingernail scrapings to known samples of DNA from Penny Beerntsen and Steven Avery. The pubic hair did not contain a sufficient amount of biological material for analysis, but the fingernail scrapings did. A portion of the specimen contained Penny

Beerntsen's DNA, but not Steve's—and both their DNA was excluded as a possible contributor to the rest. The bottom line—someone else's DNA was retrieved from underneath Penny's fingernails after the assault.

Armed with physical evidence suggesting someone other than Steven Avery committed the assault, Glynn called Judge Hazlewood's judicial assistant and scheduled a hearing on his motion. The defense would be requesting a new trial based upon newly discovered evidence under Wisconsin Statutes Section 974.06.

A few weeks later, Glynn filed a second unrelated motion. Like Jack Schairer did in Avery's first appeal ten years earlier, he alleged that the state had withheld exculpatory information. But this time, it wasn't about a mystery man on the beach or a neighborhood canvass that came up empty. This time, the allegation was more specific and it sounded like it might even have teeth.

Never accused of being overly discreet, former Detective Leo Jadowski had spilled the beans. Leo told Glynn's investigator that the sheriff's department had identified an alternate suspect from Sheboygan County early on in the investigation who matched the description of the assailant, but the prosecution never shared the information with the defense. Glynn argued that the state's conduct violated his client's right to due process under the law and entitled him to a new trial. He also wanted to ferret out the facts at an evidentiary hearing.

Jim Fitzgerald got right on it. He instructed the newly promoted Chief Inspector Gene Kusche to interview each of the detectives who worked the case back in 1985 and ask them if they ever heard about an alternative suspect from Sheboygan. Over the next several weeks, Kusche conducted a series of interviews. Although several of the detectives had retired, he managed to catch up with all of them. The settings for the interviews varied; some were at retired detectives' residences, one was at a restaurant, and another was at Leo Jadowski's pawn shop.

Kusche tape-recorded each of the interviews and forwarded the transcripts to Fitzgerald so he could prepare for the hearing. The detectives circled the wagons. "Who, me? I never heard anything about an alternative suspect from Sheboygan," was the common refrain. But years later, an independent investigation conducted by the Wisconsin Department of Justice would suggest otherwise.

On July 30, 1996, Steven Avery was back in the same courtroom where he was convicted a decade earlier. Judge Hazlewood conducted the hearing on Glynn's motion for a new trial.

Anita Lynn Matthews, the scientist from the lab in Virginia who tested the fingernail scrapings and the pubic hair, testified by phone. She explained the fundamentals of DNA science and the latest testing procedures, saying that DNA is a microscopic chemical compound found in the nucleus of every cell in our bodies. It's divided into pairs of spiraled strands called double helixes. Each cell contains about ten thousand double helixes, and each double helix contains twenty-three pairs of chromosomes, with one member of each pair coming from the mother and one from the father.

"As human beings," Matthews continued, "we share many physical traits—we all have hair and eyes and skin, for example, so we have many similarities in our DNA. But there are regions on each strand of our DNA called loci, where the number and the order of chromosomes vary from one person to another. It's these regions that scientists examine to identify the source of a particular specimen of DNA."

Then Glynn asked her how scientists test the DNA to determine who it came from.

"Police submit a questioned sample, or specimen, of biological material—blood, skin, hair, semen, saliva, that sort of thing, along with a known sample that was collected from the suspect," Matthews explained. "DNA testing is simply a comparison of the DNA patterns between the questioned sample and the known sample. If the DNA profiles are consistent with each other, then they could have originated from the same source, and we assign a statistical likelihood of that, such as 1-in-2 billion Caucasians, or 1-in-5 billion Hispanics, etcetera. On the other hand, if the DNA profiles are different from each other, then they could not have originated from the same source."

"What did you find in this case?" Glynn asked.

"In this case, there were two questioned samples—fingernail scrapings and a pubic hair—and the two known samples, one purported to be from Penny Beerntsen and the other from Steven Avery."

"Specifically, how did you analyze the pubic hair and the fingernail scrapings in this case?" Glynn asked.

"The DNA testing performed in this case involved first purifying the DNA in one-half of the evidentiary sample to remove cellular debris, resulting in a clean DNA solution. Then I used the polymerase chain reaction (PCR) technique to amplify the DNA at the specific regions, or loci, where variability is generally noted. PCR essentially copies the DNA until there is enough to analyze. Then a detection method is applied to visualize the different 'alleles,' or forms of DNA, which are present at each locus, permitting a comparison of the DNA in the evidentiary sample with that from the known samples."

Matthews explained that after isolating DNA from the preparations of the fingernail scrapings, she was able to characterize the DNA at three loci. The results of the first sample were consistent with the known sample of DNA from Penny Beerntsen. But the results of the second sample indicated a mixture of DNA from at least two individuals. And, as Matthews testified, "neither Penny Beerntsen nor Steven Avery could have contributed to the number eight allele—it had to have come from some person other than Steven Avery or Penny Beerntsen."

Jim Fitzgerald fought tooth and nail against the defendant's request for a new trial. The defendant's own expert can't say who else contributed to the DNA, he argued, only that it doesn't belong to either the defendant or to the victim. And he reminded the court that Matthews admitted on cross-examination that DNA can be transferred casually. It could have come from the victim's spouse, her children, or even the nurse who collected the fingernail scrapings at the hospital that night.

"The only new evidence the defendant really has," Fitzgerald said, "is that some of the DNA underneath the victim's fingernails came from somebody else, Judge, and that's not enough for this court to grant a new trial."

Judge Hazlewood agreed with Fitzgerald, and on September 23, 1996, he issued a written decision denying both of the defendant's motions.

While the judge agreed with Glynn that the DNA evidence was "truly newly discovered in the sense that the type of DNA testing at issue here didn't exist in a practical sense at the time of the trial," in order to warrant a new trial, the judge explained, the newly discovered evidence must create a reasonable probability that there would be a different result on retrial—and in this instance, he ruled, it didn't.

The ruling on Glynn's second motion—that the prosecution failed to disclose information about an alternate suspect from Sheboygan—was even worse for the defense. Fitzgerald had planned to call each of the detectives and former detectives that Kusche had interviewed, but Judge Hazlewood denied the motion without even granting the defendant a hearing, so the detectives didn't even have to testify.

Steve Glynn did what every good defense attorney does who loses at the trial court level but still believes in the rightness of his client's cause—he appealed. So ten years after the conviction, and five years since the initial appeal, the case of *State of Wisconsin vs. Steven A. Avery* was back in District II of the Wisconsin Court of Appeals.

As Jack Schairer did in the first appeal, Glynn began his brief by pointing out that Penny Beerntsen was the sole eyewitness against his client and the only one to identify him. Sixteen other witnesses testified that Avery was elsewhere at the time of the attack, but the jury nonetheless convicted him. Then he got to the meat of his argument.

"Given the extent of her injuries and the blood on her hands, one source of the DNA underneath the victim's fingernails was certainly the victim herself," Glynn argued. "Likewise, given her clawing at the assailant and his forcing her to stroke his penis with her right hand while grabbing that hand with his own, another source was almost as certainly the assailant. While the DNA results themselves could not show whether there were only two sources, the most likely conclusion on the facts in this record is that there were only two—the victim and her assailant."

Glynn also addressed the state's argument that the DNA could have come from someone other than the perpetrator. "It was the perpetrator whom the victim clawed at with such force as to break her own fingernails, and it was the perpetrator who forced her to stroke his penis with her right hand," he wrote. "The state's assertion that the DNA could have originated from some sort of casual contact with someone else is wholly speculative on this record."

Then he addressed the trial court's denial of his second motion, his request for a new trial based upon the state's failure to disclose that they'd had an alternative suspect in Sheboygan. He argued that Judge Hazlewood erred when he summarily denied the motion without permitting him to call the detectives who investigated the case and question them on the record.

"Evidence that the sheriff's department had identified an alternate suspect in the next county who matched the description of the perpetrator is material and exculpatory," he began. "This was an extremely close case, and the withheld information goes directly to the sole contested issue at trial—that of identification. There was a strong case on Mr. Avery's side in terms of alibi, and no physical evidence tied him to the crime. Under these circumstances, evidence that someone else from a nearby county who resembled the assailant was suspected by the police creates a reasonable probability of a different result on retrial."

But on September 3, 1997, the court of appeals sided with the state and affirmed the lower court's decision. Glynn filed a petition for review with the Wisconsin Supreme Court a few weeks later, but the petition was promptly denied. For the second time in the eleven years since he was convicted, Steven Avery came up short in his quest for a new trial.

Steve Glynn was disappointed with the court's decision, but he wasn't really surprised since he knew that the cards are stacked heavily against defendants when their cases go up on appeal. Avery, on the other hand, was more than just disappointed—he was devastated. He'd spent the last eleven years of his life in prison for a crime he swore he didn't commit, years he should have spent on the outside with Lori and the kids and the rest of the Avery clan. Instead, he and Lori were divorced and he was estranged from his children. The state had taken it all away.

PART II

FIFTEEN

Parochialism. Whether we're a big city dweller from Chicago, New York, or Los Angeles, or a small town farmer from the nation's heartland, it's a formidable part of each of our DNA. Growing up in the first ring of suburbs outside Milwaukee, I was hardly immune from the affliction, referring along with my peers to anywhere more than fifty miles north of Milwaukee as *Up North*. At only seventy-five miles due north on the interstate, Manitowoc wasn't *Way up North*, a term reserved for the northern third of the state where clear lakes and well-to-do tourists, not agriculture, reign supreme. But it was solidly within the *Up North* category. In fact, to the majority of Milwaukeeans, it might as well be north of the Arctic Circle.

So when my wife, Jody, and I moved to Manitowoc in the fall of 1991, I had barely even heard of the place, much less the name, Steven Avery. I started my career as a prosecutor in suburban Milwaukee, but a few years after we were married we decided to move closer to Jody's parents. So we kept our eyes open for an assistant district attorney position in the central part of the state. Before we knew it, two counties posted openings—one in Calumet County and the other in Manitowoc. I must have fooled the interviewers pretty well because both counties offered me the job. It was good news, but it also meant we had to choose. So we spent a weekend checking out our prospects.

One county west of Manitowoc County, Calumet County has its own kind of charm, but we fell in love with Manitowoc almost immediately. With a healthy respect for its past, the city rightly boasts of its shipbuilding heritage and is officially designated the Maritime Capitol of Wisconsin, though sixty miles to the north Sturgeon Bay still fights for the title. Visit the Wisconsin Maritime Museum and you can tour the USS *Cobia*, an authentic World War II submarine that's docked in the river. Among other things, you'll learn that twenty-eight of the 211 U.S. subs built during WWII were built right here in Manitowoc. Sadly though, the city's shipbuilding industry has been in serious decline for decades. The largest and most storied of the old firms, the Manitowoc Company, no longer even builds ships here. All that remains is Burger Boat, which was founded in 1863 and sells one-hundred-fifty-foot luxury yachts to Arab sheiks and NBA basketball players. But with the recent jolt to the nation's economy, now even Burger Boat is struggling.

During our weekend tour, we walked along the main street in the historic and touristy downtown, and then we came upon the courthouse at the intersection of Eighth and Washington. We looked up at the century-old stately stone building capped with a dome, and then we walked inside.

Listed on the prestigious National Register of Historic Places, the Manitowoc County Courthouse is just one of Wisconsin's many well-preserved historic county courthouses. When local citizens built it at the turn of the century—the one before the last turn that is—the city's shipbuilding industry was in its heyday and the county coffers must have been flush with dough. Using materials like dolomite limestone and Italian marble, construction began in 1902 and was completed four years later.

Classical architecture inspires the Manitowoc County Courthouse. Its beauty comes from its integrity, its balance, its order. Indeed, Lady Justice herself couldn't have designed a more gorgeous courthouse. Huge slabs of purple sandstone anchor the foundation on the outside. And three stories higher, the symmetrical main structure gives way to a now-oxidized copper abutment that supports a towering dome. The dome used to be made of glass, but now it consists of plain sheets of dull gray steel. Solid pillars, six to a floor, support a gigantic atrium inside, where marble stairs worn smooth by a century of climbing litigants carry visitors from one floor to the next under the light of a massive chandelier hanging precisely halfway from the top of the dome. People who work there have grown accustomed to its beauty, but if you gaze up you'll see four murals depicting classical images of the four cardinal virtues spaced across the curvature of the dome.

For fifty years, natural light filtered in through the glass dome during the day and artificial light shined forth at night, displacing the darkness like light from a cathedral. The glass, like the parties caught up in the stress and uncertainty of litigating the disputes inside, was fragile. So when a hailstorm swept through the city on June 28, 1950, the glass shattered. Construction workers did their best to restore the dome by replacing the glass with steel, but eventually even steel corrodes, and after a few decades the courthouse dome became unsightly.

But it wasn't the charm of the city or the beauty of its historic courthouse that inspired us to settle here. It was Lake Michigan. Driving north along Lake Michigan's shoreline between Manitowoc and Two Rivers, Jody gazed out the window while I snuck an occasional view from behind the wheel. The lake curves gracefully here, the vast, endless waters drawing you in. They say every lake has its own personality. Lake Michigan has several. Unruffled and undisturbed one day, it can turn wildly impulsive and agitated the next. And, like every lake, it's mostly the weather that determines the Great Lake's demeanor. If it's a clear summer day on land, then the lake looks warm and inviting, too, turning deep blue or even tropical green at times. But if the weather turns ugly, if the sky is gray and foreboding, then the lake turns ugly, too, and you can barely discern the horizon.

But the lake was neither calm nor foreboding when Jody and I drove north toward Two Rivers that day. With fog hugging the shoreline, it was full of mystery instead. It's rare to see an iron ore ship along the western shore of Lake Michigan—they generally stick to the middle—but there one was, shrouded in fog and seemingly suspended above the surface of the water. It was a monstrous iron ore ship; a ghost ship appearing out of nowhere, motionless and timeless in the choppy waters just a half mile offshore. I learned later that the brisk northwesterly wind is why the giant ship was hugging the shore that day—it was seeking shelter from the wind-driven swells. But regardless of why it was there, the ship's mysterious appearance, its romance, explains a good part of why we chose to make Manitowoc our home.

SIXTEEN

Becoming a lawyer wasn't something I aspired to when I was growing up. Like a lot of attorneys, I went to law school by default. But something strange happened a few years after moving to Manitowoc. I came to enjoy my reluctantly chosen profession. Shy and reserved by nature, to be an effective prosecutor I couldn't be either. As a prosecutor, I had to take control of the tempo, hustle the ball up the court—you name the sports metaphor—but being shy and reserved wouldn't cut it in a courtroom.

Also, I was dealing with real people with real problems. Fighting over which multibillion dollar advertising company infringed upon another's trademark, or schmoozing with well-heeled corporate clients while climbing over my peers, isn't my shtick; I'd fall flat on my face if I tried. But guiding a devastated rape victim through the trauma of a jury trial or encouraging a small-time offender to turn his life around is something I could sink my teeth into. And as a bonus, I could even try to do what I thought was right.

By the time I started working here, Steven Avery had already spent six years in prison, and many years passed before I even heard his name. Nevertheless, I did get to know most of the players involved in his arrest and conviction, many of whom gradually moved on. Sheriff Tom Kocourek retired after a distinguished career in public service and Chief Inspector Gene Kusche soon followed.

Meanwhile, three years after the court of appeals rejected his second plea for a new trial, Steven Avery continued to rot in prison. But his dad persevered and encouraged Steve to apply for legal assistance with the Wisconsin Innocence Project, one of several clinical programs at the University of Wisconsin's law school in Madison.

A dozen or so students at the Wisconsin Innocence Project, under the direction of their professors, investigate claims filed by state prisoners asserting they were wrongly convicted. Like similar programs throughout the country, much of the Wisconsin Innocence Project's work in recent years has focused on DNA.

The clinic receives several hundred applications a year from inmates claiming they were wrongly convicted. Cases are screened out based upon a careful review of the evidence, including the likelihood of actual innocence and the availability of untested physical evidence that, given advancements in DNA technology, could now be analyzed. Among the cases the Wisconsin Innocence Project accepted in 2001 was Steven Avery's.

In 1996, when Steve Glynn convinced the court to permit DNA analysis of biological material retrieved from Penny Beerntsen's fingernail scrapings, DNA science was still in its infancy and its forensic value was extremely limited. But advances in technology during the late nineties and the first years of the new century allowed scientists to examine ever smaller units of biological material for DNA. The improved testing helped police and prosecutors solve crimes and secure convictions more readily, but it also gave those who claimed they were innocent a new avenue for appeal. The faculty and students at the Wisconsin Innocence Project hoped to use the new technology to uncover hard proof that Steven Avery was innocent.

In the spring of 2001, two of those students wrote a letter to Manitowoc County District Attorney Jim Fitzgerald and asked if he would stipulate to retesting the physical evidence for DNA. Fitzgerald told the students his recollection was that there was physical evidence that directly tied Steven Avery to the crime, so why should the case be reopened? He suggested that they review the 1,029-page trial transcript and then direct him to the portions that referred to physical evidence so he could make a decision.

The students reviewed the transcript and then sent him the following letter:

Dear Mr. Fitzgerald,

We have reviewed the trial transcripts as you requested. Enclosed please find those parts of the state's case which address the issue of microscopic hair evidence.

The hair found "consistent" by Ms. Culhane (from the Wisconsin State Crime Lab) was the only physical evidence tying Mr. Avery to the victim in this matter. Testimony by Ms. Culhane about that hair consisted of approximately twenty-five pages. Testimony by three other witnesses was offered solely for the purposes of establishing a chain of custody and/or emphasizing the importance of the "consistency" testimony by Ms. Culhane.

Please let us know what else, if anything, we can provide for you.

The case languished for months without a response from Fitzgerald, and the law students eventually concluded he wasn't going to stipulate. So under the direction of Professor Keith Findley, one of the co-directors of the Wisconsin Innocence Project, they filed a motion for post-conviction DNA testing and scheduled it for a hearing in front of Judge Hazlewood.

On March 22, 2002, almost a year after the Innocence Project first contacted Jim Fitzgerald, Steven Avery was back in court for another hearing. Steve was in good spirits, grateful to be out of prison if only for a day and full of hope that he'd be given another chance to prove his innocence.

Keith Findley argued the case for the defense, and Fitzgerald objected on behalf of the state. At the end of the hearing, Judge Hazlewood said he wanted to take some time to review his notes—he'd make a decision from the bench in a few weeks. Twelve days later, with the defendant appearing by phone from prison this time, the judge granted the motion. He asked the attorneys to see if they could reach a stipulation concerning which pieces of evidence should be tested for DNA and how to ensure their safekeeping during transport.

The parties filed a stipulation a few weeks later enumerating the items they agreed to have tested. Included in the list were thirteen hairs that were recovered from Penny Beerntsen on the night of the assault. Judge Hazlewood signed an order directing the clerk to seal the evidence and release it to a deputy sheriff for transport to the state crime lab. The order included a provision that if there was a sufficient DNA profile for comparison, the crime lab was to return any remaining evidence to the clerk of courts, where it would be preserved. If there wasn't a sufficient sample, the crime lab was to contact the court and await further instructions.

But then there was a problem. The stickers identifying the exhibits had fallen off, presumably because the glue had dried out. A month later, two new students from the Wisconsin Innocence Project wrote to Steve to explain the holdup.

"We have spoken with the district attorney regarding the evidence you would like retested," they wrote. "As you may know, the labels have fallen off the exhibits, and it has now become necessary to arrange a time with the DA to relabel the evidence. Hopefully, once the pertinent evidence has been identified, we will be able to get the DNA testing process under way shortly thereafter."

With a fresh pair of law students handling his case, and after more than a year of trying to get a few damned hairs retested, the evidence in the court file couldn't even be identified. Steve was disgusted. And he wasn't the only one. Penny Beerntsen was becoming increasingly frustrated by the delay too. She had tried repeatedly to find out the status of the retesting of the physical evidence, but Jim Fitzgerald never returned her calls.

It took four more months to clear up the sticker problem, and it wasn't until September 16, 2002, six days after Jim Fitzgerald lost his bid for re-election, that he presented the court with an amended order to transport the evidence to the crime lab.

The scientists at the Wisconsin State Crime Lab analyze all manner of physical evidence—guns, drugs, fibers, fingerprints, blood, hair, semen, saliva, handwriting exemplars, and a whole lot more. Every day, police agencies and district attorneys across the state bombard the crime lab with requests to test physical evidence—especially for DNA.

But DNA analysis is painstaking work that takes time. The result is an ever-growing backlog that has become a hot button political issue in recent state attorney general elections. Add that pending trial cases receive priority over cases on appeal, and it's not surprising that it took almost a year for the crime lab to analyze the resubmitted evidence in the Avery case for DNA.

But now the results were in. Eighteen years earlier, on a warm summer night in July 1985, a nurse at Memorial Hospital retrieved thirteen loose pubic hairs from Penny Beerntsen's body, any of which could have been left behind by the man who assaulted her. The nurse placed them in a "sex crimes kit" and handed the kit to Deputy Dvorak, who transported the evidence to the crime lab, where serologist Sherry Culhane examined the hairs, doing her level best with the science and technology available at the time.

Still working at the crime lab eighteen years later, Culhane examined the hairs again, this time looking for DNA. She observed detectable amounts of

DNA on only two of the thirteen hairs. She compared the DNA profiles of the two hairs with known samples of DNA from Penny Beerntsen and Steven Avery. The DNA from one of the hairs matched Penny Beerntsen. But the DNA from the other hair—the final hope for Steven Avery—matched neither.

Culhane ran the DNA profile of the hair against the state and federal DNA databases and waited. She received a hit. The DNA profile on the final hair matched Wisconsin State Prison Inmate No. 167930, a convicted sex offender by the name of Gregory A. Allen, who was currently serving a sixty-year prison sentence for a brutal rape that he committed ten years after he assaulted Penny Beerntsen.

Three highly skilled defense attorneys had spent enormous amounts of energy and untold hours to prove Steven Avery was innocent, but after eighteen years, their efforts proved impotent. In the end, what freed Steven Avery wasn't the law. What freed him was an infinitesimally small amount of a chemical compound inside the nucleus of the cells in one pubic hair that was recovered by a nurse on the night of the assault.

Thank God for DNA.

SEVENTEEN

District attorney Mark Rohrer had been in office for less than six months when the Avery case exploded on the morning of September 3, 2003. Rohrer succeeded Jim Fitzgerald by a circuitous route. In the summer of 2002, for what I thought then and still believe were legitimate reasons, I decided to run for DA. There hadn't been a contested election for the district attorney in Manitowoc County since 1986, when Jim won a close election against Elma Anderson after the recently departed but still influential Denis Vogel threw him his support. Jody and I ran a positive but aggressive campaign, and with lots of help from family and friends, we won. But I'd worked myself to exhaustion, and when I began feeling symptoms similar to what I felt at the onset of a serious depression I'd struggled through years earlier, I decided not to take the office we'd fought so hard for. Governor Jim Doyle appointed my campaign manager, Mark Rohrer, to serve as the district attorney, and when the depression I had feared didn't materialize, I stayed on as an assistant district attorney.

In the short time Mark had been in office, we had already dealt with a couple of drunk-driving fatalities and a first degree intentional homicide when the Avery case hit the proverbial fan. He was also feeling the stress from taking over an office that had been neglected for years. With all that on his plate, he needed help or sometimes just a good ear, and since I was a trusted friend and a prosecutor with fifteen years' experience under my belt, I was often that ear.

On the morning of September 3, all three courtrooms were packed with plea dates, pretrial conferences, and preliminary examinations. Mark hurriedly approached me as I was walking out of Branch 3 and said something about the DNA test results being in on an eighteen-year-old sexual assault case. Could I join him in his office? The crime lab had called, and he had the analyst on the phone.

So when I walked into Mark's office, Sherry Culhane was on speakerphone. She was calling about the Steven Avery case. She'd completed the DNA analysis and suggested we have a seat before she told us the news. The DNA profile from one of the questioned hairs recovered from the victim matched a convicted sex offender serving time for a first-degree sexual assault in Green Bay. His name was Gregory Allen. Sherry explained that the statistical likelihood that it was not Allen's hair was 1-in-251 billion in the Caucasian population, 1-in-162 billion in the African-American population, 1-in-1 trillion in the Southeast Hispanic population, and 1-in-49 trillion in the Southwest Hispanic population. Allen is Caucasian, and although Sherry didn't use the word "match," for all practical purposes, we could treat it as Gregory Allen's hair.

Mark and I looked at each other in disbelief. Neither of us had ever heard of Gregory Allen. In fact, we knew very little about the Avery case itself, other than that it involved the brutal assault of a prominent local woman along the beach on Lake Michigan. Mark was still an undergraduate when Avery was convicted, and by the time Jody and I moved here, Avery had already spent six years in prison. Jim Fitzgerald hadn't relayed any of the issues or facts involved in the Avery case after the election, and he said nothing about a DNA analysis being done on a pubic hair that might soon prove consequential.

The Avery "file" consisted of hundreds of documents packed inside expandable file folders in three separate boxes that were still in Jim Fitzgerald's corner office, the office now occupied by Mark. I started skimming through the file while we were on the phone, and I came across some police reports and an attached criminal complaint that didn't belong in the file. What caught my attention was the name of the defendant—Gregory Allen. It was the same name that Sherry Culhane just told us was the real assailant. That's kind of strange, I thought.

Then I skimmed the criminal complaint. On August 2, 1983—almost two years to the day before Penny Beerntsen was attacked—Gregory Allen was charged with exposing himself and lunging at a woman who was walking her dog along the same isolated stretch of beach where Penny was assaulted two summers later. I flipped to the signature line on the last page to see who prosecuted the case against Allen. It was Denis Vogel. "Holy shit," I said out loud.

Sherry Culhane had given Gregory Allen's identifying information to Mark so we could run a record check on CCAP, the Wisconsin Circuit Court's website. Mark still had Allen's information up on the screen, so I asked for his full name and date of birth just to make sure. "It's Gregory A. Allen, DOB 01/17/54," Mark said. I compared it with the middle initial and date of birth of the Gregory Allen named in the criminal complaint that I'd found in the Avery file—it was the same guy. And then a sinking, sickening feeling that would return with varying degrees of intensity over the next several weeks came over me.

After Sherry hung up, Mark and I delved further into Gregory Allen's past. CCAP revealed that by the time he assaulted Penny Beerntsen in 1985, Allen had already chalked up a considerable record. And worse, because he wasn't arrested for and charged with assaulting Penny, Allen had the opportunity to commit other crimes. On June 27, 1995, ten years after he avoided prosecution for assaulting Penny Beerntsen, Allen broke into a residence on the north side of Green Bay and raped the woman inside while the woman's daughter lay sleeping in a room nearby. He was convicted of kidnapping, burglary, and second degree sexual assault "while possessing a bulletproof garment," and the presiding judge sent him away for sixty years.

The records also revealed that while he was in custody awaiting trial for the Green Bay assault, authorities in South Carolina issued a fugitive complaint asking the state of Wisconsin to return him to South Carolina once the prosecution was complete. He was wanted on "suspicion of murder" for a crime that occurred in the 1970s. That complaint was later dismissed, but regardless, Allen was one scary dude.

Mark and I gathered our thoughts and started "thinking like a lawyer," as the saying goes. By nature, lawyers are creatures of caution. It's our job to look ahead and imagine every possible way something might go wrong, and then make sure it doesn't. We take nothing for granted, knowing that if we miss anything, the consequences could be dire, and we double-check everything.

If Steven Avery was innocent, we had to get him released. That much was obvious. But before taking such a momentous step, we had to be certain that the crime lab's finding meant what it seemed to mean. The DNA results appeared to show that Gregory Allen was the assailant, not Steven

Avery, but you never know. After all, a jury had found Avery guilty and the court of appeals had twice upheld his conviction. Before undoing all that on the strength of microscopic evidence on one pubic hair, we had to be sure.

So we split the file in half. Mark focused on the physical evidence by reviewing the police and crime lab reports, and I read the trial transcript to see what other evidence the state had presented at trial. The idea was to see how the DNA results on the hair squared with the rest of the evidence, and who knows—maybe the reports would suggest some other physical evidence that could be tested for DNA.

Mark soon discovered that Denis Vogel had presented precious little physical evidence at trial, and what he did present was of questionable scientific validity and almost no probative value for the jury—in fact, it was junk. Vogel tried to link Avery to the crime, literally by a hair—though it might just as well have been a thread, when he employed the "science" of hair examination to suggest that a hair recovered from Avery's shirt was that of the victim. Even though she'd been called by the prosecution, Sherry Culhane had taken pains to spell out the limited usefulness of hair examination.

"Is it possible to prove identification by hair analysis?" defense attorney Jim Bolgert had asked.

"No," Culhane candidly replied.

"Is the hair of many people consistent with each other?"

"Yes."

"Can you give an opinion as to the probability whether the two hairs are from the same source?"

"No."

"All you can say is that it's not impossible that they're from the same source, isn't that correct?"

"That's right."

It's not the job of the scientists at the crime lab to win convictions for the state, and when Sherry Culhane worked on the Avery case in 1985, she did just what she should have: She used the tools of science available at the time to objectively analyze the physical evidence, and then she testified truthfully about the results. When she told the jury that the hair found on Avery's shirt was consistent with the hair of the victim, "consistency" meant something less than 90 percent certain. So it isn't surprising that in the years following Avery's trial, hair examination lost whatever meager standing it previously held in the scientific community, and even before the advent of DNA testing, most courts throughout the nation ruled it inadmissible.

Eighteen years later, still working at the crime lab, Culhane remained the analyst assigned to the Avery case, and it was she who isolated the DNA on the pubic hair that set Avery free. But this time the odds that the hair didn't belong to Steven Avery weren't 1-in-10, they were 1 in 251 billion.

Having satisfied himself that Vogel's hair evidence was bogus, Mark shifted gears. He kept his eyes open for any other physical evidence that the prosecution hadn't used at trial that might point to Avery's involvement despite the new DNA finding. There wasn't any. Then he meticulously reviewed the file to confirm that the pubic hair containing Allen's DNA was linked by an ironclad chain of custody all the way back to 1985. It was.

Meanwhile, I started reviewing the trial transcript—all 1,029 pages, but I decided to take it home to finish it. I knew it was going to be a long night, and I'd much rather spend it at home with Jody and the kids than in the modestly furnished gray surroundings of my government office.

I've prosecuted my fair share of sex assaults over the years, but I was struck by the brutality of this one, by the way the assailant shook the victim so violently that her head slammed into the ground and by how she crawled toward the water for help after he left, sitting there naked on the beach, dazed, and staring at her blood-soaked hands. I was impressed by the strength of her character, both in withstanding the assault and in recounting it to the jury six months later.

I was also surprised by how conspicuously the DA appealed to the jury's emotions. A trial is supposed to be about getting at the truth, at least for the prosecutor, and since it's through the mind and not the heart that the truth is generally found, prosecutors are supposed to use emotion sparingly. In fact, before deliberations, jurors are specifically instructed not to be swayed by sympathy or passion in reaching their verdict but to be guided by reason and judgment instead.

Apparently, Denis Vogel didn't subscribe to that view of prosecution. Having the victim and her husband re-enact the crime in front of the jury wasn't just bad taste, it was disingenuous overkill. And the crime-scene re-enactment with the victim up to her knees in the water while a Coast Guard chopper snapped a few photographs from the sky was ridiculous. These dramatic courtroom stunts shed no light whatsoever on the question at hand. The issue wasn't whether the assault occurred, or even how it was accomplished—it was whether Steven Avery was the assailant.

I became increasingly confident as I read the transcript that the DNA results meant exactly what they appeared to mean: Steven Avery was innocent. My focus shifted to how the sheriff and the DA could have been so certain that Avery was the perpetrator. And I didn't like what I found.

"What's with the greasy hands?" I almost said out loud. Avery's wife and his mother both testified that his hands were permanently greasy because he worked on cars every day, and it was impossible to get them clean. The clerk at the Shopko in Green Bay even noticed how greasy his hands were when he and his wife went through the checkout line.

The Avery boys worked on cars all the time and their hands were perpetually greasy. Every cop in the county knew it. And I'm sure Dvorak and Kocourek knew it, too.

But when Deputy Dvorak and Sheriff Kocourek asked Penny Beerntsen at the hospital if the assailant's hands were greasy, she was adamant. "No," she said. "The man's hands weren't greasy, they were clean." Her answer was the same a few days later when Dvorak reinterviewed her at home. "The assailant's hands weren't greasy," she repeated, "as a matter of fact, the man smelled clean."

I looked up from the transcript. Whoever attacked Penny Beerntsen didn't have greasy hands and apparently Steven Avery always had greasy hands. "Shouldn't they have paused and considered that maybe it wasn't adding up before they went out and arrested him?" I thought. "And shouldn't the jury have paused before they found him guilty?"

I kept reading. When I got to Gene Kusche's testimony, I was surprised with his meager qualifications as a police artist. He attended a course on "rapid visual perception" at the FBI Academy in Quantico, Virginia, just six months before the trial. The course was designed to train cops to teach bank tellers and others in positions likely to witness crimes to better observe facial characteristics, so they could accurately describe offenders to the police. It included a two-hour class described by Kusche as "an introduction" to drawing composite sketches. That introductory course was the only training Kusche ever received for the difficult art of drawing composite sketches, and as it turned out, the sketch in this case was the only one he ever completed that was introduced at trial.

Something else about the composite sketch didn't sound right. During cross-examination, Kusche conceded that it's not standard procedure to have a photo of a potential suspect before preparing a composite drawing. But Sheriff Kocourek had the jail bring Avery's mug shot to the hospital more than an hour before Kusche started working on the sketch—the sketch that ended up looking exactly like Avery's mug shot. The reason they had one in this case, Kusche said, was because they already "had some idea who it might be." He also admitted that someone mentioned Avery's name before he started working on the sketch, but he claimed he didn't know who Avery was, even though he'd worked with Steven Avery's uncle for years. Also, several deputies were told more than two hours before Kusche finished the sketch to get ready to pick up Avery.

Gene Kusche is no longer with us, but when he was, he was a joy to be around. I remember how he'd greet me in Russian—"Mikhail!" he'd say in his booming voice, and then continue with some well-worn Russian phrase that he thought sounded impressive. But that night I wondered how he drew such a perfect likeness of Steven Avery, one that looked exactly like Steve's mug shot, and as I kept plowing through the transcript, my suspicions grew.

Penny Beerntsen initially told Deputy Dvorak that her assailant had brown eyes, but after she picked out the blue-eyed Steven Avery from the photo array, she said, "I was mistaken, his eyes are blue."

And then there was the creepy telephone call that she received a few days after the assault. I'd seen it before—fixated on the woman he assaulted, the assailant calls her a few days later to extend the nightmare and victimize her all over again. Or sometimes the call is to intimidate her so she won't cooperate with the police. It sounded to me like that kind of call, but it couldn't have been Avery—he was locked up in jail with strict orders from the sheriff forbidding any calls or visits.

My astonishment only grew when I got to Jim Bolgert's presentation of the defense. Not only was the state's evidence flimsy, but the defendant's alibi was incredibly strong. Even though Avery and his wife hadn't spoken since his arrest, they gave the investigators the same detailed account of their day. So did his mom and dad. In fact, there were sixteen witnesses who testified that Avery couldn't have done it—he was with them at the salvage yard that day. Five of them claimed they saw him after *Divorce Court* ended at three-thirty, just twenty minutes before Penny Beerntsen was attacked ten miles away at Neshotah Park. The defense also presented a receipt from Shopko that established Avery was in Green Bay at 5:13 p.m., which virtually proved he didn't commit the assault. "How the hell did this happen?" I thought to myself. "Why did the prosecution go through with it, and how did the jury vote to convict?"

But at the same time, I couldn't help but be impressed with Denis Vogel's trial skills—how he used the brutality of the assault to engender sympathy for the victim and disgust for whoever assaulted her.

It was after midnight when I went to bed that night, but the thousand-plus pages of trial testimony were swirling around in my head and I couldn't fall asleep. When you try a case, you live and breathe it, and after a while you come to know the truth. I hadn't tried the case but I felt like I had, and I couldn't imagine how Denis Vogel could have thought Avery was guilty. Unless there was something Mark found out in his review of the physical evidence, there was no doubt that Avery had been wrongfully convicted, and tomorrow morning we'd begin the process of cutting him loose. I hoped that would be the end of it. But I knew it wouldn't be.

✳   ✳   ✳

Mark and I compared notes first thing the following morning. We were both satisfied that Avery was innocent, at least of this particular crime, and we'd have to release him. But Mark suggested that we check a few other things first. He would call Sherry Culhane and ask her to run a second DNA test just to make sure, and I'd call Keith Findley at the Wisconsin Innocence Project to discuss a time frame for Avery's release.

The crime lab had also informed Keith about the DNA test results by the time I called him, and he'd already told Steven Avery the good news. He was anxious for his client's release, but he understood our need for caution. I think he also appreciated the non-adversarial way that Mark and I were handling the case, not fighting him every step of the way when his only goal was to retest the evidence with new technology to make certain there had not been a mistake. Of course his client was anxious to be released, he'd been in prison for eighteen years for a crime he didn't commit, but Keith said he would tell Steve they had to wait until the DNA results were confirmed, which shouldn't be more than a week.

Keith also agreed to put a muzzle on his client and his family until the new DNA test confirmed his innocence. We all knew there'd be a media frenzy as soon as word of Steve's exoneration got out, and everyone wanted to have their ducks in a row before the madness began.

Mark wanted to check one other thing just to make sure. We needed to confirm that Gregory Allen wasn't in jail or prison somewhere on the day Penny Beerntsen was assaulted. So we called the Department of Corrections. Allen had served a stint in prison on a burglary conviction a few years earlier, but on the day Penny was assaulted, he was roaming the streets. Or more accurately, he was prowling the sands.

✻ ✻ ✻

Penny Beerntsen was about to learn that the man she believed assaulted her, the man who spent the last eighteen years in prison on the strength of her identification, was innocent. It wasn't going to be easy for her. In fact, it would be miserable.

I had met Penny before, so it made sense that I'd be the one to call her with the news. A year earlier she told me she had repeatedly tried reaching Jim Fitzgerald and shared with me her frustration that he wasn't returning her calls. She knew the court had ordered the hairs retested, but that was four months earlier, and since then she'd been left in the dark. This was around the same time it was discovered that the stickers had apparently fallen off the exhibits.

Someone told me that Janine Geske had called our office several months earlier inquiring about the status of the Avery case. Janine had previously served as a Wisconsin Supreme Court Justice, but had decided several years earlier not to seek re-election and was now teaching at the law school at Marquette University in Milwaukee. Janine met Penny through their work in the Restorative Justice Program in the prison system, and she had been helping Penny navigate the legal and emotional ups and downs of the Avery case. Mostly, though, Penny and Janine were good friends, and I thought she'd have some ideas about how best to break the news.

So I called Janine and told her about the DNA test results. Like all of us, she was shocked by the news. She said Penny would be devastated, that she'd blame herself and would be sickened that an innocent man spent eighteen years in prison. Janine was especially concerned about Gregory Allen and the possibility that he was in attendance at one of the restorative justice classes that Penny helped facilitate in prison. So she asked if I could check which prisons Gregory Allen was incarcerated in during the preceding six years. If we could establish that he hadn't attended one of their presentations, she could at least put that fear out of Penny's mind. Janine also asked if I could get hold of a mug shot of Gregory Allen, the closer to the date of the assault, the better. Penny would want to see what her real assailant looked like. She would want to see his face.

As our conversation progressed and I learned how close Janine was to Penny, I asked if it would be better if she told Penny about Avery's innocence rather than me. I knew Penny would eventually want to speak with someone in our office and I was more than happy to do so, but given their friendship, it might make more sense for her to break the news. I think Janine was thinking the same thing, and she promptly agreed. She told me she'd think about how best to tell Penny, and she'd call me back to let me know how it went.

Janine called me back the next day. She had tried calling Penny, but she and Tom were out of town for the weekend, so she left an innocuous message asking Penny to call her when she returned. Her plan was to drive up to Manitowoc Sunday night to tell her in person. We couldn't keep the story under wraps much longer, though, so she'd have to get Penny out of town before the media picked up the story. Janine would be her spokesperson.

* * *

Mark and I spent the next day tracking down the information that Janine Geske had requested. First on the list was finding out whether Allen could have been present during one of Penny and Janine's restorative justice classes. Tracing where Allen was housed wouldn't be easy. With the help of the Republican-dominated state legislature, Governor Tommy Thompson had spearheaded all sorts of tough-on-crime legislation during the 1990s, and with a steady stream of new offenders flowing into the system, business was booming for the prison industry. The state built new prisons as fast as it could, but the number of inmates grew so rapidly that they ran out of room and had to send some offenders as far away as Texas and Oklahoma. We knew that Allen would have been shuffled from one prison to the next—he could have been anywhere.

But we shouldn't have fretted. With the assistance of a committed records clerk at the Department of Corrections, we were able to track Allen's whereabouts from the day he was processed at Dodge Correctional in 1996 all the way to his current location. The news was good. After six months at Dodge, they shipped him from one prison to the next, but Allen was never housed at a prison on the same day Penny Beerntsen was there. It would be small comfort, but it was better than knowing she'd unwittingly been near the man who'd brutally assaulted her.

Next on the agenda was trying to find a mug shot of Allen from 1985. Mark and I went over to the sheriff's department—maybe they'd have one on file. Sure enough, dispatch found one from a March 11, 1984, arrest. It was taken almost a year and a half before Penny's assault, but it was the best they could do. Allen was listed at five foot ten and 210 pounds. Notations indicated he had scars on his nose and his forehead. He listed his occupation as a sheet metal mechanic, and the "remarks" section included the warning, "Can be violent."

Janine called a few days later to tell me how it went with Penny. Penny was struggling with a swirl of emotions—guilt, sadness, anger, fear. She flew to Colorado where their son lived to avoid the coming media storm and just to be alone for a while, but Janine gave me her telephone number and suggested I give Penny a call. She needed to be confident that the current DA's office was on top of the situation and was interested in doing the right thing.

So I called Penny and had a long conversation with her. I apologized on behalf of the office and told her this never should have happened. But Janine was right—Penny was devastated. She was angry at Kocourek and

Vogel for not telling her about Gregory Allen. But at the same time she was blaming herself for ruining Steven Avery's life.

I told Penny that I'd been doing this stuff for a long time, that I'd read the entire trial transcript and there's no way it was her fault. She was obviously convinced Steven Avery was the assailant when she testified. The identification process was ridiculous, I explained. More than anything else, it appeared designed to confirm the suspicions of Deputy Dvorak and Sheriff Kocourek. By the time she sat down with Gene Kusche to work on the composite sketch, the sheriff had already had Avery's mug shot from a prior arrest in hand and he'd already sent word to his deputies to ready themselves to bring Avery in. The whole process was designed to make sure she'd pick out Avery, I told Penny, at least that's how it looked to me. If anyone was to blame, it was the sheriff and the former DA.

And their deception paid off. For eighteen years Penny was convinced that Steven Avery was the man who assaulted her. It was always Steven Avery's face that she saw during flashbacks and nightmares. He was the person who grabbed her and dragged her over the sand dunes. He was the man who beat her and tried to rape her. Even the photo of Gregory Allen that we'd sent her a few days earlier didn't dislodge Steven Avery's image from her mind. No matter how hard she tried to imagine Allen as her assailant, it was still Steven Avery's face that Penny saw when she closed her eyes.

Apparently, the Harvard-educated lawyer and psychologist who testified at the trial, Dr. Steven Penrod, the defense expert who Denis Vogel had so derisively dismissed, was right. Memory is a strange and fickle creature, not to be trusted lightly. Memories, especially of a traumatic event like a rape or a brutal assault, are malleable. They're molded by what we experience after the trauma has passed, including by what we are told by the police. So what crime victims think they remember—even if they feel certain about it—can be completely wrong.

And that's what happened in this case. Penny said the sheriff told her they had a suspect in mind and that the suspect's photo was included in the array. That alone contaminated the identification process, even without considering the question of how Kusche drew such a perfect likeness of Avery's mug shot in the first place.

Penny shared something else with me before we ended our phone conversation. About a week after the assault she received a telephone call from a detective at the City of Manitowoc Police Department. The detective told her his department had a suspect in mind that matched the description of the assailant, and it wasn't Steven Avery. Between what the detective told her and the strange telephone call she received from the unknown male a few days earlier, she was beginning to have doubts. So she called the Sheriff's Department. She thought she spoke directly with Sheriff Kocourek, and she told him about her conversation with the detective and asked him if there was another suspect. She was told not to worry about it, that the Sheriff's Department had jurisdiction over the case, not the city police department, and they would check out this suspect. When she called to follow up a few days later she was told that they had checked out the suspect and that he had an alibi. He was with his probation officer at the time of the assault and therefore couldn't have been the perpetrator.

A few days later, I would find out otherwise.

* * *

News travels fast in courthouses. It always has and it always will. So it wasn't a surprise that word about Steven Avery's exoneration was soon on the lips of every other person in the courthouse. And the news was naturally the chief topic of discussion in the DA's office. A few members of our staff were working in the office in 1985. One of them, Victim-Witness Coordinator Brenda Petersen, had come to know Penny quite well during the course of the trial. We all talked about how horrible Avery's exoneration would be for Penny. It would be all over the media and she'd have to relive the whole thing nearly two decades after it happened.

The degree of sympathy for Steven Avery, on the other hand, varied from one person to the next. But there was one matter my colleagues in the office unanimously agreed upon: Steven Avery would be even more messed up now than he was when he went in.

Another thing about courthouses is that the people who work in them aren't afraid to speak their minds. As I said, two of the women in our office were working in the DA's office when Denis Vogel prosecuted Steven Avery in

1985, and a third was still working for the county but in a different capacity. None of them ever thought Avery was the assailant. In fact, they all thought Gregory Allen was. Allen had been in and out of court during the preceding six months for stalking, window peeping, and stealing women's underwear—not the types of offenses that go unnoticed by women, especially those who work in prosecutors' offices.

Brenda, in particular, worked closely with police agencies in the county, and she had a good sense of what was happening crime-wise in the community back then. She told us the Manitowoc Police Department had been keeping a close eye on Gregory Allen during the summer Penny was attacked and the detectives were convinced that it was Allen, not Avery, who had assaulted Penny Beerntsen. Brenda also said she watched the entire trial, and she never believed Avery was the assailant.

In fact, Brenda and two other staff members at the time were so concerned that Allen was the assailant that they went into Denis Vogel's office and told him so. But Vogel said it was impossible because Allen was on probation in Door County. He'd called his probation agent and the agent told him that Allen was in Sturgeon Bay at the time of the assault. Vogel said it couldn't have been Allen; he had an alibi.

But an independent investigation conducted by the Wisconsin Department of Justice would later find out otherwise. Gregory Allen wasn't on probation the day Penny Beerntsen was assaulted, like Denis Vogel said he was. The "Sandman," as some of the officers had taken to calling Allen, had been free to roam the beach and terrorize his next victim. And now we know that's exactly what he did, grabbing Penny and manhandling her over the dunes.

Incidentally, when interviewed by the Department of Justice several months later, Vogel told the investigators that he didn't "specifically recall" anyone from his office asking him about the Avery case, though he admitted his staff frequently discussed pending cases.

* * *

As promised, Sherry Culhane had the results of the second DNA test in less than a week. The test confirmed it—the pubic hair was Gregory Allen's, or at least there was only a 1-in-251 billion chance that it wasn't. Keith Findley drafted a Stipulation and Order vacating the conviction and dismissing the charges. Its concluding sentence was music to Avery's ears. "It is further ordered that Steven A. Avery shall be released from custody of the Wisconsin Department of Corrections forthwith," it said. Mark and I signed the stipulation and walked it down to Branch 3 for Judge Hazlewood's signature.

It was impossible to keep the story under wraps any longer. The news outlets would soon catch wind of Steven Avery's pending release and the "you-know-what" would hit the fan. So with the help of a more erudite courthouse lawyer, Mark and I whipped up a press release and faxed it to the local newspaper and TV stations in Milwaukee and Green Bay. After covering the essentials, we tried to put the best spin on Avery's exoneration, writing:

> Upon receipt of the new DNA evidence, this office conducted an exhaustive review of the original investigation, earlier crime lab reports, and the complete court record. Based upon this review, it is clear that Steven Avery did not commit this crime. It is tragic that Mr. Avery spent eighteen years in prison for a crime he did not commit, but the DNA identification technology that has exonerated Mr. Avery was not available when this case was investigated and prosecuted in 1985. Now that technological advances have established that Mr. Avery did not commit this crime, justice requires the dismissal of the charges, and it is my duty to see that Mr. Avery is immediately released from prison.

* * *

Clear blue autumn skies and comfortably mild temperatures greeted Steven Avery on the morning he was released from prison. It was September 11, 2003. Television and print reporters flocked to Stanley Correctional Institute in northwestern Wisconsin at the appointed time and mobbed the protagonist as he walked out a free man. Here's how reporter Tom Kertscher of the *Milwaukee Journal Sentinel* covered the story:

> Under a bright sun just before 9 a.m. on Thursday morning, Steven Avery took his final steps toward freedom with his sister on one arm

and his daughter on the other, his parents and his history-making legal team trailing behind.

There was a pause as the group approached the final set of locked doors at the prison. More than 17 years behind bars for a wrongly convicted man were about to end.

"I'm out!" the soft-spoken Avery cried. "Feels wonderful."

Moments later, the 41-year-old former auto salvage worker became the first Wisconsin inmate to get his conviction overturned by the Wisconsin Innocence Project and only the third state inmate to be freed from prison through DNA testing.

A day after the testing proved that another man had beaten and sexually assaulted a Manitowoc woman in 1985 Avery expressed no anger toward the victim, who had repeatedly identified him as her attacker.

"It ain't her fault," he stated simply, directing blame instead at the Manitowoc County Sheriff's Department for making him a suspect. "They put it mostly in her head."

The sheriff's department, in Avery's estimation, didn't want to pursue other leads once it had helped steer the victim toward identifying him. He claimed that after his arrest the sheriff told him he would never get bail and never get out of jail.

"They wanted somebody real bad," he said. "And I was the one."

But while expressing sympathy for Avery, Tom Kocourek, who was sheriff in Manitowoc County when Avery was arrested, defended his department's investigation of the case and called his conviction "unfortunate."

"I don't know what else we could have done at the time," he said.

Trying not to dwell on the case, Avery was cheered Thursday by the presence of one of his five children, 19-year-old Jennifer. But he shed tears over how his conviction led quickly to the end of his marriage and the estrangement of his twin sons, now 18, who were born six days before his arrest.

"There ain't no way I can make it up," Avery said of the time he lost with his family.

But after spending some time with his parents, Avery said he plans to settle in Crivitz, near where most of his children live. He urged other wrongly convicted prisoners to remain faithful.

"There's always miracles going around," he said. "Hopefully they can get out just like me and get the guilty one in."

* * *

For several days after his release, the airwaves were filled with news of Steven Avery's exoneration. Time and again it was reported that he spent eighteen years in prison for a crime he did not commit. But actually, only twelve of those years were for the wrongful conviction. Steve had cut a deal on the other charges pending against him at the time—the charges associated with his forcing a deputy sheriff's wife off the road—and he received a six-year sentence for that crime. In other words, he would have spent six of those eighteen years in prison even if he had not been wrongly convicted of the other crime.

But to the media, it didn't really matter because Steven Avery was a celebrity now. With his shaved head, twinkling blue eyes, and foot-long beard, they loved him. Given all the attention they lavished upon him, and with a special affinity for attractive young female reporters, it was apparent that Steve loved them, too.

Before long, everyone in Wisconsin knew his name, and thanks to the number of television interviews he granted, most people recognized his face, too. But what they didn't know, and what Steve himself didn't know, was that two years later he'd be at the center of a far greater media storm.

EIGHTEEN

A week had passed since the crime lab called with the DNA test results, and the Avery case was beginning to take a toll on my nerves. So late in the evening on the day Steven Avery was released I went for a run, and then put the calories I'd lost right back on as I tried to relax with the assistance of a bottle of "Spotted Cow," an apt name for a beer brewed in Wisconsin if ever there was one.

But neither the run nor the beer had the effect I'd hoped for. The discomfort I felt when I saw the complaint charging Gregory Allen in Vogel's file had returned over the past few days with varying degrees of intensity, and now the questions were staring me straight in the eyes: Did they know? Did Vogel and Kocourek know that Gregory Allen was Penny Beerntsen's assailant? What else could explain the presence of the Gregory Allen complaint in the Steven Avery file?

I couldn't shake the feeling that something went horribly wrong back in 1985. Two summers before he assaulted Penny Beerntsen, Allen had lunged at another woman on the same beach who was walking her dog. And Vogel had filed the criminal complaint charging Allen with that crime.

It didn't make sense. Why was the Allen complaint in the Avery file? Did it mean that Vogel knew Steven Avery was innocent and that Gregory Allen, a psycho-sociopathic rapist that the police had been tracking for months, was the actual perpetrator?

To answer these questions, I needed to find out more. So the next day at work I retrieved the police reports concerning Allen's earlier crime. Mark and I instinctively knew to leave the originals in the file in case somebody outside the office had to later investigate, so we made copies and returned the originals to the file.

Reviewing the reports didn't make me feel any better—in fact, it only made it worse. The victim was walking her dog on the beach when a man wearing blue shorts and a tank top—who we now knew was Gregory

Allen—suddenly ran over the sand dunes and began walking right behind her. He pulled his shorts half way down his legs and began masturbating. And then he lunged at her, just like Penny Beerntsen's assailant had two summers later. Fortunately, in this case the victim was able to escape Allen's grasp and run away. This was way too similar to the assailiant's MO during the Penny Beerntsen attack to be just a coincidence. And it happened on the same stretch of beach! What are the chances of that? Vogel had to have made the connection. Why else was the complaint in the Avery file?

Then it got even worse. The victim in the first attack had told police she recognized the man—he used to come into the convenience store where she worked, and a co-worker even knew his name. It was Gregory Allen. Later she called the police again to report that Allen had called her a few days after the incident. She was scared. She'd moved to Green Bay, but somehow Allen found her telephone number, which meant he also knew where she lived.

I couldn't believe it. Allen used the exact MO two years later when he assaulted Penny Beerntsen—right down to calling her after the crime. How could Vogel not make the connection? And if he didn't, why were the Allen reports in Avery's file?

Then I looked at the criminal complaint. Maybe Vogel just signed off on the complaint and someone else handled the case from there, as frequently happens amidst the chaos in district attorney's offices. But that's not what I found. Vogel had personally prosecuted the file, from start to finish. He appeared for the state at the bail hearing and successfully argued for $500 cash bail. He met with Allen's attorney at the pretrial conference. He subpoenaed the state's witnesses for trial, he cut a plea agreement with the defense a few days before the trial, and on February 28, 1984, with Gregory Allen in court to enter his plea, he amended the charge to disorderly conduct. The judge accepted the plea agreement and ordered a fine of $100 plus costs—not a bad deal for running over a sand dune to accost a woman walking along a beach.

Given his full knowledge of Allen's crime and Steven Avery's sixteen alibi witnesses, it's especially ironic that two years later Vogel noted in Avery's file that "the defendant may have alibi."

* * *

Mark and I devoted much of our time to the Avery case in the week after the crime lab call, but our regular caseload didn't disappear. The other attorneys in the office were swamped, too, but they pitched in and somehow we muddled through. But bombshells were exploding every other day, and now it was time for another.

Mark asked me to join him in his office, and by the look on his face I knew it was serious. One of the other prosecutors in the office had called Gene Kusche the day before Avery was released. Gene was retired by then, but for some reason, our colleague called him about the Avery case. Mark caught wind of it and asked him what they discussed.

He said he called Kusche to see if he knew about Avery's exoneration and that he would soon be released from prison. Apparently, he thought Kusche should know about it before he found out through the media. Nobody's ever accused either Gene or our fellow prosecutor of being men of few words, so the conversation covered other ground, too.

Kusche told him about an incident that occurred ten years after Avery was convicted. A detective from Green Bay called the Manitowoc County jail to report that an inmate in their jail was claiming that he had raped a woman jogging on a beach in Manitowoc County ten years earlier. The inmate claimed that someone else had been convicted of the assault and was presently serving time in prison for a crime he didn't commit. Kusche told the ADA that Andy Colborn was the corrections officer who spoke with the Green Bay detective and that Colborn got word of it to Sheriff Kocourek. But according to Kusche, the sheriff told Colborn and a detective to stay out of it—they already had the right guy. Andy Colborn doesn't recall if the Green Bay detective mentioned the confessing inmate's name, but Gregory Allen was in the Brown County jail at the time awaiting trial for raping the woman in Green Bay ten years after Penny Beerntsen was attacked on the beach.

Kusche told the assistant DA something else that was even more disturbing. He said he withdrew the composite drawing from the court file several years earlier. It was at his home, and he was planning to keep it there.

It went right over my head then, but Penny Beerntsen said something similar during our phone conversation a few days earlier. She told me she ran into Kusche a few years before at the grocery store, and he said something odd, something that really disturbed her at the time. He said he had the composite drawing from the Avery trial hanging on his living room wall, and asked her if she wanted to come over to see it. Penny was startled by his offer and she politely declined. And now, Kusche just told one of my colleagues that he still has the composite drawing and he planned to hold onto it. What the hell was going on?

Nobody removes evidence from a court file without a judge's permission, not even cops. So I assumed that Judge Hazlewood must have released the drawing to Kusche. Later that day I checked, and sure enough, on October 14, 1998, thirteen years after Steven Avery's trial, the judge had signed an order releasing the composite drawing to Inspector Gene Kusche. The order also released the original of Avery's mug shot that was moved into evidence at trial, the one that Penny picked out from the photo array that night in the hospital.

I suppose Kusche looked at the composite drawing as a trophy—his masterpiece that helped send a sex predator to prison. But it still struck me as odd. Trophies are for sports competitions, not for attempted murder trials.

❊ ❊ ❊

Another bombshell exploded a few days later. In the summer of 1989, a professional snitch by the name of Ray Crivitz was serving time at the state prison in Green Bay when he struck up a conversation with an inmate in the adjoining cell. The inmate went by the name of "Stivers," but his real name was Steven Avery. Crivitz memorialized their dreary conversation in the following sworn affidavit, dated June 14, 2000, eleven years after the conversation supposedly occurred.

AFFIDAVIT OF RAYMOND E. CRIVITZ:

I, Raymond E. Crivitz, do hereby swear and attest to the following:

1. My name is Raymond E. Crivitz.
2. As of the date of the signing of this affidavit, I am an inmate at Green Bay Correctional Institution in Green Bay, Wisconsin.
3. During a previous period of my incarceration I lived here from fall of 1988 to the summer of 1989.

4. During this period of incarceration I was housed in the North Cell Hall, C Tier, in cell C-73.

5. While I was living in C-73, I came to know another inmate who was housed in C-72 right next to my cell.

6. This inmate was Steve Avery (approximately five feet five inches tall with sandy/dirty blond hair and ice blue eyes), who also went by the nickname "Stivers."

7. During one of several conversations I had with Steve Avery (while each of us were sitting in our cells), in the spring/summer of 1989, I asked him what he was in for.

8. Steve Avery told me that he was arrested and convicted for raping a woman on a beach near Manitowoc, Wisconsin.

9. I responded that I was also in for assault (even though I wasn't) just to get his trust and so he would talk to me.

10. Steve Avery told me that he was "set up by this bitch," that he was on the beach and saw a woman jogging. He said he "wanted some." I asked him if he got some.

11. Steve Avery then told me that "yes he got some," that he "fucked the bitch" and that "she loved it."

12. I asked him if that was a small town and if he thought he would see her again. He said it was and that if he did see her again that he "would finish what he started" because he felt he had been "set up by the bitch" and that he thought she was working with the police or was some kind of policewoman.

13. About three weeks later I was transferred out of Green Bay Correctional Institution.

Here's the strange part: Sheriff Kocourek kept a safe in his office, and the only thing left in it when Ken Petersen, the new sheriff, took over in 2001 was Raymond Crivitz's affidavit.

To me, it sounded like Avery was engaging in typical inmate bravado to an equally typical jailhouse snitch. Crivitz told Avery he was in for assault even though he wasn't, "just to get his trust," and Avery was very likely doing the same thing. That's if the conversation even occurred.

But why was the affidavit the only thing the sheriff left in the safe? Did he really believe Avery was guilty and held onto the affidavit in case he had to prove it? But why hide it? Why not add it to a follow-up police report and send a copy to the DA? That would be standard procedure, and Tom Kocourek is certainly a standard procedure kind of guy. Or was it his trump card? If the truth ever came out, he could hold up the affidavit and say, "See, I thought he did it."

Who knows? But what we do know is that the affidavit was prepared eleven years after the conversation supposedly occurred, and Sheriff Kocourek kept it securely hidden in a safe. It was just one more odd fact in a series of increasingly odd facts in a case that was becoming more disturbing by the day.

✳ ✳ ✳

Events were beginning to spin out of control. Each revelation was more disturbing than the last one and, taken together, they suggested that Kocourek and Vogel might have knowingly sent an innocent man to prison while letting a guilty one go free. We had to get a handle on it, someone would eventually have to investigate this mess, and it sure as hell wasn't going to be us since there was an obvious conflict of interest. So the following day, Mark put out what he referred to as a "gag order," prohibiting discussion of the Avery case with anyone outside the office. It was a pretty ambitious directive and I'm fairly confident that that no one followed it precisely.

Late that afternoon Mark and I called the state attorney general's office in Madison to see if they would conduct an independent review. We didn't know it at the time, but Keith Findley of the Wisconsin Innocence Project had made the same request. But citing what she perceived to be an absence of legal authority to conduct such an investigation, Attorney General Peg Lautenschlager declined. Then, a few days later, she changed her mind.

Lautenschlager had recently rolled out her brand-new "Public Integrity Unit," and she belatedly decided that Steven Avery's wrongful conviction was just the sort of case her initiative was designed for. So an appointment was scheduled for the following day.

As Mark and I drove to Madison the next morning, the Avery case was already on its way to becoming the most notorious wrongful conviction in Wisconsin's history. The state's major newspapers ran several front-page stories about his exoneration and the electronic media continued to saturate the public with coverage of every new development. It was also the subject of an AM radio talk show out of Milwaukee that aired on our way to Madison. It was impossible to escape it.

Most of the coverage was quite good. "Quick Action in Avery Case May Have Left Man Free to Continue Crimes," read the headline in the *Milwaukee Journal Sentinel* the day before our appointment with the AG. Reporter Tom Kertscher, who served as the *Journal Sentinel's* point man on the wrongful conviction story—and who would do so again when an even more incredible story concerning Steven Avery broke two years later—informed his readers that even though Gregory Allen was convicted of lunging at a woman along the same beach two summers earlier, the police apparently never considered him a suspect in the second assault. Kertscher also noted that because Allen wasn't arrested for assaulting Penny Beerntsen, he was free ten years later to break into a Green Bay residence and brutally rape the woman inside.

One of the Green Bay TV stations ran a segment about the Avery case the night before, complete with a live interview of the protagonist himself, on location at the Avery Salvage Yard. During his tenure in prison, Steve had affected a Mansonesque appearance with long hair and scraggly beard hanging half way down to his belly button. But now he was all cleaned up. He kept the mangy beard but his hair was buzzed and his icy blue eyes twinkled like Santa Claus.

Steve told the television reporter that he wasn't angry at anybody for his plight. He just hoped an investigation would be conducted so nobody else would have to go through what he did. He planned to live with his parents for now, and, oh yeah, he was keeping his options open about filing a lawsuit.

When Mark stopped to gas up halfway to Madison, I picked up the latest edition of the *Journal Sentinel*. Sure enough, the Avery case had made the front page again. "Manitowoc County DA Requests Avery Case Review—Wants the Attorney General to Look for Safeguards," read the headline of that day's edition.

Tom Kertscher had contacted some of the main players. Mark's pretty tightlipped with the press, so after noting he had requested the independent investigation, he said he couldn't comment further because he wanted "to ensure the integrity of any independent review." Denis Vogel was identified as the former district attorney who had prosecuted the case, but Vogel couldn't be reached for comment.

Steven Avery, on the other hand, was more than willing to talk. He thought the police suspected him because he had a few run-ins with the law, he explained during the interview, and the sheriff's department didn't like him. His uncle Arland was a deputy at the sheriff's department and so was one of his neighbors, referring to the husband of the woman he ran off the road six months before he was arrested for the attack on Penny Beerntsen. Toward the end of the interview, Steve added that Sheriff Kocourek told him when he was taken to jail that he would not be released on bail and that he'd never get out of jail.

Surprisingly, Kocourek also agreed to be interviewed. Here's that part of the story:

> Sheriff Tom Kocourek, who retired in 2001, called Avery's conviction "unfortunate." But he expressed confidence that his department had aggressively pursued all leads and that the "vast majority" of evidence had pointed to Avery.
>
> "I don't know what else we could have done at the time," he said. "We didn't leave any stones unturned."

Tom Kertscher's story concluded by noting that according to the New York-based national Innocence Project, Steven Avery was the 137th wrongfully convicted person in the United States to be freed from prison through DNA testing.

* * *

The city of Madison lies on an isthmus between Lake Monona and Lake Mendota. But while Madison isn't quite an island geographically, it may as well be, given its politics and cultural identity. As the state's capitol and home to its largest university, the city is crawling with attorneys and university professors with social and political views that are foreign to the rest of the state that, with the exception of Milwaukee and a few other holdouts from the days of "Fighting Bob" La Follette, tends to vote red.

Mark and I arrived in Madison three hours after leaving Manitowoc, just in time for our 10 a.m. appointment with the attorney general. I'd met Peg Lautenschlager before. She's blessed with a personable and engaging style. Peg warmly greeted us and then introduced us to Deb Straus and Amy Blackwood-Lehman, the two special agents she'd assigned to handle the investigation.

We walked into a conference room where ten to fifteen agents and attorneys were waiting to grill us about why we were there. But it didn't take long to see that they were sincerely interested in the case, and they asked intelligent and insightful questions that showed they cared. We walked out two hours later, confident that the Wisconsin State Attorney General's Office would conduct a fair and thorough investigation, which is all anyone could ask for.

After leaving the AG's office we walked up State Street, which runs between the capitol building and the university. We had lunch at an Afghan restaurant and then walked back to the capitol building and wandered through its maze of hallways in search of State Representative Mark Gundrum's office. A Republican legislator from suburban Milwaukee and the chairman of the State Assembly's Committee on Courts and Corrections, Gundrum had called for hearings two days earlier to explore what led to Avery's wrongful conviction. He must have caught wind that Mark had requested an independent investigation because he called the previous day to see if we'd stop by after our meeting with the attorney general.

We weren't sure how much to share with Representative Gundrum. For one thing, we didn't want to say anything that would compromise the attorney general's investigation. But also, Democrat Peg Lautenschlager and Republican Mark Gundrum were ambitious politicians on opposite sides of the aisle and we weren't interested in becoming pawns in a political chess match between them.

So when we arrived at Gundrum's office, we expected to be met by a self-serving politician hoping to make some political hay out of Steven

Avery's wrongful conviction. But we were pleasantly surprised. It was clear from the beginning that Mark Gundrum actually cared. He was knowledgeable about the criminal justice system in general and deeply concerned how it had failed in the Avery case so miserably. The State Assembly eventually heeded Gundrum's call for legislative hearings, and he was appointed the chairperson of what would later—if temporarily—come to be known as the Avery Task Force. By all accounts, Representative Gundrum did an excellent job.

*   *   *

On our way home from Madison, Mark and I were beating a few more dead horses about the Avery case when I began nodding off—despite drinking a 24-ounce cup of coffee I'd picked up on our way out of town. I had just finished reading the latest article about the case in the *Manitowoc Herald Times Reporter* when I fell into a deep sleep. The reporter had covered the same ground as the *Journal Sentinel* piece. Mark's request for an independent review was there, along with a few interviews of some of the same main players. But it was a quote from Steven Avery himself that, had I not been half asleep when I read it, would have jolted me from my seat.

In his interview with the *Herald Times Reporter*, Steve discussed the composite sketch of Penny Beerntsen's assailant that was prepared by Gene Kusche on the night of his arrest. He claimed it was a fraud. He accused Kusche of drawing his police artist sketch straight off of Steve's earlier mug shot, the one the sheriff's department had on file from his arrest six months before Penny was assaulted. He told the paper that one of his relatives told him so, which I assumed at the time, and later confirmed, was his uncle, Deputy Arland Avery.

I had previously heard from several people that Kusche's composite sketch of Penny's assailant looked suspiciously like Steven Avery's mug shot. In fact, I'd been told, they were nearly identical. But seeing it in print gave the claim an authenticity that it previously lacked, even though it was Steven Avery who was making the claim. Now it was a public accusation, an allegation the newspaper considered credible enough to put in print. It was no longer just a few insiders who had speculated about the composite drawing, it was front-page news and would soon be all over town.

Did Gene Kusche really forge the composite drawing? I was staggered by the possibility and desperately worried that it might be true.

NINETEEN

It was one of the strangest telephone conversations I've ever had. On the morning we presented him with the stipulation and order granting Steven Avery's release, Judge Hazlewood suggested that I call Denis Vogel. He thought it was only fair that we should give the former DA a heads-up to give him time to digest the news before the media started hounding him. That sounded reasonable to me, so I called Denis at his law firm in Madison. We had met on a few prior occasions but we didn't really know each other so our conversation was brief. I gave him the short version, that the crime lab had retested some evidence and the DNA results made it clear that Gregory Allen, not Steven Avery, had been Penny Beerntsen's assailant. But Denis Vogel didn't even try to feign surprise. I had just finished telling him that he'd sent an innocent man to prison for eighteen years, but he wasn't bothered in the least, or if he was he sure didn't show it.

Now it was a week later. I was in court all morning and Vogel had left a message on my voice mail asking me to give him a call. It must have been serious because he called again that afternoon before I had a chance to return his call. Again, he was all business. He said an analyst from the crime lab had testified at the trial and his recollection was that her examination of some hairs had tied Avery to the crime. "Yeah, right, Denis," I thought. "You're still relying on the 'science' of hair examination." Then, almost mechanically, Vogel asked me a question I'll never forget.

"Is there anything on Allen in the file?" he said.

I feigned ignorance and mumbled something inconsequential about the case instead. Then I told him Mark and I had turned the whole Avery file over to the attorney general the previous Friday, which I'm sure wasn't news to him since the media had already extensively covered Mark's request for an independent review.

I hung up the phone and just sat in my office for a while, reflecting upon our conversation. Vogel's question—was there anything on Allen left in

Avery's file—implied he knew that Allen, not Avery, was the assailant, didn't it? He was covering his tracks and he must have thought I'd go along. How else could I take it?

Despite their well-known reputation, most attorneys possess as much integrity as the next person—maybe even more. But Denis Vogel appeared to be one of the exceptions. How could he prosecute someone he knew was innocent? And how could he let somebody as dangerous as Allen go free?

Being sanctimonious is an occupational hazard for prosecutors, one I'm not immune from, so I tried to temper my judgment about what Vogel had done with an understanding of why he did it. Part of the problem, I thought, was that by rushing the decision to arrest Avery without consulting the district attorney, the sheriff had put into play a course of action that would have been difficult to reverse. Vogel could have cut Steve loose at the bail hearing and summoned him in later if he thought the case was strong enough to charge. But with such a prominent victim and with the media paying such close attention, letting Avery go free would have been politically difficult. After all, back then district attorneys had to run for re-election every two years. Besides, I thought for a moment, it's possible he didn't know.

But the more I tried to convince myself that Vogel didn't know, the more convinced I became that he did. And the more I thought about why he did it, the more I realized there was nothing that could possibly justify it. No doubt, the office of district attorney is fraught with political pressure, but you can't play politics with a case as serious as this one.

Then I recalled my conversation with some of the office staff, about how all three staff members who worked there at the time thought that Gregory Allen and not Steven Avery was the assailant. They even approached Vogel with their concerns, but he told them they were mistaken, that he had checked with Allen's probation agent who said that Allen had an airtight alibi, a statement that, like so many other statements made by the authorities in the Avery case, turned out to be a big fat lie.

The next morning I called Tom Bergner at the Manitowoc Police Department. Bergner called me "Ayda," pronounced with a long "a" because of the way I signed off on memos to his department: "ADA Griesbach." And since Tom was the deputy chief, I called him DC. He's retired now, but for years Tom Bergner was a great detective and a great DC.

I asked if he could do me a favor. I wanted to find out why the staff in the DA's office in 1985 was so convinced that Gregory Allen, not Steven Avery, was Penny Beerntsen's assailant and why Denis Vogel was so worried that something on Allen remained in Avery's file. I didn't know how far back the department's records went, but I asked if he could send me whatever he had on Allen from the last twenty five years or so. Tom uttered one of his more imaginative obscenity-laden insults and then replied of course he could, he'd have the files on my desk later that day.

He was true to his word and the minute I came back from court late that afternoon I started paging through Allen's rap sheet. It didn't take long for me to realize that Steven Avery wasn't the only bad guy the cops were keeping their eyes on in 1985. In fact, he was a model citizen compared to what Gregory Allen was up to.

Allen's crime spree started in January of that year, and as the months went by, the police were just waiting for a strong enough case to bring him in. At six-thirty in the morning on January 26, 1985, a woman on the south side of Manitowoc reported a suspicious man in her neighbor's backyard. The man had a ski mask on and it was still dark out, but the woman was able to see his outline as he moved a cement block brick underneath the neighbor's bathroom window, stood on the brick, and peered inside. Police later found out that the neighbor's teenage daughter was in the bathroom getting ready for school. She'd just gotten out of the shower when she looked outside and let out a scream.

The girl had told her parents a few weeks earlier that she had a strange feeling someone outside was watching her when she was in the bathroom, but they didn't make much of it at the time—maybe it was just her imagination.

But this time the man's face was right up to the window and he was staring at her from out in the darkness. She managed to keep her wits about her long enough to remember what the man looked like so she was able to give the police a good description of him. Later at the police station, she picked out Gregory Allen from a photo array, and the investigating officer referred the case to the DA's office for prosecution. But an assistant DA sent it back a month later. He wouldn't be filing charges against Allen, he explained, because it was just a prowling incident and in his opinion the suspect's behavior didn't constitute a crime—though I'm not sure why at least disorderly conduct didn't come to mind. The city of Manitowoc had an ordinance that covered prowling, so the officer issued Allen a municipal court citation instead but two months later the city attorney even dismissed that charge.

Untouched by the authorities, Gregory Allen remained on the prowl, striking usually just before sunrise. He was especially active in the months of June and July, when he engaged in increasingly violent and deranged behavior that culminated in his brutal assault of Penny Beerntsen on July 29.

His first victim that summer was 24-year-old Tina Hansen, who also lived on Manitowoc's south side. Tina kept late hours. As a bartender at the Main Event, she didn't have a choice since in Wisconsin, closing time for taverns is 2 a.m. At four-thirty in the morning on June 23, she was in her kitchen making posters for her parents' upcoming anniversary party. Nearly the longest day of the year, a faint morning light had already appeared when Tina heard tapping on her window. When she looked outside, she saw a man with a red T-shirt wrapped around his head. His erect penis was exposed, and he was masturbating. It seemed like he was staring straight through her.

Her heart jumped—she'd left the front door open. She ran to lock it, but the man saw her and he ran toward it, too. She beat him there by seconds and quickly locked the screen door, but the man continued masturbating in front of her. He asked her to lift up her shirt to expose her breasts, a request she obviously denied.

"What difference would it make, you'll never see me again," the man pleaded.

"Get out of here, I'm calling the police," Tina yelled, hoping he'd leave. Then the man said he'd be back for more tomorrow, and then he scampered away.

Frightened, but not sure what to do, Tina waited ten minutes and then called the police. The responding officer advised her to call 911 immediately if the man returned.

A few days later than promised, but true to his word, the man struck again on June 26 at 2:31 a.m. Tina was sleeping on the sofa when she heard knocking at the front door. The man with the red T-shirt wrapped around his head had returned, and just like the first time, he exposed himself. He had opened up the outside screen door to try to get in, but Tina screamed, and with his efforts frustrated for the second time in three days, the man fled.

Less than ten minutes after Tina's call into dispatch, an officer stopped Gregory Allen driving his motorcycle at 14th and Hamilton—just four blocks from Tina's home. Allen was wearing a red T-shirt, and other than having a mustache while Tina thought he was clean shaven, he matched her description.

Later, Tina discovered that twelve Phillips screws had been removed from the frame of her bedroom window. Not coincidentally, Allen had two Phillips screwdrivers in his possession when the officer stopped him that morning.

A detective assembled a photo array that included a picture of Allen, and asked Tina if she recognized the man who had now twice appeared outside her home. Although she got a good look at Allen's eyes and his nose this time, the rest of his face was concealed by his T-shirt so she wasn't able to identify him. But the detective was sure it was Allen, and alarmed at how reckless he'd become, he noted the following at the end of his report:

"It would appear that this is getting very serious in regard to the suspect, Gregory A. Allen. He is in all probability the suspect involved; however, at this point the victim could not make a positive identification. Allen will have to be caught in the act as he is starting to become very bold."

It was getting serious all right. Just three weeks later, on July 14, 1985, Allen was the prime suspect in an even bolder crime. Asleep and alone in her south side residence, Megan Riley was only seventeen years old. Her parents were up north with her younger sister—they thought she'd be fine. But just after 3 a.m., she woke up to find a man holding a knife to her throat. With the exception of her one-piece bathing suit that had been hanging on the clothesline, but was now wrapped around his head, he was nude.

"Say anything and I'll kill you," he said as he sat on top of her with one hand on her breast and the other over her mouth.

"Take off your clothes," he demanded. "Take off your clothes, or I'll kill you."
Megan managed to tearfully tell him she was having her period.

"Where's your younger sister?" the man grunted.

"Up north with my parents," she unwisely replied.

Then he put her hand on his penis and forced her to rub him until he ejaculated. After that, he took her by the arm, and with the knife to her throat again, he pushed her to the back door. As he left he told her he'd come back and kill her if she called the police.

When Megan looked down, she noticed a stain on her nightgown where the man had ejaculated. Sick to her stomach, she threw up in the bathroom and then walked into the kitchen to settle down. She knew she had to move fast—what if he came back? She checked the phone, but it was dead. He must have cut the line. But she couldn't wait any longer, and after looking out every window to make sure he was gone, she made a dash to her car, locked the doors, and sped off to the police station. Still shaking when the detective interviewed her thirty minutes later, she wasn't able to give a very good description. The man was about five eight with a solid build, she said, but that's all she knew. She thought he had a beard, but she wasn't even sure about that since he'd had her bathing suit wrapped around his head.

A neighbor told the investigating officer that she saw a man park his motorcycle nearby at about two-thirty that morning and then walk toward Megan's house. She had watched as the man carried a picnic bench between her house and Megan's. Another neighbor said he saw a man duck into the bushes in Megan's yard about a month earlier just before dark. He also had noticed a motorcycle parked in front of a house nearby.

The police immediately suspected Gregory Allen. He had a motorcycle and the crime matched his MO, but without a better description, the investigation led nowhere. At the end of the report, a detective wrote, "This department has compiled several complaints recently concerning prowling, window peeping, indecent exposure, and sexual assault, ranging from January 1985 through July 14, 1985. In each case, Gregory A. Allen has been listed as a suspect. Past record and intelligence concerning Gregory Allen reveals he is a dangerous individual with a potential for violence."

That note was entered on July 17, just twelve days before Penny Beerntsen was attacked and nearly murdered.

The Manitowoc PD began monitoring Allen's whereabouts, logging his location in an ongoing report. With each incident more serious than the last, they knew he'd strike again—the only question was when. The log was included in the stack of reports that Tom Bergner delivered to me, and as I examined them closely, I noted two entries for the day Allen attacked Penny Beerntsen. The first indicated that Allen's motorcycle was at an address on the south side of town, and tragically, the second entry, made just over an hour before Penny was assaulted, merely stated: "Unable to check due to other calls."

After escaping prosecution for attacking Penny Beerntsen, Allen was still up to no good three months later—a fact that should have given Vogel and Kocourek pause, especially because his next crime was so similar to some of his prior activities.

On October 17, with Steven Avery securely locked up in the county jail, the city police department received a call from the concerned parents of two teenage girls. The girls, ages thirteen and fifteen, had told them several times that they saw "eyes looking at them" through the bathroom window in the early morning hours before it got light outside. The parents didn't know what to make of it—maybe the girls were just making up stories? But that morning the dad noticed a large block of wood underneath the bathroom window, and his fifteen-year-old daughter said she thought she saw someone staring at her when she got out of the shower. Police immediately suspected Gregory Allen, who had frightened the daylights out of another teenage girl in the same manner nine months earlier.

TWENTY

There's an Italian deli on the north side of Manitowoc called Maretti's. Trays of fresh, cold pasta dishes and an assortment of salads are displayed behind glass counters and large blocks of Italian and Wisconsin cheeses line the shelves behind them. There's a small dining area to the side where comfortable booths surround six or seven tables and hundreds of bottles of wine are neatly arranged in cubby holes along the walls.

Pasta dishes with expertly seasoned Italian meatballs smothered in red tomato sauce, hot or cold subs and sandwiches with generous layers of shaved beef stuffed with green peppers and onions highlight the menu. Then there's our favorite: thick-crust pizza with a hint of well fermented beer loaded with cheese, sausage, mushrooms, and onions. But it's the atmosphere of the place that keeps us coming back to Maretti's. With a bottle of Merlot on the table and Frank Sinatra crooning in the background, life is good as we sit together in a booth recounting the day's events.

I'd spent the last hour and a half at work poring through police reports recounting Gregory Allen's violent, sex-crazed episodes in the months leading up to Penny Beerntsen's assault, and I was exhausted from trying to reconcile how Kocourek and Vogel could have missed that Gregory Allen, not Avery, was Penny Beerntsen's assailant. And after another week of running the kids all over town and meeting all the other demands of a mother of four, Jody also was tired and in need of a reprieve. So dinner at Maretti's was the perfect antidote for both of us on that first Friday night after the Avery case hit the fan.

But there was no escaping the story. The previous occupants of our booth had left behind that day's edition of the *Milwaukee Journal Sentinel*, and someone had opened it to yet another article concerning the Avery case. Well past obsession by that point, I began skimming the article, reading out loud the few parts we didn't already know about.

Tom Bergner was quoted extensively. As always, he was open and honest with what he knew. He said he thought from the very beginning that they had arrested the wrong person, that Allen was the assailant, not Avery. In fact, he had walked over to the sheriff's department a few days after Steve was arrested and told Sheriff Kocourek he thought he had the wrong guy. He asked Kocourek if he knew how dangerous Allen had recently become, that Bergner's department was even tracking him around the clock, but they lost sight of him the afternoon Penny was assaulted. Bergner told the reporter he had the impression that the sheriff knew all about Allen's recent conduct, but Kocourek told him they had already ruled Allen out.

The reporter interviewed Kocourek, too, but the former sheriff said he couldn't recall having such a conversation with Detective Bergner. Months later he would claim to investigators from the AG's office that he wasn't even aware of Gregory Allen in 1985. He claimed this despite the fact that the investigators had found a copy of the criminal complaint charging Allen for the previous beach incident in the sheriff's own files.

"Yeah, right," I mumbled to myself.

"What's wrong?" Jody replied.

"Tom Bergner sent me copies of the reports on Gregory Allen today," I said. "There's no way Kocourek didn't know about Allen."

I told Jody how dangerous Allen had become that summer, recounting some of his more bizarre behavior—tapping on windows at three in the morning and then exposing himself to the woman inside, removing screws from windows so he could later break in. I told her about young girls getting out of the shower and seeing eyes peering in at them through the darkness—all the demented, dangerous behavior of a predator on the loose. Then I told her about the incident just two weeks before Allen attacked Penny Beerntsen—the night when he broke into a house and tried to assault the girl inside while her parents were up north.

Jody couldn't believe it. "He had a swim suit wrapped around his head?"

"That's right, and he had a knife to her throat."

"Why did he leave?"

"'Cause she told him she was having her period."

"Smart girl," she said.

The pizza came just in time. We were both starving, and at least for a little while we were more interested in the food than discussing the Avery case. We looked outside at Buffalo Street between mouthfuls and watched some of Manitowoc's nightlife, such as it is, walk by. There was an early season chill in the air, but it was warm and cozy in the brightly lit deli with its black-and-white checkered floor.

I poured us each a second glass of wine, and with Jody patiently putting up with my rambling, I tried to unpeel more layers of what went wrong in Steven Avery's conviction.

"So why didn't they check out Allen?" Jody asked, resuming our conversation.

"I don't know," I responded, "the sheriff told Bergner they ruled him out, and Vogel said he had an alibi."

"But he didn't have an alibi," Jody objected.

"I know."

Then I told her that Penny Beerntsen had called the sheriff a few days after the incident and told him a detective from the city police department had called her expressing doubts that they had the right guy.

"What did the sheriff tell her?"

"'Don't listen to the police department,' something along those lines," I said. "'My department has jurisdiction, not the city PD,' you know—that sort of thing."

"Turf war, you mean that's what this was about?" Jody interjected.

"Partly, but it was more than just turf war."

"Like what? What are you suggesting?"

I stared out the window and wondered the same thing. Why were Kocourek and Vogel so confident in the face of so much doubt? Sixteen witnesses had given a consistent, detailed account of Steven Avery's whereabouts, and most of them were interviewed within hours after his arrest. There's no way they could have coordinated their stories with Steve. He was already locked up in jail, not allowed calls by order of the sheriff himself. And their timeline was confirmed by the receipt from Shopko. But none of that mattered to Vogel and Kocourek. They had made their arrest and they sure as hell weren't going to back down now.

In their drive to convict, they ignored any information that ran contrary to Steven Avery's guilt. It meant nothing, for instance, that it took Penny ten minutes to identify him in the lineup. And some of the red flags were impossible to miss. Like when Penny received that disturbing telephone call a few days after she was assaulted, which was consistent with Gregory Allen's MO when he had exposed himself and lunged at the woman on the beach two summers earlier. Both times, Allen inexplicably knew personal information about his victim and called them to make sure that they knew it.

I'd drifted off in thought and Jody repeated the question she'd asked me several minutes earlier. "If it wasn't just turf war, then what was it?"

"Avery was on bail for a violent confrontation with a woman who lived down the road from him," I began. "He rammed his pickup truck into her car and held her at gunpoint, intending to assault her."

"Did he?"

"No, he let her go—the woman had her baby with her."

"So he was on their radar screen, is that what you're saying?"

"Exactly, and the woman he pulled over was married to a deputy, and don't forget, his uncle was a deputy at the sheriff's department."

"Not real smart—he chooses as his victim a deputy's wife?"

"It gets better. The first deputy to interview Penny at the hospital the night she was attacked, her name was Judy Dvorak. She lived across the street from Avery and she knew all about him and the family. She even saw him tether one of his kids to a tree one time. She also knew he was on bail for pulling over and pointing a gun at the wife of one of her colleagues at the sheriff's department. Judy Dvorak despised him."

"So, what are you saying? Deputy Dvorak just assumed it was Avery because he was a pervert and a child abuser with another case pending against him at the time?" Jody asked. "That doesn't make sense without any evidence supporting her suspicion. There are all sorts of sex offenders out there—you guys prosecute them all the time."

"Tell me about it. But that's how I think it started. Even though Penny's description of the assailant wasn't even close to matching Avery, other than the long hair and the beard, Deputy Dvorak assumed it was him, it's like she wanted to believe he was the perpetrator."

Jody cut right to the point. "Who matched the victim's description of the assailant better, Avery or Allen?"

"Allen did. Penny said the assailant was short to medium in height, stocky—I think beer belly is the term she used—and that he had brown eyes and long hair with a scraggly beard. Avery's only five foot one, his eyes aren't brown, they're blue, and believe it or not, he didn't even have a beer belly back then," I said. "Allen, on the other hand, at five ten with brown eyes and plenty of heft may not have been a perfect match, but he fit Penny's description a whole lot better than Avery did."

"Okay, so Deputy Dvorak didn't like Avery," Jody replied. "But what about the sheriff and the other officers who worked the case that night. Why were they so certain it was him?"

"I don't know, but they jumped right on the bandwagon and then the whole thing took on a life of its own. It's kind of human nature, don't you think? If someone comes up with a plausible suspect, others are inclined to agree until information arises to the contrary."

"But information did arise to the contrary," Jody replied. "You just said Steven Avery didn't match the description, and I thought his alibi was solid. It sounds like they turned a reasonable suspicion into much more than they should have."

Jody was right. Dvorak and Kocourek's initial suspicion of Steven Avery was reasonable, given Avery's previous behavior. But a reasonable suspicion is just that, a suspicion. Instead, with absolutely no hard evidence, they drew an unreasonable inference and concluded that Avery was the assailant. And when they learned information to the contrary, instead of discarding their assumption and starting over, they pressed on, heedless of the consequences. They worked the case in the exact opposite way police are trained. Instead of gathering and analyzing facts in order to learn the truth, they assumed the truth, and then, believing in the rightness of their cause, they adopted the facts that fit their assumption and discarded the rest. That wasn't police work—that was garbage!

I had been quiet for a while when, after I poured myself another glass of wine, Jody broke the silence. "Maybe Vogel and Kocourek felt there was no harm in sending Avery to prison even though he was innocent of this particular crime. He was severely disturbed and was bound to victimize other women."

Jody was probably right about their intention, but it's not an excuse. It's rare, but what happened here is a good example of what happens when cops and prosecutors lose sight of their calling, when they're so convinced that what they're doing is right that they don't care about how they get the outcome they're seeking.

It's classic arrogance by government officials and a serious abuse of power. They exhibited a complete lack of respect for the most basic constitutional rights, and their mind-set is shared by more people than we'd like to admit. "Society would be better off with this kind of riffraff behind bars," the thinking goes, "it's just too bad we have to spend taxpayer money to house lowlifes like Steven Avery in prison."

I was good and worked up as Jody and I left Maretti's that night. Our conversation had brought the pieces together, and it looked to me like Vogel and Kocourek knew Avery was innocent, which means they also probably knew that Allen was the true assailant.

The identification process at the hospital on the night of the assault was at the very least suggestive, and it might have been a complete scam. Once Kusche completed his masterpiece, the die was cast and a chain of events was set in motion where the machinations of law enforcement took over and the drive to convict never slowed down. Kocourek and Vogel ignored the statements of sixteen separate witnesses whose timelines were consistent with the receipt from the Shopko store in Green Bay. It was virtually impossible for Steven Avery to have committed the crime.

Worse, given all I knew then and learned later, it was hard for me to imagine that they didn't know that Gregory Allen was the real assailant. It was bad enough that they ignored their oath as elected officials to defend and protect the Constitution, but they also failed to discharge their primary duty as law enforcement officials to protect the public, as the woman in Green Bay found out ten years later when Gregory Allen broke into her apartment and raped her while her daughter lay sleeping in a room nearby.

TWENTY-ONE

I paid much less attention to the Avery case as the next several months went by. New challenges replaced old ones at work, and it wasn't long until another Thanksgiving and Christmas were over. The intensity I felt about what happened in 1985 gradually subsided. But the aftershocks of the wrongful conviction were far from over. Investigators from the attorney general's office were hard at work trying to sort out the events that led to Steven Avery's wrongful conviction, and in late-December, having interviewed dozens of witnesses, Attorney General Peg Lautenschlager released her report, faxing a copy to our office just minutes before releasing it to the media.

Mark and I read it with great anticipation, wondering what her conclusion would be regarding "what, if any errors occurred during the investigation, and whether any criminal or ethical violations were committed by anyone involved in handling the case," as the report described its goal. Seeing Vogel and Kocourek's misconduct summarized in an official report, in a document authored by the Wisconsin Department of Justice no less, gave the revelations a weight and a substance that they previously lacked. The thirteen-page Summary of Facts was divided into eight sections that detailed conduct by Vogel and Kocourek that I was certain would strike the media and the general public as shocking and inexcusable.

Most of the report covered ground that we were already aware of, but there were a few surprises. It turns out, for instance, that Penny Beerntsen received more than just one disturbing phone call while Steven Avery was locked up in isolation at the jail. Here's the language from the report:

> Penny Beerntsen received harassing phone calls following her assault, even after Steven Avery was arrested. Many of the phone calls were of a sexual nature, some of which occurred five minutes after she would return home, indicating she might be being watched. Such stalking

behavior and post-crime contact was consistent with Gregory Allen's past-offense history.

I knew that Vogel's file for the Avery case had contained a copy of the police reports and the criminal complaint charging Allen for the beach incident two summers earlier, but the investigators from the AG's office also found copies in the sheriff's file. In an interview with the *Milwaukee Journal Sentinel* the day after Avery was released from prison, Kocourek claimed he didn't know anything about Allen's crime on the beach two summers earlier. When the investigators from the AG's office later interviewed him, he denied knowing anything about Allen at all. So what was the complaint doing in his file?

The next revelation was just as disturbing. Shortly after Steven Avery's exoneration, some of our staff told me that they had doubted all along that Avery was the assailant, that they thought it was Allen. They had even approached Denis Vogel at the time, but he assured them that they had the right guy and that Gregory Allen couldn't have been the assailant because he checked with Allen's probation agent and Allen had an airtight alibi. But the AG's investigators did some checking of their own and found out that Allen wasn't even on probation on the day Penny was assaulted. In fact, he wasn't on probation at all that summer. Vogel, of course, didn't recall having such a conversation with the three members of his former staff, even though all three of them independently told the investigators what their boss had said.

But the report's conclusion was hugely disappointing. Given the facts uncovered by the investigators, I thought at the very least the attorney general would conclude that Vogel and Kocourek had engaged in ethics violations. But she concluded the opposite.

Her report cited "poor communication between law enforcement agencies" as one of the primary reasons for the wrongful conviction. But blaming it on poor communication was nonsense. Tom Bergner from the Manitowoc Police Department spoke in person with the sheriff about Allen and it's hard to imagine how he could have been any clearer. He even explained that his department was tracking Allen and had the impression that Kocourek already knew. And the Two Rivers Police Department's incident report concerning Allen lunging at the woman walking her dog on the same beach two years earlier was in the sheriff's file. So how did the attorney general conclude that poor communication among police agencies was to blame? It didn't make sense. As far as I was concerned, the report was a whitewash.

Using words without meaning and answering questions by merely restating them, the report opined that "the underlying problem in this case was that the investigators responsible for the investigation into the assault of Ms. Beerntsen never deemed Allen a suspect." No kidding, I thought, everyone knew that the sheriff and the DA didn't treat Allen as a suspect; the real question was, why not? It was classic bureaucratic doublespeak, and it was hugely disappointing. It's as if the two investigators wrote the findings of fact, and then some politico wrote the conclusion, the dichotomy was that extreme. The investigators had uncovered egregious facts, but the attorney general ignored them. She effectively whitewashed the entire affair.

TWENTY-TWO

Snowbirds, they call them. Thousands of retirees from Wisconsin flock south after the holidays for the rest of the winter. To Arizona, to Florida, to anywhere it's warm. For the rest of us, though, for those who must stay, the exhilaration of December's snowstorms and the excitement of winter's first blast of arctic air have been driven away by the doldrums of mid-winter blues. Cold gray skies alternate with sub-zero temperatures, and like bears hibernating in their dens, we settle in for the long haul.

Lest you end up like Jack Nicholson in *The Shining*, though, you must occasionally bundle up and get out in the cold. Kids build snow forts and ride sleds and toboggans, some like snowmobiling, and others go ice fishing. But my family's preference is cross-country skiing. With the right snow conditions, the groomed trails at Point Beach State Park are excellent and it's our favorite place to go.

Our first time out that year was later than usual. It was a Sunday afternoon in late January. A winter storm had churned northeast from Oklahoma and, having tapped abundant moisture from the Gulf of Mexico, dumped a foot of snow in the Upper Midwest. It left a Canadian air mass with brilliant sunshine and clear, crisp air in its wake.

The deep green and pure white of the partly snow-covered pine trees contrasted sharply with the clear blue winter sky. Gone were the hustle and bustle of work and the daily concerns of life; a quiet calm gradually filled our souls.

Four months earlier, Jody and I had dined at Maretti's, and with Steven Avery's wrongful conviction fresh on our minds, our conversation had been intense. I'd held forth sanctimoniously about Vogel and Kocourek's blatant abuse of power and even questioned what I do for a living.

But over the intervening months I had come to accept what happened to Steve Avery as an aberration unlikely to ever be repeated, at least in Wisconsin, thanks in part to the Avery Task Force's anticipated reforms.

Besides, we all make mistakes, I considered, sometimes even serious ones like Vogel's and Kocourek's, and we wouldn't want others to judge us so harshly if we were in their shoes. It's like a saying I once heard: "There are only two kinds of people, sinners who think they're saints and saints who know they're sinners."

TWENTY-THREE

Like all former offenders who have done their time, Steven Avery faced a number of difficult decisions in the days immediately after he was released from prison, some of them more significant than others. Try going to a restaurant and ordering from the menu when for the last eighteen years you've eaten whatever the prison cooks slop on your tray.

But there were larger questions, too: Where was home? Who would he live with? What about work? These are good questions for any former offender as he transitions from prison to life on the outside, and they were especially good questions for someone who went in with problems as deep-seated as Steven Avery's.

"Home" turned out to be back at the Avery Salvage Yard with Mom and Dad. Appearing on a local TV station's nightly news program the day after he was released, Steve was all smiles as he relaxed in his house trailer and popped open a beer. It was the first time I got a good look at him since his release, and by the looks of his girth, the prison food must have agreed with him.

But Steve didn't last long in the house trailer. A person grows accustomed to his surroundings after a while, and having spent eighteen years in an eight-by-twelve-foot prison cell, he felt the need for smaller confines. So that winter he moved into an ice shanty—that's right, an ice shanty. Its close quarters made it feel just like home. "I wanted somethin' small," he told a reporter, "everything was, I don't know, just too big. It didn't feel right."

But it was unlikely Steve would live in an ice shanty for long. His lawyers were seeking compensation for what everyone agreed was a horrible injustice, regardless of whether it was by accident or by design, and if he played his cards right, Steven Avery would be a millionaire.

Keith Findley of the Wisconsin Innocence Project led the injustice-by-accident effort by seeking payment from the State Claims Board. Under Wisconsin law, those who are wrongfully convicted may petition the state for compensation for the time they spent behind bars. But the law dates back to 1913, and rewards are limited to $5,000 per year with a cap of $25,000. Nevertheless, shortly after Steve's release from prison, Findley submitted a massive document entitled "Steven Avery's Petition for Compensation for Wrongful Imprisonment." Not only did he ask the claims board to increase the out-of-date limits, but given the egregious circumstances in this case, he also suggested that they ignore any limits at all.

Keith found a receptive audience in the person of Mark Gundrum, the state legislator that Mark and I met in Madison after our visit with the attorney general. Not a member of the claims board itself, but the chair of the courts and corrections committee, Representative Gundrum proposed to raise the limits from $5,000 to $25,000 per year and reset the cap at $450,000.

"I think that's a much more reasonable number," he told the *Milwaukee Journal Sentinel*. "The government has been negligent per se in the administration of justice in this case. That's my opinion."

Steve told the press the day he walked out of prison that he wasn't angry with anyone and wasn't really thinking about monetary compensation, but from the looks of the petition he filed with the claims board, he'd obviously changed his mind. The special damages alone—loss of income, pension, future earning capacity, those sorts of things—added up to an amount "conservatively estimated" at $1,097,200. Steven Avery may not have been thinking money when he got out, but it hadn't taken long for him to come around.

Even the most fiscally conservative politicians found persuasive the petition's account of the hardships suffered by Steve from spending eighteen years in prison, though I'm sure there was disagreement over the amount he had requested. He was a 23-year-old auto mechanic when he was convicted, and now he was 42 and trying hard to overcome the emotional trauma of his wrongful incarceration and to start his life over. He lost his wife and the ability to develop a relationship with his children.

"For more than eighteen long years," the petition asserted, "Mr. Avery lost his freedom, his civil rights, and his dignity, and through no fault of his own, he was denied the chance to live the American dream—to enjoy the company of his family, to parent his children, to own a home, to advance in a career, and to choose how to live his own life."

The petition went on to describe the immense injuries Steve suffered in terms of "emotional, relational, and personal injuries, social stigma, and the staggering loss of freedom he endured." It tallied economic losses, including eighteen years of lost income, Social Security earnings history, retirement savings, "and more than eighteen years in which to acquire skills, increase his level of education, and seize financial and personal opportunities." An actuary put the losses at $1,097,200, and that didn't even include pain and suffering. By granting the request, the petition concluded, the state legislature could diminish the "terrible injustice" suffered by Steve and give him "the financial independence with which he may begin his life anew."

* * *

Keith Findley and the Innocence Project staff weren't the only ones seeking compensation for Steven Avery. Despite the ambivalence he initially expressed about bringing a civil action, Avery soon retained attorneys Walt Kelly and Steve Glynn, the attorney who handled his second appeal, to represent him in a $36 million wrongful conviction lawsuit. That's a lot of zeroes, but how else do you try to make whole someone who lost his freedom for eighteen years? The legal system hasn't figured out a better way than to award them money, and that's exactly what Steve's attorneys set out to accomplish.

Unlike the negligence theory upon which Keith Findley's petition to the claims board rested, Kelly and Glynn alleged intent. They filed what lawyers call a 1983 Action, where the plaintiff claims that his or her civil rights were violated—in this case, their client's right to due process under the law. Tom Kocourek and Denis Vogel were named as defendants, both individually and in their official capacities, along with Manitowoc County. In order to succeed, Glynn and Kelly would have to prove that the government officials acted intentionally, or at the very least, with gross negligence, when they convicted Steve Avery and sent him off to prison.

* * *

On a Friday morning, almost two years to the day after Steven Avery was exonerated, Mark and I were both subpoenaed to appear for depositions in his wrongful conviction lawsuit at the local branch of a large Milwaukee law firm. Walt Kelly would be our inquisitor that day. Whether at trial or in depositions, when it comes to grilling reluctant witnesses, Walt is one of the best. He's an aggressive attorney, but he's never just a hired gun. Walt passionately believes in his client's cause, and that's why he pushes the limits of civil advocacy to some extent. His gray beard and piercing blue eyes well-match the personality of this aging but still vibrant 1960s activist, and although we'd never before met, I liked him immediately. Besides, my feelings about what happened in 1985 weren't a secret. I'd been open with the Wisconsin Department of Justice and I intended to be the same the day I was deposed.

I walked into a conference room where a flock of red-eyed and weary attorneys were sitting around a table with pens and legal pads poised in front of them, ready to have at their next victim. Since each party had his own attorney, including two each for both Vogel and Kocourek, I started adding up the legal fees in my head. I gave up when I reached over $2,000 an hour.

I sat down in the witness chair—the one with the video camera positioned three feet in front of my face—and readied myself for battle. Steven Avery was sitting right beside me, and he appeared to be in good spirits. Who wouldn't be? His $36 million case was picking up steam.

Walt methodically covered the basics first—my name, occupation, dates of employment at the DA's office, that sort of thing. Then he zeroed in on what I knew about his client's wrongful conviction. So I told him about finding the Gregory Allen complaint in Vogel's file and about my telephone conversation with Vogel a few days later.

But I couldn't add much to what the lawyers already knew. I'd been forthcoming with my answers, so when Walt turned me over to the defense, they had very little to hone in on and I escaped pretty much unscathed. They'd each received a summary of my interview with the investigators from the AG's office, so they already knew where I was coming from. I noticed as I walked out that a few of the defense attorneys seemed none too pleased with my answers, but what did they expect?

I gathered from one of the attorneys that they were approaching the end of the witness list for depositions and things weren't going well for the county, or for its former sheriff and district attorney. Glynn and Kelly had been zeroing in on Kocourek and Vogel for months, and the two of them were on deck to be deposed. There was little doubt—Steven Avery was about to become a millionaire.

TWENTY-FOUR

Pessimism permeates the trenches of the criminal justice system, and if you thought too much about what happened in the Avery case, it was easy to become discouraged. But Steven Avery's wrongful conviction also brought out the best in people and as in a surprising number of more ordinary criminal cases, its tragedy was overcome by redemption—at least for a while.

News of Steve's exoneration brought smiles to the faces of those who had believed so firmly in his innocence and fought so tenaciously for his release over the years. These included assistant public defender Reesa Evans-Marcinczyk and attorney Jim Bolgert at the trial court level, private investigator James Stefanic, attorneys Jack Schairer and then Steve Glynn on appeal, and, of course, Professor Keith Findley and his students at the Wisconsin Innocence Project, who accomplished the ultimate goal—their client's freedom. Some of their efforts fell short, but each of them kept up the drumbeat that Steven Avery was innocent. And for that they had reason to be proud.

The exoneration was especially welcome news for Jim Bolgert. Steve's conviction had worn heavily upon him since the jury handed down the guilty verdict in 1985. At times, he testified at his deposition, he felt "grief stricken" over the whole thing. In 2000, he had a conversation with Denis Vogel and told him they had to do something about the case, that it was "a travesty" that kept him up at night. But Vogel replied that he never lost any sleep over it.

For Penny Beerntsen, the emotional aftermath of the exoneration was full of complexity. Penny is conscientious, maybe to a fault, and compassionate beyond belief, so it wasn't easy for her. A few days after Steve's release from prison, Penny sent him an extraordinary letter.

"There are no words sufficient to express how deeply sorry I am for what has happened," she wrote. "Your wrongful conviction has taken away eighteen years of your freedom—something that can never be given back to you. I wish it was in my power to restore those years, but it isn't. The only thing I can offer now is a sincere apology that I identified you as my assailant when you were not.

"I work for peace and justice and I feel I'm doing some good," Penny explained, "and then I find out that I'm part of a huge miscarriage of justice. When I testified in court, I honestly believed you were my assailant. I was wrong. I can only say to you, in deepest humility, how profoundly sorry I am. May you be richly blessed, and may each day be a celebration of a new and better life."

If only Steve could have lived up to Penny's hopes for him. Two years later, the entire state of Wisconsin fervently wished that he had.

And it wasn't just those who were directly involved in Steve's case that were moved by his exoneration. There was something about his personality, his renegade appearance and the easy laugh and good cheer he exhibited in public that engendered an extraordinary amount of sympathy for him in the community at large too. Many felt moved by his plight and reached out to help him in any way they could. After seeing a feature story on TV about his ice shanty abode, a few especially sympathetic souls set up a charity fund for him and collected close to $3,000 from like-minded donors in no time at all.

Attorney General Peg Lautenschlager made the most of it, too. By agreeing to conduct an independent investigation of the wrongful conviction, she had taken on a dicey political endeavor. As the state's "top cop," she could lose the support of her most natural constituency—law enforcement—if she came down too hard on Vogel and Kocourek. Her conclusions concerning what led to the wrongful conviction were disappointing, to say the least, but at least she focused attention on the value of DNA evidence for the state's justice system.

"DNA evidence has gained acceptance in the criminal justice system as having forceful, potentially irrefutable probative value," she announced in her report. "Had the investigation into the assault of Penny Beerntsen been conducted using currently available technology, it is reasonable to believe that the trial of Steven Avery never would have occurred."

And Steven Avery's exoneration wasn't only followed by a strong emotional response from those who were personally involved and self-congratulations by some of us in government. It also brought reform.

Keith Findley's petition to the state legislature to raise the outdated caps on compensation for wrongfully convicted state prisoners was picking up steam. Governor Jim Doyle advanced the likelihood that the proposal would become law when he enthusiastically endorsed it without passing judgment on the specific amount of money requested by Steve's attorneys.

But the most significant reform would come from the Avery Task Force. It hadn't exactly started off with a bang. Politicians were in charge and the media was constantly on hand—always a bad combination for getting anything of substance done. But the hearings were in full swing by the middle of February, and Mark Gundrum and the other members of the task force were getting down to business and addressing the issues with the urgency they deserved.

One of the most widely publicized hearings took place at the state capitol in Madison with both Steven Avery and Penny Beerntsen in attendance. The hearing was held in front of the judiciary committee, and many of the heavy hitters in Wisconsin's criminal justice system, along with a few nationally known experts, would be on hand. Wisconsin Supreme Court Justice Louis Butler would address the committee. So would Chief Deputy Bob Donohoo from the Milwaukee County DA's office, nationally known DNA guru Norm Gahn, and several state senators and circuit court judges with an abiding interest in criminal justice system reform.

The hearing would focus on the perils of eyewitness identification, but it was clear from the agenda that other issues would also be confronted. In fact, one of the main things to come out of the task force—a requirement that police officers either audio record or videotape interrogations of juvenile suspects and a strong incentive that they do the same with adults—had nothing at all to do with Steven Avery's wrongful conviction. But the most anticipated testimony would come from Penny Beerntsen. Here's how *Milwaukee Journal Sentinel* reporter Tom Kertscher covered that part of the story:

> The sexual assault victim who falsely identified Steven Avery as her attacker, helping send him to prison for more than seventeen years, is to appear Tuesday at the Capitol before a task force. The Manitowoc woman plans to cite a lack of "moral courage" on the part of top

Manitowoc County officials who investigated the 1985 assault. She plans to blame law enforcement authorities for not telling her that Gregory A. Allen—whom DNA testing linked to her attack in September—had been identified, with Avery, as a suspect.

The woman, 55, is to urge the task force to review ... the need for investigators "to commit to writing discussions about other potential suspects."

She also plans to tell about the guilt she has experienced since Avery was exonerated five months ago. "Of all the people I need to learn to forgive in this whole process, forgiving myself will be the most difficult," the woman says in a statement she plans to make in Madison. "Not a day goes by that I don't think about Mr. Avery, his family and the suffering they endured."

The hearing was held two days later, and in a dramatic moment for all those who witnessed it, Penny Beerntsen embraced Steve and apologized. Later, she described his response—that she needn't worry and that it wasn't her fault—as "probably one of the most grace-filled things ever said to me."

Longtime *Milwaukee Journal Sentinel* columnist Bill Janz covered the story. He noted Penny's restorative justice work in the prisons and described how inmates admire her courage and appreciate her efforts to help them. Some of them had recently written to her and defended her in the assault case, "as she has defended them as human beings, not monsters," Janz wrote.

TWENTY-FIVE

My sons and I go salmon fishing at the end of every summer—how often depends on how the fish are biting that year. Running from mid-August through late September, the salmon run is a blast. Chinook, sometimes called "King" Salmon, aren't native to Lake Michigan—the Department of Natural Resources stocked them for sport fishermen thirty years ago. Bellies bulging with eggs, the twenty-pound behemoths stage just offshore before swimming upriver to spawn. Charter boats take well-heeled tourists from Milwaukee and Chicago into the deeper waters all summer long. But when the spawn is on, in August and September, local anglers like us along with some diehard pier fishermen from Minnesota and Iowa, take part in the fun.

We went out on the last Saturday in September 2005, the day after I was deposed in Steven Avery's wrongful conviction lawsuit, and after stopping for a "healthy" breakfast at Kwik Trip—soda and candy bars for the boys, and coffee and donuts for me—we were at the Two Rivers pier by a quarter to six.

Two or three more serious fishermen beat us to the most coveted spots at the end of the pier, but there was plenty of room, so I set up about thirty yards beyond the boys and started casting. Green and silver three-quarter ounce Champs are the standard fishing lure during the spawn, but anything that makes the salmon angry will do. Not particularly caring if anything with gills struck my lure, but hoping I could at least avoid a snag by staying off the bottom, I casted over the water and watched the Champ arc far over the waves.

It was warm for that time of year, feeling more like August than the end of September. A late summer thunderstorm had passed through an hour earlier, leaving dark scraggly clouds in its wake as it moved out over the lake. The sky turned from pink to red and then to purple as the sun rose triumphantly over the departing storm.

I was happily lost in a fisherman's reverie with my thoughts drifting off in all directions—until they settled on the Avery case. Maybe it was because I'd seen him just the day before while being deposed, but whatever the reason, the events surrounding his wrongful conviction were once again on my mind.

Like the storm's high winds that had downed trees and knocked out power a few hours earlier, Kocourek and Vogel's actions had severely damaged the local justice system. The media had forever linked Manitowoc County with Steven Avery—the innocent man who spent eighteen years in prison for a crime he didn't commit. And if that wasn't enough, local citizens who already mistrusted the police distrusted them even more, and those who did trust them started to wonder why.

But now the storm was over. Avery's exoneration had overcome the injustice of his wrongful conviction, and like the dark clouds drifting off to the east, the turmoil wrought by the Avery case was slowly receding. Smart lawyers and committed government officials were trying to restore his life to what it was before—or at least to salve the injury with a boatload of money—and to prevent something similar from happening again. They were doing their best to repair the damage, and a measure of justice was being restored.

But their efforts would fall tragically short. The original injustice was about to explode. The first storm was about to spawn a second one, a storm so powerful that it would shatter the atmosphere and lay waste to parts of the land.

PART III

TWENTY-SIX

On October 31, 2005, Halloween day, 25-year-old freelance photographer Teresa Halbach drove east on Highway 10 toward the Avery Salvage Yard. Teresa worked for Pearce Photography in Green Bay and one of her accounts was with Auto Trader Magazine, a company that listed used cars and trucks for sale in classified ads. Her last assignment that day was to snap a few pictures of a maroon Plymouth Voyager that Steven Avery was putting up for sale.

Teresa had graduated with honors from the University of Wisconsin-Green Bay where she majored in photography. She specialized in taking children's portraits, but she also took wedding pictures for friends. Her brother Mike later told a reporter that his sister had a gift for making people feel comfortable, and it showed in her photography.

One of five children, Teresa grew up near the village of St. John in Calumet County, one county west of Manitowoc, where her parents ran a dairy farm. She had recently moved back home from Green Bay so she could start saving up for one of her dreams: opening her own studio.

Steve had hired Teresa before, and on her last assignment he came out of the shower wrapped only in a towel. She was a little unnerved by the incident and mentioned it to a friend, but with all the publicity surrounding Steve's exoneration and the sympathy he garnered from so many in the state, she didn't give it much thought. Besides, every other assignment with him had gone off without a hitch.

Teresa loved singing along with the radio and she was probably doing just that as she drove east down Highway 10. She especially loved karaoke, and a friend said later that when it was Teresa's turn to take the stage, she became the life of the party.

Three days later, on November 3, Teresa's mother started worrying when she hadn't heard from her daughter. Teresa was never out of touch that long. So she called the police and reported her missing.

* * *

After forty hours of scraping and painting someone's house, the last thing a professional painter wants to do at the end of the day is to scrape and paint his own. It's the same with prosecutors. We deal with enough of society's ills during the day that we don't want to read more about them at night. So like most of my colleagues, I don't pay much attention to crime in the rest of the state, or in the rest of the country for that matter. The nation's obsession with JonBenét Ramsey's disappearance, for instance, passed me by. The O.J. Simpson case was an exception but who didn't become obsessed with that one?

So I missed it when news first broke that Teresa Halbach had gone missing.

But my ignorance didn't last long. Mark Rohrer called me at home on Saturday morning, and from the tone of his voice I knew it was serious. Could I meet him at the Avery Salvage Yard, he asked, right away? A volunteer search party had just found the SUV of a young woman from Calumet County who was reported missing three days earlier, and the police needed a search warrant for what they feared would be her remains.

"Where'd they find the SUV?" I asked.

"At the edge of the junkyard near the woods, whoever did it threw a bunch of branches on top to conceal it."

"Do we know anything else yet?"

"Well," Mark replied, "her final shot that day was of a used car for sale at the salvage yard. And guess who called to set up the appointment?"

"Oh shit," I replied.

Mark was right. It proved to be Teresa's final shot all right, for she never left the Avery Salvage Yard that day, and in fact, she never would-.

Within minutes I hopped in our van and sped out to the scene. Media helicopters circled overhead as more than a hundred police officers from several jurisdictions, including sixty state troopers, conducted a massive search for what nearly everyone feared would be Teresa's remains. I remember gathering information from detectives for a search warrant and wondering where in the midst of the countless skeletons of junked cars—each surrounded by tall grass and weeds—the killer had hidden the body. As darkness fell, a light drizzle that started in mid-afternoon turned into a cold driving rain. A mobile unit from the state crime lab equipped with a few floodlights and a space heater served as the command post and a refuge from the dark, wet cold. The rain got heavier as the night wore on, and the flimsy transparent plastic that served as the canopy for the crime lab unit flapped noisily in the gusty wind. I'll never forget the eerie feeling evoked by the shrill sound of police dogs loudly barking as the search continued late into the night.

Still, no body ... until finally one of the dogs, a Belgian Shepherd named Brutus, zeroed in on a burn barrel just outside Steven Avery's trailer. Half a dozen detectives converged on the scene and began sifting through the contents of the burn barrel. It didn't take long. They found pieces of charred bones and teeth fragments that a forensic anthropologist would later identify as those of an adult human female.

Hours later, Calumet County Sheriff Gerald Pagel and Calumet County District Attorney Ken Kratz held a makeshift late-night press conference. It was well past midnight. Television and print reporters from Milwaukee and Green Bay flocked to a municipal building in the nearby village of Valders and covered it live.

That Steven Avery was the last person to have seen Teresa alive had been widely reported for several days, and with all the police activity at the salvage yard that day, the media had rightly assumed that there'd been a major break in the investigation. But the authorities had been extremely tightlipped about what, if anything, they found, so the reporters had no way of knowing the gravity of what they were about to learn.

Sheriff Pagel said it was the worst crime scene he had investigated in his 33-year career.

"You can probably tell I'm a little bit shook up today, with the evidence we've discovered," he told the reporters. "And I think I have a right to be."

For me, the press conference was almost as extraordinary as the ghoulish scene at the salvage yard. The unprecedented sight of big city television and newspaper reporters descending upon the tiny village of Valders, population 962, at one in the morning left a lasting impression on me.

The reporter's questions and the official's responses were predictable enough.

"Has anyone been taken into custody?" shouted one reporter. "Did you obtain any other physical evidence?" asked another. "Is Steven Avery the prime suspect now, or still just a 'person of interest'?"

Sheriff Pagel and the Calumet County DA artfully responded, releasing just enough information to satisfy the reporters but withholding anything that might compromise the investigation.

But as ordinary as the back-and-forth between the media and the government officials was, even among the most jaded reporters the mood was uncharacteristically somber. Beneath their professional exteriors, they were parents, siblings, or dear and trusted friends, and most of them were genuinely disturbed by the profound evil that must have befallen Teresa Halbach.

The ghoulish atmosphere at the salvage yard was now replaced with a new, though no less intense, mood—and every person in the room instinctively felt it. We were witnessing the initial reports of an unspeakable evil, though evidence uncovered by investigators in the coming weeks ensured that the evil would remain anything but unspoken.

Caught up in the immediacy of what was happening at both the salvage yard and the press conference, I failed to appreciate the gravity of the events until I got home. For one thing I had been busy gathering information for search warrants. But that wasn't all. When people are caught in the middle of a catastrophe—a serious car accident, a tornado, or, tragically and increasingly more often, a terrorist bombing—it feels like a dream. Their sense of sight, smell, and sound are heightened while their higher brain functions are dulled. It's a survival instinct dating back millions of years. The intellect, the ability to process information, to analyze what happened, doesn't catch up until the trauma from the event has run its course.

I wasn't in any danger at the salvage yard that night and I wasn't traumatized in the classic sense. But I was affected enough that the enormity of what had occurred did not begin to register with me until I got home. And that's when the analyzing began. A young woman's life had ended in what would prove to be an exceptionally brutal, even sadistic, fashion at the hands of a violent killer. The worst fears of her loved ones had become a reality. By now her parents had received the most dreaded news a parent can ever receive: their missing child had almost certainly been murdered.

I tried to imagine what it was like for the Halbachs after they were told about Teresa's charred remains. Did they think of how she was murdered, of whether she fought back? What kind of suffering did she face in her final moments? Was she crying? Screaming? What were her final words? Despite the unshakable faith that would inspire so many others during the months that followed, such thoughts undoubtedly crept into their minds.

And the enormity of what transpired didn't stop with the violent end of Teresa's life. Steven Avery, the legendary survivor of an imperfect court system, a formidable feather in the cap of the Wisconsin Innocence Project, and the inspiration for one of the state's most ambitious criminal justice reform bills in years, was the No. 1 suspect in Teresa's murder.

What if what was suspected was true? What if Steven Avery was the perpetrator?

Mark and I had paved the way for Avery's efficient release just two years earlier. We offered little resistance to freeing an ex-con who had racked up a considerable record long before he was wrongly convicted. Did we do the right thing or should we have put up a fight? Steven Avery was a seriously disturbed individual long before he was wrongly convicted as evidenced, for instance, by his repeatedly running naked in front of a neighbor's passing car. When Penny Beernstsen was attacked, he was out on bail for ramming into that same neighbor's car with his pickup truck and then holding the female driver at gunpoint. And he had a well-documented history of deranged behavior long before then, including dousing a cat with gasoline and then lighting it on fire.

Had the system failed, had our office failed, not by wrongly convicting Steven Avery two decades earlier, but by releasing him two years ago? Maybe Kocourek and Vogel were right all along: Who cares that a depraved sociopath like Steven Avery was wrongly convicted of an earlier crime—look what he did to Teresa! He was a dangerous deviant then and is apparently no less of a dangerous deviant now.

But I'd been an attorney for too many years to so cavalierly discard my respect for the rule of law.

"It's better to let a hundred guilty go free than to convict one who is innocent," thus boldly proclaims one of our oldest and most cherished principles of law. No one could blame Teresa Halbach's family if they rejected the idealism of this lofty legal view—I'm sure I would if it had been my daughter who'd died at Steven Avery's hands. But the principle dates back to thirteenth century English legal theorists and is the cornerstone of the criminal law provisions of our Constitution. It goes to the very heart of our justice system.

Besides, I considered for a moment, maybe he didn't do it? By assuming guilt without knowing all of the facts, wasn't I repeating the same mistake that Tom Kocourek and Denis Vogel made twenty years earlier?

TWENTY-SEVEN

Along with most people in the state, Steve Glynn and Walt Kelly first learned of developments in the Teresa Halbach case on the morning after the press conference. A missing person story, transformed overnight into the Steven Avery story, was the lead story in newspapers and television reports across the entire state. The lawyers tried desperately to get hold of their client, but Avery was at his parents' cabin up north.

Steve and Walt are compassionate men who care deeply about their clients, regardless of how despicable the crime is they are alleged to have committed. Never assuming guilt unless admitted by the defendant in a plea or proven by the prosecution at trial, and doing their best to find good in the worst of their clients, I'm sure they approached Steve gingerly. But about one matter they had to be clear. Under no circumstances, they told him, was he to talk about the case. Not to the media. Not to the police.

But Steve ignored them on both counts and spoke freely to anyone with a microphone or a pen. Thanks to the attention lavished upon him two years earlier, he wasn't a bit shy of the cameras and enjoyed being in front of the klieg lights again. He granted several interviews with newspaper and television reporters from his family cabin up north and repeatedly claimed he had nothing to do with Teresa's murder.

Yes, he conceded, she was at the salvage yard that day, he'd hired her to take some pictures of a minivan he was putting up for sale. She'd been there several times before, he explained, doing the same thing. He told them he saw a pickup truck that he'd never seen before in the area a little after 2 p.m. It pulled up right behind Teresa as she turned off Avery Road and headed back to the main highway.

In response to one reporter's question about how Teresa's RAV4 ended up on his family's land, Steve said he was worried the police were trying to set him up again—just like the last time. "Maybe the Manitowoc County cops planted it there," he said.

Two nights later, 250 people held a candlelight vigil near Teresa's hometown. They feared the charred bones and teeth fragments found in the fire pit were Teresa's, but DNA tests were still under way so there was nothing definitive. They held a prayer service and tied blue ribbons on trees—Teresa's favorite color was blue—at first as a sign of hope that she would come home, but later as part of her tear-filled memorial.

Teresa's brother Mike, who worked as a video assistant for the Green Bay Packers, would serve as the family's spokesperson. Trying hard to remain hopeful, Mike spoke to a reporter after the vigil.

"We hope Teresa will come home, but we don't know where she is," he said in a calm and poised tone of voice. "But at the same time we are preparing for the worst. Until we know where she is, we definitely think she'll come home to us."

But Teresa never did come home. A few days later, DNA tests confirmed what most people suspected all along. The bone and teeth fragments were Teresa's.

Mike Halbach spoke to the media again after receiving the news.

"We braced for the worst, hoped to God it didn't happen, but it seems the worst did happen. It hurts to know that we won't see Teresa on Earth, you know…, as far as we know, but we'll move on. It will take a while to move on, but we'll see Teresa again."

Sheriff Pagel informed the media that in addition to the teeth and bone fragments, investigators also found evidence that "someone attempted to dispose of a body by incendiary means, but was not completely successful." The evidence had been sent to the crime lab for DNA testing to determine if it matched Steven Avery's DNA.

Steve Glynn put it best after being reached for comment by the media. "Steven Avery finds his life once again in the hands of a DNA analyst," he said. "That's pretty strange to happen to the same guy in two years."

❊ ❊ ❊

In a heartfelt letter to Steven Avery eighteen months earlier, and during a later public embrace, Penny Beerntsen had apologized and expressed hope and encouragement for his future well-being. It was an act of atonement, an incredibly dignified one, offered not by the system responsible for the injustice—the system rarely atones—but by a second victim of the same injustice.

But that was a year and a half ago and Penny was moving on with her life, again. She had learned a lot from the Avery case, including how to strike the right balance between acknowledging the bad stuff life throws at you and holding onto the pain for too long. It would be impossible for her to entirely forget Steve's wrongful conviction, nor would she have wanted that, but for Penny it was time to let go and move on.

That's what *should* have happened. It would have happened twenty years earlier had Kocourek and Vogel done their job. But the pain that had intermittently plagued Penny for the last twenty years was about to return. The final stage of her nightmare was about to begin.

Janine Geske, who had made a similarly difficult telephone call to Penny two years earlier, called her again a few days after Teresa Halbach went missing with some potentially dreadful news. Janine and her husband had stopped for gas in Manitowoc County on their way back from a weekend getaway up north. Nearly every gas station and grocery store in the county had a missing person poster with Teresa Halbach's picture on it by that time, and the gas station where Janine had stopped was no exception.

Sadly, missing person investigations aren't all that uncommon in Wisconsin or in any other region of the United States, so Janine didn't think much of it. Until she happened to notice where the attractive young woman on the poster was last seen alive.

Janine wasn't sure if she should call Penny or not. That the missing girl was last seen at the salvage yard didn't mean that Steven Avery had killed her, or even that she had met foul play. There can be other explanations for these things. Why worry Penny about what very well might turn out to be nothing?

But Steven Avery had racked up an impressive record before his eighteen-year unlawful hiatus in prison, and blessed with an excellent memory, Janine remembered almost all of it. There was the cat-burning incident. And the case when he rammed his pickup truck into the deputy's wife's car and then held her at gunpoint, clearly intending to rape her. He'd pled guilty to that charge at the same time he was wrongly convicted of attacking Penny, and six of his eighteen years in prison *rightly* resulted from his conviction for that offense. Janine also knew that with his exoneration came complete free-dom, which for a disturbed soul like Steve's, meant no freedom at all. He was left unsupervised, with no parole, and had no doubt been drifting aimlessly, imprisoned this time by his own violent and perverted untreated proclivities.

So, like many of us who knew of Steven Avery's past, the moment she first learned that a young woman who'd gone missing was last seen alive at the Avery Salvage Yard, Janine thought reflexively that Steve was likely involved. She hated to alarm Penny, but in the end she decided to call.

Penny had put plenty of emotional distance between herself and Steve's wrongful conviction, but in just three weeks she was scheduled to be deposed in connection with his lawsuit and had recently met with Steve's lawyers in order to prepare. So when Janine called with the news, with Steve's inno-cence and Vogel and Kocourek's role in wrongly convicting him fresh on her mind, it wasn't easy for her to switch gears from Steven Avery, the vic-tim, to Steven Avery, the villain.

Steven? Murder? No way. His wrongful conviction lawsuit was reaching a critical point, she explained confidently to Janine, and from everything she understood an award well into the millions was nearly a sure thing. Finan-cially secure, he could start rebuilding his life, hopefully even his relationship with his children. The same question Penny asked Janine would become a common public refrain: With all that going in his favor, why would Steven Avery throw it all away?

Penny might have been overly optimistic about Steve's commitment to building a good life and his wherewithal to succeed, but she was right about his lawsuit. Having already deposed dozens of lesser witnesses, and with Kocourek and Vogel on deck, his lawyers were progressing steadily up the food chain. They had solidified the facts about which they already knew and even uncovered some new ones that would be very difficult for Kocourek and Vogel to plausibly deny.

One of those new facts came from Penny herself. She wasn't planning to mince her words at her deposition, nor should she have. She would be testi-fying about some previously unknown activities engaged in by the sheriff's department and the prosecution that were bound to make the case against Vogel, Kocourek, and the county all the stronger.

They came to light during a meeting she recently had with Steve Glynn and Walt Kelly in preparation for her deposition. On the night she was assaulted Penny had given the police a very specific detailed description of the leather jacket her assailant was wearing. It was a worn-out waist length black leather jacket with buttons or snaps down the front. Kocourek and Vogel had little, if anything, to work with, but they did everything they could to tie the leather jacket to Steven Avery, at least figuratively.

They found a leather jacket when they executed the search warrant at Steve and Lori's house the morning after Penny was assaulted, but it was nothing like the one Penny had described. And there was another problem. Despite seeing him every week for as long as he could remember, Steve's uncle, Deputy Arland Avery, never saw Steve wearing a leather jacket. Never.

But a week before trial Vogel sent Steve's lawyer a note informing him that three officers who had prior contact with Steve "will be in a position to testify" that they had personally seen him wearing a leather jacket exactly like the one Penny had described. A week later Vogel paraded the three officers in front of the jury and each of them claimed they'd seen Steve wearing a leather jacket like the one Penny said her assailant was wearing, never mind the vagueness of their recollections. Vogel had to call Arland Avery to the stand later to prove some other point, but conveniently he never even asked Arland if Steve wore a leather jacket.

Steve Glynn and Walt Kelly already knew that much about the leather jacket. But when Penny met with them to prepare for her upcoming deposition, she shared with them some additional information about the leather jacket, information that if turned over to the defense by Vogel and Kocourek could very well have led to a different result at the trial.

Maybe you've never heard of a leather jacket lineup, I know I hadn't, but Sheriff Kocourek conducted one a few days after Penny Beerntsen was assaulted. Kocourek's officers had found a leather jacket at Steve and Lori's house the morning after they arrested Steve. Lori told them Steve never wore it, a claim later backed up by deputy Arland Avery, and it didn't look anything like the jacket Penny had described. But the sheriff thought maybe she was mistaken, so he had some tables set up in a conference room and displayed some leather jackets on top of each table, including the jacket they found at Steve's residence. Then he called Penny in and asked her to examine each jacket very carefully and let him know if she recognized the one her assailant was wearing. Penny took her time, but she was certain—none of the jackets looked anything like the one her assailant was wearing. The leather jacket line up was a bust!

The results of the leather jacket lineup fall squarely within the definition of exculpatory evidence, which is evidence tending to negate the guilt of the accused, and not disclosing them to the defense was serious prosecutorial misconduct. How much significance would the jury have attached to the results had they known them? Given the weakness of the state's case in general, would the leather jacket lineup's failure have tipped the balance in favor of an acquittal? We'll never know. But the criminal justice system is about process, not results, and Vogel and Kocourek's failure to disclose this and other exculpatory evidence to the defense illustrates at the very least a lack of respect for the process. At its worst, it reveals outright contempt.

TWENTY-EIGHT

Although they denied it, from the moment police got word that Teresa Halbach's vehicle had been found at the Avery Salvage Yard, they considered Steven Avery the No. 1 suspect for her murder. And like the last time they investigated him for a serious crime, at least in the beginning, their suspicion was reasonable.

He was the last person known to have seen Teresa alive, after all, and her car was concealed on his property. And when he called her employer to set up an appointment that morning, he specifically asked for Teresa, and not some other employee.

News of Teresa's disappearance had already garnered some national media attention, but when it became known that the man suspected of killing her had spent eighteen years in prison for a crime he did not commit, the story reverberated through the Midwest and beyond. It was the first time in the nation's history when an exonerated person was later accused of murder, and the *Deliverance*-like crime scene and grisly details of the murder guaranteed it a national audience.

In what must be one of the show's strangest episodes ever, Steven Avery called in to the *Nancy Grace* show on CNN a few days after the human remains in the fire pit were identified as belonging to Teresa Halbach. Still holed up at the family cabin up north, he again proclaimed his innocence, telling America that he was being set up by the Manitowoc County Sheriff's Department in revenge for his $36 million lawsuit.

"Mr. Avery," Nancy Grace asked. "Why do you feel that you're being framed?"

"Because every time I turn around, the county's out here doing something to me."

When asked about the tooth fragments and bones that were found in his fire pit, Steve said the salvage yard isn't usually locked and anyone could just drive right in.

"I worry about it every minute," he said. "I look out the window, is a squad car here, are they going to pick me up? When are they going to pick me up? When I'm sleeping, are they going to come in? I always have that fear," he said.

"I think Manitowoc County is trying to set me up real good because they're taking everything," he said, "but they don't seem like they found anything because there ain't nothing there. They've been watching us. They've been sitting up by the end of the driveway. But I'm done talking to them."

Two days later Calumet County District Attorney Ken Kratz charged Steve with first degree intentional homicide and mutilation of a corpse. Kratz was appointed special prosecutor after Mark Rohrer—citing a conflict of interest because of Avery's pending lawsuit against the county, including its former DA—bowed out. Ken's a very good prosecutor, but he loves the limelight, so he was more than happy to prosecute the case. Also, Teresa was from Calumet County and Ken had been working with his sheriff's department since the investigation into her disappearance began.

Dressed in a black-and-white striped jail jumpsuit, his wrists handcuffed and attached to a belly belt, Steve was escorted into court by eight uniformed deputies. Judge Patrick Willis set $500,000 cash bail.

In a strange bit of irony, his arrest occurred on the same day the governor was scheduled to sign into law the "Avery Bill" in the same courtroom where he had been wrongfully convicted twenty years earlier. But with news of the bill's namesake's arrest, the ceremony was promptly called off and the legislation was rather blandly renamed the "Criminal Justice Reforms Package."

Self-serving proclamations of innocence or not, somewhere along the line, the innocent man had turned into a cold-blooded killer. Or had he?

TWENTY-NINE

Somebody mentioned at work the next day that Nancy Grace was supposed to cover the Avery case again that night, so I made sure to tune in.

Sitting in for Nancy, guest host Harris Faulkner opened the show with a video clip of a somber-looking Ken Kratz conducting another press conference.

"It's no longer a question, at least in my mind, of who is responsible for the death of Teresa Halbach," Kratz said, pushing well beyond the limits of what prosecutors are supposed to say to the media.

Trying to deflect any leftover sympathy for Avery from those who couldn't accept that the "innocent man" could have committed such a heinous crime, Kratz reminded the viewers that there was only one victim in the case—and that was Teresa Halbach.

Faulkner turned to former prosecutor Wendy Murphy after a commercial break—presumably for her expertise.

"Wendy," she asked. "If you're prosecuting this case, what does all this evidence tell you?"

"Well, this doesn't take rocket science," the former prosecutor began. "It doesn't get any closer to a slam dunk, even without knowing yet that it is, in fact, this woman."

Apparently, facts didn't matter to Wendy Murphy.

"I mean, I've got to tell you something," she said with disgust in her voice. "The sympathy for this guy, the idea that he's filed this lawsuit, I just want to reach through this camera and grab the guy and shake him and bang his head on the wall because I'm not convinced at all that he was wrongly convicted of the first crime!

"I will not deny for a minute that the DNA evidence that wasn't available at the time of his trial kind of affected his ability to have a fair trial," she continued. "But let's not confuse this with innocence. I'm not persuaded at all that this guy was innocent with regard to that earlier rape!

"So let me say this to the people who helped him get out. Good job!" she said. "You let the guy out by claiming he's innocent. And now look what he did. He killed a woman! Thanks a lot!"

"But he was exonerated," Faulkner interjected.

"That doesn't mean he's innocent," she snapped back. "I'm sick of these DNA lies. The Innocence Project and these people who falsely claim that 150 men have been exonerated and proved actually innocent with these new DNA tests on old cases is nonsense.

"I don't care how many shows he goes on and claims he's not the type of guy that does this sort of thing," she continued. "How does he explain the bucket of blood from his body in her car?"

"'Bucket of blood'? What's she talking about?" I said out loud. "I thought it was a few stains."

Next, they brought in a forensic psychologist who opined the obvious—that whoever committed the murder was "a stone-cold sociopath."

"To put a dead body in a barrel," the expert said, "to light it on fire, the sights, the smells, the sounds, to watch it burn. That says that this is a man who has no care for human life."

Following Steve's arrest, considerable—and irrational—anger was directed at anyone associated with his exoneration two years earlier. Rabble-rousing hosts of radio talk shows, incensed citizens in letters to the editor, and web surfers in Internet chat rooms espoused sentiments not unlike those expressed by the prosecutor on *Nancy Grace*. Keith Findley from the Wisconsin Innocence Project and his family even received death threats.

Locally, Steven Avery's arrest for Teresa's murder wasn't just a bizarre news story that would capture national attention for a week before Nancy Grace and others in the media moved on to some other salacious crime story. It was the talk of the town, and sometimes the entire state, and it would remain so for months, if not years, ahead.

Everybody, of course, was shocked by the news. Some couldn't bring themselves to believe that their former hero was a killer. Why would he ruin his life by murdering Teresa Halbach? He was about to become a millionaire—there's no way he would do such a thing! But a majority assumed he was guilty—why would the police have arrested him if he wasn't involved?

Being a prosecutor, I thought he was probably guilty, too. I'd seen it happen before, how an offender can swing from trying his hardest to stay on the straight and narrow one day to committing a horribly violent crime the next. And given my prior obsession with Steve's wrongful conviction, I was more familiar than most with his sordid past, going all the way back to when he was a juvenile.

But on the other hand, I had personal contact with him on two separate occasions since his release from prison, and in neither instance did it seem like he was capable of committing such a heinous crime.

The first time I saw him was in connection with the arrest of his then-newfound girlfriend, Carla Schwartz, for drunken driving. The case came up for trial almost a year after the incident, and Steve was the star witness for the defense.

Carla had put her car in the ditch out on Reifs Mills Road. She crawled out of the car after the crash and walked up to a nearby farmhouse to call a friend for a ride home, but when they pulled into Carla's driveway, a county sheriff's deputy was patiently awaiting her arrival. Carla started crying. "Yes, I was driving," she told the officer, "I was alone at the time." She said she got into an argument with her boyfriend and she was driving around to clear her head. "I went in the ditch because it was so damn foggy," she blurted out.

It was the fifth time she'd been busted for drunk driving, which even in Wisconsin is a felony, and she had six other criminal convictions on her record, too—disorderly conduct, resisting an officer, misdemeanor theft, and other similar petty offenses. Her blood alcohol concentration this time was a healthy .285—more than three times the legal limit—and it was the drunken driving charge that would net her the most time.

I knew the case was coming up on my trial calendar, but I hadn't given it much thought until I received a letter from Steven Avery. The letter was handwritten and it wasn't easy to read, but the gist of it was that Carla didn't put the car in the ditch; he did. If the cops would just do their job and investigate, Steve wrote, they'd know what happened and he and his sweetheart wouldn't be in such a pickle. He said he didn't want to get involved, but he couldn't take Carla being in jail anymore—he loved her and wanted to marry her.

The day for trial arrived and there was Steve, in the same courtroom where Judge Hazlewood sentenced him nearly twenty years earlier. We hadn't yet met, but I knew what he looked like and I think he knew who I was, too. His girlfriend's attorney and I exchanged a few pleasantries and then the judge called in the jury.

Steve told the same tall tale at trial as he did in his letter to me. He and Carla met each other for the very first time at the Uni-Mart out on Highway R that night, and after some small talk, Carla asked him to go for a ride. He said he didn't have anything else to do that night, so he took her up on the offer. Even though it was Carla's car, he drove. He told the jury they aimlessly drove around the county for a while, and then Carla asked if he would take her out to the salvage yard to show her around. A junked vehicle was blocking the entrance, so he used Carla's car to push it out of the way, but he hit the gas too hard and the car slipped off the bumper and rammed into the front end of the junked car. With Carla's car still drivable, Steve continued, they went for another ride, but then the fog rolled in, and after missing a turn he put Carla's car in the ditch. He said he called his sister to come get them, but Carla said she was going home and she started walking the other way.

But his story wasn't believable, and the jury didn't buy it. Carla had already told the arresting officer several times that she was the driver, and she never said a word about anyone else being with her. So she was convicted, and a few months later Judge Hazlewood placed her on probation and gave her nine months in the county jail.

Steve and I crossed paths again a few weeks later when I was deposed in his $36 million lawsuit against the county. He was seated right next to me and we nodded to each other when I walked in and did the same when I left. He sat politely and listened attentively as the lawyers asked their questions and I did my best to answer.

There was nothing about his appearance on either occasion to suggest that his sexual deviance—which was so evident when he was younger— was about to explode. On the contrary, his demeanor both times was non-threatening and even calm.

THIRTY

The Manitowoc County Circuit Court operates under a monthly intake cycle. Whether it's civil or criminal, traffic or juvenile, or any other type of dispute that can be settled in a court of law, if you're the intake judge, it's yours. You'll start it and you'll see it through to its hopefully satisfactory end.

Judge Patrick Willis was on intake when the murder charges against Avery were filed. Since assuming the bench seven years earlier, Judge Willis had drawn more than his fair share of high-profile trials. And now, by good luck or ill, he drew the Avery trial, the hands down most sensational trial in the county's history.

The case passed predictably enough through the usual mile-markers of the criminal justice system with the press covering each hearing more than its significance deserved. The initial appearance, the preliminary examination, the arraignment—front-page headlines and nightly news reports covered each of them to satisfy the public's appetite for the latest news.

During the months that followed, the parties filed every motion under the sun and, as always, Judge Willis dug in and rose to the challenge. Some of the motions had more merit than others, but he plowed through them one at a time and methodically disposed of each according to law.

Having already invested hundreds of pricey hours in a civil lawsuit that had abruptly lost most of its value, neither Steve Glynn nor Walt Kelly were inclined to defend Steve against the murder charges. Besides, there was probably a conflict of interest.

So Assistant Public Defender Erik Loy was appointed instead. Like Glynn and Kelly before him, Loy tried gagging his client, but true to form, Steve ignored him and granted one interview after another from the Calumet County jail, claiming more boldly each time that he was being set up by the sheriff's department.

"Whoever killed Teresa Halbach ain't got a right mind," he told one reporter. "There's no way I could kill somebody—that would be too hard.

"They know what to look for," he said, referring to the police, "so they know what they should plant and where they should plant it."

Delores Avery, Steve's mother, echoed his claim. "I don't know why the hell they do that stuff," she told the reporter. "They must like wrecking people's lives.

"He's innocent, I know it in my heart," she said.

Allan Avery, Steve's dad, told the reporter that the cops were wrong before and now they're wrong again. "Now it's starting all over again," he said.

Kratz responded. He told reporters that Steve and his family's allegations of planting evidence were "absurd." He said someone would need a vial of Steve's perspiration to plant his DNA on Teresa's car keys. As it turned out, Ken's choice of the word "vial" turned out to be an unwise one.

Steve Glynn and Walt Kelly were deeply disappointed when the investigation into Teresa's murder increasingly pointed in the direction of their former client. "This case has blown us away," Glynn told a reporter from the *Journal Sentinel*. "I haven't taken that hard a punch in a long, long time."

"This lets down so many people," he went on. "It became something that could have had an enormously positive effect on the criminal justice system in this state, but now that's up in the air."

Penny Beerntsen was disappointed too. At first it was difficult for her to square the light-hearted and forgiving Steven Avery she met two years earlier with the perpetrator of such a horrible crime. But as more evidence was released by the authorities, she accepted the likelihood of Steve's guilt and her thoughts and compassion turned more and more to Teresa Halbach and her family.

News of Steve's likely involvement in Teresa Halbach's murder was especially difficult for the Wisconsin Innocence Project. Its brochure described its mission as not just to release the innocent, but also "to find the truth and properly punish those truly responsible for crimes."

"This is a very emotional time and a very emotional event," Director Keith Findley told a reporter, "but this should not affect what we do."

And it didn't. In the intervening years the Wisconsin Innocence Project has steadfastly continued its work, winning the release of additional wrongfully convicted inmates along the way.

* * *

With twenty-five years of experience under his belt and the typical heart of a public defender, Erik Loy is an excellent attorney. But like so many criminal defendants ignorantly say when they decline the free services of the public defender, Steve wanted a "real" lawyer instead. So he turned to the big leagues. He promptly settled his lawsuit against the county for a fraction of its worth—$400,000, to be precise—and retained a talented but pricy legal defense team from Madison and Milwaukee. In a classic good cop/bad cop routine, Dean Strang of Madison and Jerome Buting of Milwaukee would tag-team the prosecution from the day they were hired until the end of the trial.

Responding to Kratz' frequent and sometimes over-the-top interviews with the media, and aware themselves that nearly everyone in the state had their attention glued to the case, Buting and Strang tried much of their case in the press. They methodically shot down the state's key pieces of evidence one at a time and then leaked a bombshell or two of their own.

They started dribbling out a few weeks after Steve was arrested. A series of quirky circumstances—coincidences I thought at the time—that made some people start to wonder whether the police could have set up Avery again.

Exhibit A was Teresa Halbach's RAV4. Investigators from the Calumet County Sheriff's Department learned early on that Steve was the last person known to have seen Teresa Halbach alive, so it made sense that they began their search at the Avery Salvage Yard. But when they searched the property, they found nothing. The RAV4 wasn't found until four days later by the volunteer search party organized by her family and friends. The salvage yard stretches over forty acres of grassy hills and is littered with more than a thousand skeletons of junked cars, so many people assumed that either Steve moved it, or the police just missed it. But others weren't so sure.

Buting and Strang masterfully seized upon the circumstances of the RAV4's delayed discovery. Calumet County investigators didn't find it because it wasn't there—it must have been planted. The deputies didn't murder Teresa Halbach, they'd never do such a thing, but they probably found her car somewhere nearby after she was reported missing and then drove it to the salvage yard to make it look like Steve killed her.

It was all part of the effort to frame their client and wrongfully convict him again. Their motive: revenge for Steve's $36 million lawsuit against the county that made the sheriff's department look bad.

The second shoe dropped a few weeks later. It had to do with how Teresa's keys, including the ignition key to her RAV4, were found. Among the locations the police searched on the first night of their investigation was Steve's bedroom inside his house trailer. The initial searches of the room conducted by Calumet County officers yielded nothing.

But a few days later, two Manitowoc County Sheriff's Department officers, Detective Jim Lenk and Sergeant Andy Colborn, searched the bedroom again. It was the third time the room was searched, but they wanted to check behind a bookcase. They moved it away from the wall and a set of keys fell out, landing on the floor right in front of them. They were Teresa's keys and one of them, the key to the RAV4, was later discovered to contain some skin cells that matched Steven Avery's DNA.

I knew Lenk and Colborn. They're two of the most honest and ethical cops I've ever worked with, and I knew in my heart and my mind that they'd be the last ones in the world to plant evidence. I didn't know why the other officers missed the keys on the previous searches, but I assumed I'd find out soon enough.

But Buting and Strang cried foul. Lenk and Colborn had both been deposed in Avery's wrongful conviction lawsuit just a few weeks before Teresa disappeared, and Steve's lawyers had roughed them up pretty good.

They surmised that Colborn and Lenk, angry that they'd been dragged into the lawsuit and accused of participating in Avery's wrongful conviction, were out for revenge.

Jim Lenk was understandably upset that his name was appearing in headlines all across the state recounting allegations that he was a dirty cop who had planted evidence. "Isn't there something I can do?" he asked me one day. "I've always followed the rules, and now Avery's lawyers are dragging my name through the mud. This is ridiculous."

But the truth is there was nothing Jim could do. A person charged with a crime has a constitutional right to defend himself, and that right has been interpreted broadly. And, short of disclosing confidential information, like the identity of a juvenile offender, the media has a right to cover the story completely. "No, Jim," I said, "it stinks, but there's nothing you can do."

Neither Colborn nor Lenk had anything to do with Steven Avery's 1985 wrongful conviction. They did exactly what they should have when they received the call from the Green Bay detective informing them that an inmate there, probably Gregory Allen, himself, was claiming that he, not Avery, was Penny Beerntsen's assailant: They passed the information up the chain of command, all the way to Sheriff Kocourek. But the coincidence of the timing of their depositions and their finding Teresa's car keys in Avery's bedroom was awfully strange, and before long the number of people who suspected the police set up Steve again rose sharply.

The news got even worse a few months later—much worse. In one of the most dramatic turn of events since Teresa Halbach went missing, Jerome Buting called a press conference that shocked the state and propelled the case back in front of the national spotlight. By the time it was over, the defense had stolen the ball and pushed it up court so explosively that the prosecution of Steven Avery for Teresa's murder was in serious jeopardy.

As part of his trial prep, Buting had requested several months earlier to see the court file from his client's 1985 wrongful conviction case. It was the same file—actually a box full of court records and exhibits—that the deputy clerk had found in the courthouse basement during Avery's second appeal ten years earlier. Buting walked into the clerk's office at the appointed time and saw the file just sitting there, unattended on the counter. He rifled through the box and quickly came upon an unsealed vial of his client's blood. It was the blood specimen Sherry Culhane used to compare Steve's DNA to the fingernail scrapings taken from Penny Beerntsen on the night of her assault.

A few drops of Steve's blood had been found in Teresa's car, and now the defense had an explanation for how they got there. It was the cops! They must have stolen some of Steve's blood from the vial in the clerk's office and placed a few drops inside Teresa's car. Buting described to the media how the box was just sitting there, unattended on the counter, available to anyone with the inclination to pilfer through at will.

But if you're going to allege a police conspiracy, it better be credible— though it helps if the alleged conspirators had previously conspired. So how did the police get their hands on the blood specimen?

Coming up with a plausible explanation was easy. The courthouse bailiffs are employed by the sheriff's department. They have keys to the clerk's office, and thereby access to the vial. They could have snuck in after hours and retrieved some blood from the vial and then handed it off to one of the detectives, who could have sped out to the salvage yard and placed a drop or two in Teresa's car.

The situation had me on edge. Either Buting had stumbled upon the mother of all red herrings, or there was something to the conspiracy theory. It was bad enough that the Calumet County investigators didn't find Teresa's RAV4 when they initially searched the salvage yard and that Colborn and Lenk were the ones to find her keys in Steve's bedroom. But now, with the sensational blood vial defense, there was a legitimate chance that Teresa Halbach's killer—or the person I and most other people assumed was her killer could go free!

THIRTY-ONE

Half a block from the courthouse, right downtown, Warren's Restaurant has been the pulse of the community in Manitowoc for almost fifty years. It's one of those greasy spoons that grace most every American small town. With bottomless cups of coffee and a menu of breakfast items that are more than just passable, it's an early morning gathering spot for local lawyers and anyone else who enjoys shooting the bull. Local, state, national, or beyond—there's no problem too large or too small for the folks at Warren's to solve. Mostly, though, it's a place of friendship and fellowship where just like at *Cheers*, everyone knows your name.

As a morning person and a hopeless coffee addict committed to non-recovery, I'm one of the regulars at Warren's, or at least a semi-regular, stopping in a few mornings every week. It opens at six and I like to get there around six-thirty to join the earliest of the early morning crowd.

The Avery case was naturally the chief topic of discussion at Warren's from the date of Teresa Halbach's disappearance until the end of the trial. From Mike the window washer to the county executive, everyone at Warren's had an opinion about the case, and given what I do for a living, they inevitably asked about mine.

For the most part, their opinions didn't evolve. Some thought from the start that Avery was guilty as sin, that the conspiracy theory was nothing but a pack of lies spewed out by a couple of high-priced, out-of-town defense attorneys. And their opinions didn't change when Lenk and Colborn found the keys—just more conspiracy theory nonsense as far as they were concerned. Take Joe, for instance—every time I'd walk by, he'd shake an imaginary blood vial and ask me if I'd been out at the salvage yard with the coppers lately. What a card.

Tammy, on the other hand, was the complete opposite. She bought the defense wholeheartedly. Of course the cops set him up—every one of them is a lying stinking bum. Just last month they nailed her teenage son for writing another forged check, and this time he didn't even do it—he only took the plea bargain to avoid going to jail. She was absolutely convinced that the conspiracy theory was true.

And it wasn't a surprise, given its extraordinary events, that a sizable number of people outside Wisconsin and even overseas were following developments in the Avery case. Many of them expressed their opinions in online chat rooms but, owing to the relative anonymity of the forum, unlike the folks at Warren's, their conversations were anything but tame.

Laquisha started off one of the threads:

> I just can't see someone who just served time for a crime he didn't commit coming home and committing the horrifying crime he is accused of.

Here is Vennetta's less than reasoned reply:

> The whole Avery family proved to be a bunch of liars .... I mean really does the whole Avery family suffer from low IQs.

Predictably, a sizable number of chatters "liked" Vennetta's comment.

And then there's Patricia, whose failure to list her place of residence may have been wise given how the conversation unfolded:

> This young man was set up by three police officers who committed the crime and the planting of evidence.

Norman, whose profile stated he was attending UCLA didn't exactly exhibiting the tolerance espoused by the university he attends when he waxed poetic:

> Patricia, you're an idiot.

And badly misstating the facts of the 1985 case, "Top Commenter" Michael from New York City butted in with unmistakable New York charm:

Yes, is she kidding? He did the first one, too, but they found another
guy's hair on her jacket?

The hair he is referring to wasn't found on Penny's jacket; she was wearing a swimsuit. What's more, it was Gregory Allen's pubic hair, which was
combed from Penny's vaginal area during a forensic exam. But Michael
obviously doesn't allow the facts to get in the way.

Lois, who announced to the world that she was earning her degree
online, and Michael from New York City are apparently cut from the
same cloth:

The justice system never should've released this monster back into
society. It is a shame the monster did not get the death penalty. I hope
(he) rots in hell for what they did to that poor girl and her family!

Rich from Colorado tried to inject some reason into the conversation:

They shouldn't have released him? He was innocent!

But cherry-picking one fact among a dozen, Michael would have none of it:

No, he wasn't. They found someone else's hair on the victim? That
means nothing. Avery is the SCUM of the earth.

Evidently there's more than one "Top Commenter," because Norman from
Los Angeles shared the designation with Michael. Here's Norman again:

But he was a life-long criminal. He should've been locked up for life
on the other crimes. That's why the whole "don't execute because
they may be innocent" is a scam. If they didn't do the crime they're
accused of, they ALWAYS have committed other crimes in the past or,
in this case, they will commit crimes in the future.

Rich tried one more time:

Don't you get it, he was innocent. Regardless of what he did later you can't keep an innocent man in prison cause he MIGHT do something later. That's insane.

Proving the point, Norman got the final word:

No, Rich, most of us are OK with that.

Here's hoping that Norman from UCLA isn't shooting for a degree in constitutional law.

THIRTY-TWO

Meanwhile, *State of Wisconsin vs. Steven Avery* continued to wend its way through the court system. By the time it was over, it would become the most thoroughly litigated criminal case ever held in Manitowoc County, and with the state's case resting almost entirely upon complex circumstantial and physical evidence, the vast amount of litigation was warranted. Besides, short of a capital murder case—Wisconsin doesn't have the death penalty—the stakes for both sides were incredibly high.

Steven Avery's predicament was obvious. If convicted, he would spend the rest of his life behind bars, it was that simple. But for Ken Kratz and the other members of the prosecution team it was more complicated. Their first duty, of course, was to bring to justice the man they were convinced had murdered Teresa Halbach. Additional suffering would be heaped upon the shoulders of Teresa's family if they failed to gain a conviction, and the Halbachs had already endured more emotional pain from Teresa's murder than most people do in the course of their lifetime.

But an acquittal would also be tragic for the public—at least for those who believed the defendant was guilty—who saw in Steven Avery a man who had to be put behind bars for the rest of his life, if nothing else than for the protection of potential future victims.

And there was something else at stake for the prosecution. The wound caused by the wrongful conviction twenty years earlier had been reopened by the defense, and depending on the outcome of the trial, the local criminal justice system would either be restored to health or injured even more severely. Add to all of that the winner-take-all stakes of a jury trial, and no wonder both sides fought so ferociously both before and during the trial.

The first skirmish occurred a few weeks after the charges were filed. The state crime lab had already conducted forensic tests on a tremendous amount of physical evidence, including DNA tests on the blood spots found in Teresa's SUV and some sweat residue from one of her keys that was

found by Colborn and Lenk in Avery's bedroom. Since it was clear that testing would continue, probably right up to trial, the defense filed a "Motion
to Assure Fair Forensic Testing," arguing that the defendant had a constitutional due process right to observe all testing performed by the state
and even to conduct its own independent tests, provided enough material
remained to be tested.

But the defense cited no legal authority supporting their position, because
there wasn't any, and noting that he was unaware of any authority granting
an accused this supposed constitutional right, Judge Willis quickly disposed
of the motion. Motion denied.

Next, the defendant moved to dismiss the entire case on the grounds that
extensive pretrial publicity generated by law enforcement had made a fair
trial impossible. They specifically complained about a two part news segment in which the sheriff himself had participated in an interview.

Judge Willis had previously issued a limited gag order at both parties'
request, and now he ruled that given the length of time that would pass
between the sheriff's interview and the date that the trial was scheduled to
begin, which was approximately nine months, the order had not been violated and the defendant could still receive a fair trial. But the judge issued a
new gag order with considerably more teeth to head off any future problems.

"Members of the Manitowoc County Sheriff's Department, the Calumet
County Sheriff's Department, and the defendant, Steven Avery," the gag
order directed, "are to refrain from making any statements regarding this
case until its conclusion."

To their credit, for the most part, all parties followed the gag order.

The defendant's next motion was to "Exclude Manitowoc County Sheriff's Officers from Testifying and from Overseeing the Jurors," an unusual
motion to say the least. Knowing they didn't stand a chance of keeping key
witnesses for the state off the stand, Buting and Strang eventually withdrew
that portion of their motion, and the parties reached a stipulation for the
other part. It was agreed that the sheriff's department would not be providing the jury bailiff and that no one from the department would have
contact with prospective jurors, which also wasn't a surprise.

A few months later the court began taking up the more substantive motions
filed by the defense, including their motion to suppress evidence based upon

what they alleged was an illegal search by the police of the Avery Salvage Yard. Whether the police violated a defendant's constitutional right to be free from unreasonable searches and seizures, essentially to be left alone, is by far the most commonly litigated issue in criminal courts throughout the country. Spawning ever evolving legal concepts like reasonable suspicion, probable cause, plain view, and my favorite, "fruit of the poisonous tree," there's so much case law interpreting the Fourth Amendment that you wonder if the Framers didn't own stock in a New England paper mill or two.

The text of the Fourth Amendment is straightforward enough. Here it is, straight from the mouths of our Founding Fathers:

> The right of the people to be secure in their persons, houses, papers, and effects, against unreasonable searches and seizures, shall not be violated, and no Warrants shall issue, but upon probable cause, supported by Oath or affirmation, and particularly describing the place to be searched, and the persons or things to be seized.

Having helped draft the initial search warrant after Teresa's RAV4 was discovered at the salvage yard, I was more than a little concerned about how the defendant's motion would fare. If the court were to grant the motion, then most of the physical evidence would be suppressed – the state couldn't use it at trial – and the defendant would very likely go free. So I watched the proceedings with frayed nerves.

Buting and Strang first argued that *all* the evidence had to be thrown out, including Teresa's charred remains in the burn barrel and what the prosecution claimed was their client's blood in her car.

Their argument was that when the volunteer search party went onto the salvage yard they were actively assisting the police in an investigation of probable foul play. As such, they were acting as agents of the police, and their search should be treated that way. And since the police did not have a warrant to search the salvage yard, all the evidence found there, including Teresa's SUV, her bone fragments, and her keys (the "fruit of the poisonous tree"), had to be suppressed.

But the argument was a tough legal row to hoe because the law doesn't lightly attribute an agency relationship between police and private parties.

The non-police entity, the search party in this instance, must be functioning as an "instrument or agent of the government," and whether they are depends upon two factors.

Lawyers love it when courts give them a laundry list of factors, choosing which ones to hang their hats on depending upon which side of the argument they happen to be on that day. In this case, with only two factors to consider, the list is shorter than usual. It includes the following: (1) Did the police play a role in instigating or executing the search? and (2) Did they have the ability to direct and control the private party's actions?

In a 1949 case called *Lustig v. United States*, the U.S. Supreme Court put it this way:

> While a search that is orchestrated by an officer will certainly qualify, so might a search in which the officer's role was more roundabout or subtle, maybe even if he merely "had a hand in it."

So, did the police "have a hand" in the volunteer search party's activities at the salvage yard? If they did the evidence would be suppressed because the search was conducted without a warrant, and without the evidence, Steven Avery would go free.

But the defense fell short.

The woman who organized the volunteer search party testified that she told someone at the sheriff's department that her group would be searching the Avery property that day. But she stated that no one in law enforcement asked them to conduct the search or assisted them in any way. As a result, the motion was denied.

But Steve's lawyers weren't finished. They argued the evidence should be suppressed on other grounds, and this time their argument appeared to have merit.

"Serial searching." That's what they called it. The police had made multiple entries into Steven Avery's trailer home looking for evidence. In fact, six times over three days they went in without obtaining a new warrant. These multiple executions of the same warrant, they argued, surely can't be right.

And they had a point. More often than not, police obtain a search warrant late at night after waking up a prosecutor and a judge. Then they drive to the residence and knock on or break down the door, depending upon whether they think the occupants might be armed, search the place, and leave a few hours later, hopefully with the goods.

But "that's not how it's usually done" rarely gets you very far under the law. The warrant in this case authorized a search of the entire salvage yard and pretty much everything on the premises, including Steve's and others' trailer homes and outbuildings. It wouldn't be reasonable to expect the police to wrap up their search after a few hours.

So Judge Willis concluded that the search constituted a reasonable continuation of the original search. He also ruled that the evidence was admissible under the "inevitable discovery" doctrine, meaning the police could have applied for and received additional warrants after finding the initial evidence anyway.

Dean Strang and Jerry Buting were earning their fee but in the end, the law was not on their side and they came up empty. The state lost nothing of value, and it was time to move on.

THIRTY-THREE

It was the most dramatic turn of events since Jerry Buting found the unsecured blood vial in the clerk of courts office. Ken Kratz made the announcement at a press conference carried live on TV. His words were unlikely to reach the tender ears of children since they were broadcast in the early afternoon during soap opera hours, but it didn't matter to Kratz. Ever the advocate for the kids, Ken had a warning for the viewers. What followed would be graphic, he warned, you parents might want to have the kids leave the room, or at the very least, cover their ears.

The details couldn't have been more horrid, and Kratz didn't hold back.

Police had long suspected that Steve's sixteen-year-old nephew, Brendan Dassey, had accompanied his uncle in Teresa's murder. And now, as cops and prosecutors refer to defendants' confessions, Dassey had "puked all over himself."

Brendan said something in a recent police interview that caught the attention of one of the investigators. "We believed he knew more than he was telling us," Calumet County Sheriff Pagel later said at the news conference. So they interviewed him again, and this time Brendan confessed to participating with his uncle in Teresa's rape and murder.

It was the stuff of a cheaply made horror film—it even happened on Halloween—except it was true. Sparing none of the gruesome details, Kratz recounted the events as Brendan described them to the investigator, one step at a time.

Brendan got off the school bus at the usual time, about 3:45, and found a letter for his Uncle Steve in the mailbox. As he walked up to Steve's trailer, he heard a female voice inside screaming, "Help me!"

When he answered the door, Steve was "covered in sweat." He invited Brendan inside and asked him if he wanted to "get some of that stuff," pointing to the bedroom. Brendan walked in and saw Teresa Halbach naked and bound face up on the bed with handcuffs and leg irons.

Steve told him he already raped Teresa and wanted to continue, encouraging him to join in. Teresa cried and pleaded with him, begging him not to do it, to let her go, and to get his uncle to stop. But instead, Brendan got on top of her and raped her for about five minutes while Steve watched from the side.

After that it got even worse. The two of them went into the living room and watched TV for 10 to 15 minutes. "That's how you do it," Steve said, telling Brendan he was proud of him. While the TV played, Steve talked about killing Teresa and burning her body. He returned from the kitchen a few minutes later carrying a knife with a six- to eight-inch blade. Then they returned to the bedroom, where Steve told Teresa he was going to kill her. He stabbed her in the stomach and handed the knife to Brendan and told him to cut her throat. Brendan obeyed, and Steve told him to cut off some of her hair.

Brendan did that, too. Then Steve went over to Teresa and strangled her. They took off the shackles and tied her with a rope and took her to the garage where—even though Brendan believed she was already dead—Steve shot her about ten times with a rifle, including a few times on the left side of her head. He and Steve threw Teresa's body into a fire pit that had already been burning when Brendan got off the bus. They put tires and brush on top to accelerate the fire, and while Teresa's body burned, they drove her RAV4 to the edge of the salvage yard and hid it from view. Steve returned to the fire pit a few days later and broke up some of Teresa's bones with a shovel, and then he buried them in areas scattered around the premises.

Kratz concluded his remarks by telling the viewers that Brendan admitted that he should have done something to stop his uncle Steve, but he forced him to do it and threatened to stab him if he told anyone. When one of the detectives asked why he participated, Brendan replied, "I wanted to see how it felt ... sex."

I watched Ken Kratz' press conference with the rest of the office on a television set in our conference room, and like the rest of the state, we were horrified by the account of Teresa Halbach's final hour. That she'd been raped by her assailant was a safe assumption, but the details of the assault and her subsequent torture went beyond what anyone had imagined. I couldn't help wondering as I drove home that night how Teresa's family could possibly take anymore.

THIRTY-FOUR

The gruesome details of Brendan Dassey's confession shocked the public and even changed the views of some of the most conspiracy-minded people in town, convincing them that their former hero was guilty after all. But for those with an unshakable conviction that the police were corrupt, Brendan Dassey's confession only solidified their views. If what he said was true, they reasoned, there'd be blood all over the place—especially in Steve's bedroom where the victim was supposedly stabbed. But the police didn't find any blood in the bedroom—not even a drop. All this butchery and not one drop of Teresa's blood in the bedroom—how could that be? The cops must have psychologically tortured Brendan until he made it up, he's barely seventeen, and rumor has it he's slow.

As for me, I felt much better about the prospects for a conviction after Dassey's confession. Kratz added charges of first-degree sexual assault, kidnapping, and false imprisonment to the murder and mutilation of a corpse charges. If convicted on all counts, Steven Avery faced life imprisonment plus 128 years. That ought to do it, I thought.

But there was another part of me that felt like the system had failed, and I wondered if we should have seen it coming. I was familiar with the direction of Steven Avery's life in the months leading up to Teresa's murder, and the trajectory wasn't a good one.

It's almost universal. Despite their initial idealism, most people who work in the criminal justice system develop an edge of cynicism after a while—we see too many repeat offenders, I guess. So it wasn't surprising that from the moment Steven Avery walked out of prison, the courthouse crowd started taking bets on when he would be back in. They knew what he was like before he went to prison, and if they didn't, one of the oldtimers filled them in. The cat burning incident, the threats to burn down his girlfriend's parent's house, the crimes of domestic violence against his fiancée, ramming into the wife of a deputy's car and accosting her at gunpoint—these incidents became part of courthouse lore, and they still resided in the long-term institutional memory of the local justice system.

And Steve had another strike against him, one not shared by most former offenders trying to stitch their lives back together after serving their time. Because his conviction and sentence had been vacated, when he walked out of prison, he wasn't placed on parole. That meant no supervision, no counseling, no weekly meetings with a parole agent who kept tabs on him, and no support.

So the joy of freedom faded after a while and things started taking a turn for the worse. While he beat the predictions of the most pessimistic of the courthouse prognosticators, it wasn't long until the "innocent man" had a few brushes with the law.

The first one was just a speeding ticket. The officer clocked him at seventy-nine in a fifty-five-mile-per-hour zone. The rookie ADA handling the case must have figured the county owed him one, because he amended the ticket to defective speedometer and Avery promptly paid the fine.

Later it got more serious. Steve had taken up with a similarly lost soul by the name of Carla Schwartz, the woman whose drunk driving charge Steve later tried to derail. They met at a convenience store and apparently it was love at first sight. But the honeymoon didn't last long because a few months later, Carla had to call the police. She had moved in with Steve, and one weekend when he was up north, he found out she was out at the races but she hadn't let him know she was going out. When Carla came home a little after eleven that night, she and Steve got into an argument. She told him "to pack his shit up and move out," at which point he pushed her, causing her to fall into a chair and hit her head. Avery got on top of her and started hitting her, telling her he should kill her. Carla was able to get up to call 911, but before she could talk to the dispatcher, Steve ripped the phone out of the wall and began choking her to the point where she lost consciousness. When she came to, he dragged her out to the car by her arms and said, "I should get the gun and kill you."

In light of the conflict of interest stemming from Avery's wrongful conviction lawsuit, Mark farmed out that case to a local attorney who agreed to serve as a special prosecutor. Due to discrepancies between Carla Schwartz's original version of the events and what she told the officer a few days later, as well as her request to drop the charges, the special prosecutor directed the police to issue a disorderly conduct citation instead of issuing criminal charges. Somehow the media never got wind of it, and as far as the public was concerned, Steven Avery was still a hero.

There was also some evidence that Steve was trying to warn the world that he was in trouble and that his life was heading dangerously downhill. In an interview with the *Milwaukee Journal Sentinel*, just three months after his release, he described how he was often depressed and full of frustration and anger.

"Sometimes it'll last all day," he said. "That's when I try to stay away from everybody. Sometimes I cuss them out, sometimes I just go for a ride—it ain't nothing to put on a hundred miles."

He confided that he cried sometimes because his twin boys didn't want anything to do with him, and "there's probably too much going on inside my head—brain can't put it all in."

He complained about the state not providing him with counseling or other help in the transition—"they just let you out the door." But he also admitted that he would have refused to see a psychiatrist even if one was offered. "I can't tell him my problem. I'll sort it out myself," he said. "What can he do that I can't?"

He gave assurances that he didn't really want to return to prison, but when he reflected about how he used to sit on a picnic bench in the prison yard and count the jets that flew by, his words didn't sound very convincing. "Sometimes," he said, "I feel like it's easier in there. Some days, just put me back there, get it all over with."

THIRTY-FIVE

The defense team had been suspiciously quiet. The conspiracy theory was the cornerstone of their defense, but they hadn't filled in the blanks yet. Any day, I feared, they'd start leaking the embarrassing, no, the inexcusable details surrounding the defendant's wrongful conviction twenty years earlier, and the public would be shocked all over again—this time by the conduct of the police. I dreaded how effectively they would manipulate those events and tie them to the murder charges.

Transforming a juror's anger against an accused murderer to sympathy for him instead wouldn't be easy, but if anybody could pull it off, it would be Buting and Strang. If the jury became mired in the details of the wrongful conviction, who knows what would happen. All it would take is one out of twelve, one conspiracy-minded juror who thought like half the folks at Warren's did, and Steven Avery would go free. Forget about convicting him—by the time the defense was finished spinning their tale, the jury would be ready to hang the prosecution instead.

But maybe my fear was misplaced. Maybe I was attaching more significance to the details surrounding the wrongful conviction than they deserved. I'd been consumed by those events for a long time, but whether they were relevant to the murder charges and thereby admissible at trial, was far from certain. I knew that sooner or later the parties would have to address the issue head on, and Judge Willis would have to decide.

I tried to take comfort in the fact that the law was on our side on this one, and when it comes to rationally and objectively applying the law to the facts at hand, Judge Willis is one of the best.

The rule is straightforward enough: Relevant evidence, assuming it's not excluded on some other grounds, is admissible at trial unless its probative value is "substantially outweighed by the danger of unfair prejudice." The police weren't on trial for wrongfully convicting Steven Avery twenty years earlier; he was, for murdering Teresa Halbach. If the defense were permitted to harp on the details of the wrongful conviction, the jury might become confused with what they were deciding and acquit for the wrong reasons. I could almost hear Kratz summing up the state's argument. "The objective of a jury trial is to find the truth, Judge, not to muddy the waters."

But where the prosecution would see prejudice and confusion of the issues, the defendant's attorneys would see critical evidence necessary for his defense. I imagined how effectively Dean Strang might argue the point. He'd point out that a police conspiracy was the cornerstone of the defense, and however fantastic it might appear to some, the defendant had marshaled some credible evidence in support of his claim. "Remember, Your Honor," he would implore the court, "our client is charged with a crime that could deprive him of his liberty for the rest of his life. He must be allowed to present his defense!"

But as it turned out, my musings about the rules of evidence were unnecessary and my fear was misplaced because a week before trial, Judge Willis accepted a stipulation that had been hammered out by the parties. The fact that the defendant was wrongfully convicted of first-degree sexual assault and attempted murder in 1985 would get in, as would the fact that he had a $36 million wrongful conviction lawsuit pending against the county. But that's as far as it would go. There'd be no mention of the details of the wrongful conviction—nothing about a suspiciously created composite drawing or about an affidavit hidden in the sheriff's safe. The jury wouldn't know about Gregory Allen's sexually deviant sociopathic behavior leading up to his attack on Penny Beerntsen or about his lunging at the woman who was walking her dog on the same isolated stretch of beach two summers earlier. Nor would they hear about Denis Vogel's inaccurate claim that Allen's probation agent said he had an airtight alibi.

I was hugely relieved. Without its details, the conspiracy theory lost most of its punch. The connection between Steven Avery's wrongful conviction in 1985 and the allegation that he murdered Teresa Halbach twenty years later would strike the jury as speculation, at best, and the spotlight would be squarely where it belonged: on the accused.

❊ ❊ ❊

The legal maneuvering of the parties accelerated rapidly in the final month leading up to the trial. Lawyers on both sides were working on nothing but the Avery file. They were living and breathing the case, and like most trial lawyers, occasionally waking up late at night to jot down a note or two for fear of forgetting something important in the morning.

Given the circumstantial nature of the evidence that tied Steven Avery to Teresa's murder, I knew there was a good chance that Buting and Strang would launch a "*Denny*" defense, named after a 1984 Wisconsin Court of Appeals case bearing the same name. Under *Denny* and similar cases in other states, the defense is allowed to present evidence to the jury that a specific person, or persons, other than the accused could have perpetrated the crime. In other words, they get to name names.

But the defense can only do so under very strict criteria. They must be able to show that the other party had motive, opportunity, and at least some evidence connecting the third person to the crime "which is not remote in time, place or circumstances." The rule is called the "legitimate tendency test," and while it sounds like a legal mouthful, it actually makes sense.

Hoping to stop that part of the defense in its tracks, Kratz and his team had filed a "Motion Concerning Third Party Liability" six months earlier. Filing the motion so early was a preemptive strike by the prosecution since the defense had strategically not tipped its hand by naming the person or persons they planned to blame for Teresa's murder. In fact, it wasn't until January 10, 2007, less than a month before trial, that Buting and Strang filed their "Statement on Third-Party Responsibility."

In it they identified "every customer of the salvage yard, every family friend, and every member of the Avery extended family who was present at the salvage yard during the hours in question" as possible third-party perpetrators.

The defendant's pleading was broad, perhaps impermissibly so, but the motion itself carried some weight. Steve wasn't the only member of the Avery clan to have had trouble with the law. His older brother Chuck had a violent past, most notably an incident six years earlier when his former wife accused him of rape and attempting to strangle her with a telephone cord.

Steve's younger brother Earl had potential, too. He pled no contest to battery and sexual assault charges in 1992 stemming from an attack on his wife.

Apparently wives don't fare well in the Avery family. I had prosecuted "Earl the Pearl," as we called him in the office, for that assault and I remembered some of the details. What Earl did to his wife was bad enough, but it was nothing compared to what his brother was alleged to have done to Teresa Halbach.

Nevertheless, Chuck and Earl both worked at the salvage yard and very well could have been on the premises the day Teresa was murdered. So they both had "opportunity" as required by *State v. Denny*.

But did they have motive? If the court found they did, the floodgates would open. The defense lawyers would spend days deflecting the jury's attention away from Steven Avery toward one or more of his similarly disturbed siblings. Or anyone else, for that matter, with an unsavory past who happened upon the salvage yard on the day Teresa was murdered.

They wouldn't have to *prove* that Earl or Chuck or someone else was the perpetrator. The defense never has to prove anything; that would be shifting the burden of proof to the accused. All they would have to do is convince the jury that someone else was just as likely as Steve to have been the assailant. One or two jurors is all it would take, and the defense would be well on its way to an acquittal.

With so much riding on the court's decision, Judge Willis decided to take the matter under advisement. He wanted to think about it for a while.

✳ ✳ ✳

A few weeks before the start of what was expected to be a six-week long trial, the parties gathered in court for the final pretrial conference. Shackled in handcuffs and leg irons, and clumsily clad in a bulky stun belt, Steve was escorted into the courtroom by five deputies standing ready with side arms and Tasers just in case. Security outside the courtroom had been ramped up, too.

Judge Willis took up Buting and Strang's "motion regarding courtroom security" first, appropriate given the defendant's attire. Calumet County Sheriff Pagel, who would be in charge of security, and special agent Tom Fassbender from the Division of Criminal Investigation (DCI) wrote letters to the court explaining why the stun belt, in particular, was necessary during the trial.

Steven Avery was a disturbed and dangerous individual even before he was wrongly convicted twenty years earlier. But let's face it: he isn't Hannibal Lecter material when it comes to his intellectual powers, and this wasn't *The Silence of the Lambs*. There was no danger that Steve would *will* himself out of his shackles, put a spell on everyone in the courtroom, and slip outside.

So while conceding the need for tighter security than usual, Buting and Strang strenuously objected to fitting their client with a stun belt. They were concerned about the impression it would leave upon the jury, not to mention the discomfort it would cause the defendant during the six-week long trial.

Noting that nothing other than the severity of the charges had been offered by the State to justify using the stun belt, the judge sided with the defense. Besides, he reminded the lawyers, two armed Calumet County deputies would be positioned right next to the defendant during the entire trial.

It was less than a week before trial, and two major issues remained unresolved. The first was whether the court would allow the defense to present their third-party liability theory—the argument that some specific person or persons other than the defendant could have been the murderer. A few weeks earlier Judge Willis had taken the matter under advisement and now he was ready to release his decision.

His ruling wasn't good news for the defense. Conceding that the persons identified by Buting and Strang may have had the opportunity to murder Teresa, there was nothing to demonstrate that any of them had a motive to kill her. And without evidence of motive, the judge explained, the evidence failed the legitimate tendency test under the *Denny* case.

Not allowed to blame someone else for Teresa's murder, Steve's lawyers would be left with arguing the conspiracy theory and harping on reasonable doubt. The jury would never learn about Chuck or Earl Avery or any other violent miscreant who happened to be roaming the salvage yard that day.

The other unresolved issue concerned the blood vial. Would the court permit the defense to argue that members of the Manitowoc county sheriff's department had planted the defendant's blood in Teresa's car? How the defense played that card and how the prosecution reacted could very well determine the outcome of the trial. No wonder each side tried desperately to shape how the issue would evolve.

Nine months had passed since Jerry Buting discovered the vial inside the unattended file at the clerk's office and the parties had been playing cat and mouse with it ever since. Actually, since each side was waiting for the other to make its move, it was more like a game of chicken.

The state blinked first by filing a motion to prohibit the defense from making any mention of the blood vial at trial. That would be the state's preference. But in the alternative, Kratz asked to adjourn the trial so he could have the FBI conduct further analysis of the blood.

But since the defense was still sitting on its hands and hadn't requested the admission of any "frame-up" evidence, including evidence about the vial, it was premature for the court to rule on the state's motion. Also, permitting the state to conduct further analysis of the blood this late in the game would mean adjourning the trial and that's one thing Judge Willis wouldn't allow. So the judge did the only thing he could do. He reserved ruling on the motion to exclude the blood vial evidence pending receipt of the defendant's frame-up motion, ordered that it be filed in a week, and denied the state's motion to adjourn the trial. And in a bid to put an end to their cat-and-mouse game, he also ordered that neither party could make reference at trial to the other side's failure to pursue further analysis of the blood.

A week later, under seal but on time, the defense filed its "Statement on Planted Blood." Then, giving the conspiracy theory a major shot in the arm, Judge Willis agreed to let the blood vial evidence come in. He also allowed the state to pursue further analysis of the blood to try to disprove the claim that the police had planted it. But the state had to move fast, because the trial would not be adjourned.

* * *

I was a basketcase on the eve of the trial. I thought the chances of a conviction were better than even, but better than even isn't good enough for the prosecution. Shouldering the burden of proving the defendant guilty beyond any reasonable doubt, the prosecution's evidence must be overwhelming in order to succeed.

The quirky circumstances of the investigation scared me—especially how Colborn and Lenk were the ones to find the keys. If only Kratz could get Dassey's confession in front of the jury, I thought, the defense wouldn't stand a chance. But given Dassey's Fifth Amendment right not to incriminate himself, the state couldn't force him to take the stand.

There was one more option, though. It strikes some as unseemly, but we do it all the time. We use little fish to get bigger fish by cutting them a deal. Kratz could offer Dassey a plea agreement in return for his testimony against his uncle, maybe a reduction in the charges, or more likely, an agreement to recommend a parole eligibility date that would get him out of prison say, when he was fifty years old.

But getting Dassey to accept a plea agreement wouldn't be easy. The close-knit Avery family is fiercely loyal to each other, and Allan Avery would undoubtedly pressure his grandson not to cut a deal with the prosecution and not to testify against Steve. Also, Kratz had to be careful. You don't offer much leniency to a cold-blooded killer, even if he's a seventeen-year-old boy with diminished mental capacities whose role model is Steven Avery.

So it wasn't a surprise when in the end the parties failed to strike a deal—Brendan Dassey would not be taking the stand. Without his confession, the jury would not be allowed to consider the most damning evidence against Steven Avery, and the outcome of the trial was far from certain.

THIRTY-SIX

Steven Avery's trial—this time for murder—was set to begin on February 5, 2007. The astonishing twists and turns of the past eighteen months were about to culminate in a fascinating six-week trial. The Green Bay and Milwaukee TV stations had decided weeks earlier how they would cover the proceedings. Key moments, like the opening statements and closing arguments, would be broadcast live, while the rest of the trial would be available online, and all three local stations would cover the lawyer's daily press conferences on their evening news shows. The newspapers started running daily stories. "Defense Gearing up to Argue Blood was Planted," read one of the headlines in the *Manitowoc Herald Times Reporter*.

No one outside of law enforcement and the court system knew at the time, but on the night before the trial began, and a day after the *Herald Times* reported that the defense would be allowed to present evidence about the blood vial and the defendant's wrongful conviction lawsuit, former Chief Inspector Gene Kusche died unexpectedly, sitting in his favorite living room chair in the comfort of his home. The official cause of death was listed as acute myocardial infarction—a heart attack—and although friends said Gene wasn't a religious man, he had a Bible at his side.

Gene had obviously been in denial. I ran into him in the courthouse parking lot a few weeks before he died and we spoke briefly about the Avery case in the midst of television trucks with their live feeds and antennas rising thirty feet into the sky. It was a shame you guys released Avery from prison, he said with a straight face, because he and Allen could have both assaulted Penny Beerntsen on the beach that day. The not-so-subtle inference: If we hadn't cut him loose, Teresa Halbach would still be alive.

Kusche had expressed similar doubts at his deposition in the wrongful conviction lawsuit a few months earlier. "Yes," he replied to one of the plaintiff's attorneys, "I've heard that DNA evidence supposedly exonerated Mr.

Avery, but I don't know that on personal knowledge because I haven't seen the reports. I don't believe everything I read in the newspapers.

"Who knows," he suggested, "maybe the DNA evidence was fabricated. Or maybe they both did it."

It's admittedly mostly speculation, but did Gene Kusche's death have anything to do with the fact that the Avery trial would start the next day? Was Gene afraid that Avery would be acquitted because of what happened twenty-two years earlier? Or was his death just another odd coincidence in a case that was chock full of odd coincidences from the very beginning?

* * *

Judge Willis is no Lance Ito—in fact, he's the opposite. Despite its complexity, he was determined that the trial would be concluded in six weeks or less. But given the amount of pretrial publicity, as well as the strongly held views of some on the panel, it took a full week just to select the jury.

By week's end, though, the 144 prospects on the panel had been winnowed down to the chosen sixteen—eight women and eight men, four of whom would serve as alternates.

The first day of trial finally arrived. Kratz delivered a three-hour opening statement that, if predictable, was also compelling. Using a PowerPoint presentation with photographs and high-tech schematic drawings, he drew a picture in the jurors' minds of the Avery Salvage Yard with its cluster of trailer homes and outbuildings that served as the offices, garages, and living quarters for the family. And speaking in his pleasant low-key comforting way, he laid out a convincing account of Avery's guilt, and the jurors, especially the older ones, took to him immediately. "I promise," he assured them, "by the end of this case you will have no doubt who murdered Teresa Halbach."

Dean Strang hit a home run for the defense. With his sincere and thoughtful demeanor, he asked the jurors not to prejudge his client's guilt. Once they heard all the facts, he told them, they would have serious doubts about the state's evidence, including how the victim's keys got into Avery's bedroom and how his blood got into her car. He said the sheriff's department focused almost entirely on the defendant in the investigation because of their disdain for him, calling their technique "tunnel vision."

"The police didn't kill Teresa Halbach," he said, "they have that in common with Steven Avery; but they wanted to believe he did." He told the jurors he was going to ask them at the end of the case "to get it right this time."

Kratz and the rest of the prosecution team started presenting their case the next day. With Tom Fallon from the AG's office and nationally known DNA guru Norm Gahn from the Milwaukee County DA's office assisting, he began by laying out a timeline leading up to Teresa's death, with phone calls and a paper trail detailing her whereabouts on Halloween 2005.

They presented a steady stream of physical evidence, starting with the human remains and some blue jean rivets found inside the fire pit outside Steven Avery's trailer. The rivets came from a pair of Daisy Fuentes jeans similar to a pair owned by Teresa Halbach, and the bone fragments included a skull section that remained intact enough for an expert to determine that the deceased had been shot twice in the head.

Sherry Culhane, still a DNA analyst at the Wisconsin State Crime Lab and testifying in yet another case involving Steven Avery, said the chances were one in a billion that the teeth and bone fragments found in the fire pit did not belong to Teresa Halbach. She also tested the blood stains lifted from Teresa's car, and they matched Avery's DNA profile, as did some skin fragments on Teresa's keys.

Jerry Buting turned the state's presentation of the physical evidence upside down by suggesting in one blistering cross-examination after another that the evidence was planted. Playing the bad cop, he attacked the investigating officers for what he perceived as their lack of caution in following procedure. He questioned how four Calumet County deputies failed to find a bullet fragment containing Teresa Halbach's DNA that a Manitowoc County detective allegedly discovered a few months later in Avery's garage, terming it the "magic" bullet.

"Did you see a bullet on November 6?" he asked one of the officers from Calumet County, who swiftly responded in the negative.

"Because if you had, you would have collected it, right?" Buting asked rhetorically. "Because it would have been an extremely important piece of evidence, right? There were four of you in that garage, and not one of you found a bullet or a bullet fragment!"

"Correct," the officer replied sheepishly.

And Buting pulled no punches when he challenged how Teresa's car keys ended up in Avery's bedroom, all but accusing Colborn and Lenk of planting them there. It turns out the bedroom was searched six times, not just three, like I had thought, before the two Manitowoc County officers found the keys "in plain sight," according to Buting.

Kratz tried to soften the blow by suggesting the keys weren't discovered earlier because the initial searches of the expansive buildings on the Avery property, including Steve's trailer, were cursory sweeps and not detailed examinations. But the explanation rang hollow to many.

He also called a Calumet County deputy who was in the bedroom with Lenk and Colborn, for at least part of the time. "Based upon your positioning a couple feet away from that key, did you believe that either Lenk or Colborn had an opportunity, out of your eyesight, to place, or what's called plant, that key there?" Kratz asked.

"No, they did not," the officer replied.

But on cross-examination, Buting beat up on him and he had to retreat from his statement that Lenk and Colborn could not have planted the keys.

"My actual observations," the deputy testified, "I would have to say that it could be possible, as in I was doing other things, I was taking photographs, I was searching the nightstand."

A television reporter interviewed Allan Avery outside the courthouse a few days into the trial. "We're sick and tired of them saying bones were found on Avery's Auto Salvage," Allan said. "They found nothing. All they found is somebody put a car there.

"Brendan Dassey is innocent and my son is innocent," he continued. "If you start from the beginning, they plugged the highway off and kicked us out of our houses for eight days so they could plant evidence. This is not right. We need to give our justice system a good goin' over."

Kratz called Bobby Dassey, Brendan's older brother, the following day. Bobby testified that he saw a girl walking toward his uncle Steve's trailer at 2:45 p.m. on Halloween day. He also said a few days after Teresa Halbach went missing, his uncle jokingly asked him if he wanted to help hide a body, and then he kidded that she probably went to Mexico.

Bobby's brother, Blaine, also testified, telling the jury he saw a huge bonfire burning when he returned from trick-or-treating the night Teresa disappeared. He said he saw someone near the fire but claimed he couldn't remember who it was.

But as they neared the end of their case, the prosecution still hadn't dealt effectively with the blood vial defense. They hoped the jury would instinctively see through what they considered to be a preposterous claim, but they needed something more than just hope. They needed proof. Hard, objective, and undeniable proof.

So they turned to science.

Chemists add a chemical compound called ethylenediamine-tetraacetic acid, EDTA for short, when they test a blood specimen for DNA so that the specimen doesn't degrade. In its natural form blood doesn't contain EDTA, so you wouldn't expect to find any, not even a trace, in the blood stains lifted from Teresa's car—unless, of course, the blood had been planted.

Judge Willis had already granted the state's motion to test the blood stains for EDTA, but it wasn't clear whether a sufficiently reliable test existed. So with the assistance of the U.S. Attorney's office, Kratz contacted the FBI and enlisted their help.

Dr. Marc Lebeau, head of the FBI's chemical analysis unit, dropped everything, and working round the clock for two weeks, he and his colleagues developed a new protocol. As the prosecution expected, Lebeau's analysis indicated that while the specimen of Avery's blood in the vial from the clerk's office contained EDTA, the blood stains lifted from the RAV4 did not. If Judge Willis found the test sufficiently reliable, Dr. Lebeau could testify and put an end to the blood vial defense once and for all.

The next day Kratz told the court he wanted to put Lebeau on the stand. It would be one of the most crucial decisions Judge Willis would make, and it might well determine the outcome of the trial. Noting that the defense had known about the blood vial before the state did and they could have pursued testing themselves, Judge Willis sided with the state. Dr. Lebeau could take the stand.

With his curriculum vitae and the EDTA results in hand, the state's newfound star witness walked up to the witness stand, took the oath, and then waited for a gloating Ken Kratz to start his direct examination. Dr. Lebeau explained to the jury how he and his colleagues used blind testing to make sure their protocol was valid before they tested the two specimens. The results of the tests showed that the blood in the vial contained EDTA, but the blood stains lifted from the RAV4 did not. It was safe to assume, Lebeau said, that the blood inside Teresa Halbach's car did not come from the vial.

Buting established during cross-examination that EDTA testing was last done thirteen years earlier during the O.J. Simpson trial, and scientists discovered errors in the protocol during the trial. He also admitted his test couldn't measure how much EDTA was in the vial, and that there was no test that could determine the breakdown rate of EDTA in an 11-year-old vial of blood. During a news conference later that night, Buting called the EDTA testing "voodoo science," and Dean Strang likened it to "palm reading" or "astrology."

Trying to put the best spin on what many at the time considered to be the nail in Steven Avery's coffin, the defense lawyers continued their attack of LeBeau's testimony with the assembled reporters. We view this as a hail Mary pass by the state," Buting told a reporter from The Marquette Tribune in Upper Michigan. "They feel their case was weak enough that they needed to take a chance to build a ready-made appeal issue into the case."

Dean Strang suggested that in the future scientists would develop a reliable protocol for testing EDTA that would prove the blood in this case was planted.

"I hope as fervently as I can that Steven Avery either is acquitted now, or if he goes to jail you may be looking at the man who has the misfortune of twice going to prison for something he didn't do only to have advances in science clear him later," Strang said.

But Norm Gahn, a member of the prosecution team and a national expert on DNA forensic evidence, saw it differently. He told the reporters that in his opinion the results of LeBeau's EDTA test vindicated the officers accused of framing the defendant. "It's just a dastardly thing to think about or even conceive, police officers doing this," Gahn said.

Despite Buting and Strang's attempt to mitigate the damage, the EDTA test dealt a serious blow to their frame-up theory, and the defense was completely deflated— at least that's the way it looked to me. With the blood vial defense discredited, the other claims of evidence-planting would lose their credibility, too, and the entire conspiracy theory would collapse.

***

With the state having rested the previous evening, it was finally time for the defense to begin presenting its side of the case. During the past three and a half weeks the prosecution had called 53 witnesses to the stand and moved 496 exhibits into evidence. But during the next day and a half, Buting and Strang would call just seven witnesses.

They opened up with Janine Arvizu, a laboratory quality control auditor from New Mexico, who questioned the accuracy of Dr. Lebeau's test results. She said the FBI's hastily developed protocol could not rule out the presence of EDTA in the bloodstains from the victim's car because the limits of the analysis machine weren't low enough to detect it in such a small amount of blood. "The fact that EDTA was not detected in the stains does not mean EDTA was not in the stains," she said. "It certainly is quite plausible that the blood stains swabbed from the RAV4 contained EDTA, but the lab simply was not able to detect it."

Next for the defense was Dr. Scott Fairgrieve, chairman of the forensic sciences department at Laurentian University in Ontario. He'd reviewed the reports of the state's forensic anthropologist who evaluated the charred remains from the fire pit as well as dozens of photographs of the scene. Fairgrieve told the jury that the bones were not all burned in one place and some of them might have even been moved.

The defense also called a school bus driver, who testified that she saw a woman photographing a van at the salvage yard when she dropped off Brendan Dassey between 3:30 and 3:40p.m., though she couldn't remember the exact day. The inference the defense hoped to leave upon the jury, of course, was that Teresa was just fine when she left the salvage yard that day.

And a propane deliverer who fills his truck at a coop near the salvage yard testified that he saw a green SUV not unlike Teresa's leave the Avery property at about 3:30 p.m. on the day Teresa Halbach disappeared, though he didn't see who was driving.

Buting and Strang wrapped up with three less consequential witnesses and then, without calling the defendant to the stand, they abruptly rested. When Judge Willis asked Steve outside the presence of the jury whether he wanted to testify, he replied "The decision is I'm an innocent man and there's no reason for me to testify, everybody knows I'm innocent." With the blood vial defense on the ropes and Steven Avery deciding not to testify, I thought his chance for an acquittal had withered away.

At least, that's what I'd hoped at the time.

* * *

With much of the public tuning in by television or online, the jury listened attentively as the lawyers presented their closing arguments. Six weeks earlier in his opening statement Kratz had told the jurors he was showing them the cover of a jigsaw puzzle; now, addressing them at the end of the trial, he said he would help them put the pieces together. He spoke of "the clues and the secrets" found in Teresa Halbach's car and inside Steven Avery's trailer. "Teresa, by her DNA and where it was found, is telling you a story," he said. "She's telling you 'this is where I was,' she's telling you 'this is what happened to me,' and she's telling you 'this is how I was killed.'"

Ken was extremely effective. "Cases are decided on facts, at least from the state's perspective," he said, taking a not-so-subtle dig at the defense. "You know, the funny thing about facts is: Facts are stubborn. Facts don't change. You can twist them, you can beat 'em up, you can try to massage, if you will, the facts. But facts don't change."

Jerry Buting and Dean Strang shared duties in presenting the closing argument for the defense. Continuing their good cop/bad cop routine, with Buting hammering home the police conspiracy theory and Strang reflecting more broadly about burdens of proof and the meaning of "beyond a reasonable doubt," they were every bit as convincing as Kratz.

Buting argued that there was plenty of evidence, but it all pointed to a frame-up by the police. "Let me make one thing very clear right here at the outset," he said, "we do not and have never claimed the police killed Teresa Halbach, and at least in that respect, they have something in common with Steven Avery. However, the person or persons who did kill Teresa knew exactly who the police would want to blame for this crime."

He reminded the jury that Manitowoc County sheriff's deputies were guarding Teresa's car for the first four hours after it was found and suggested that the police could have taken Avery's blood from the vial at the clerk's office after normal working hours and then planted some in her car. Yet, investigators did not find the defendant's fingerprints in the victim's car, he said, "because fingerprints are very difficult to plant."

The shrill tone and sarcasm in his voice reached fever pitch when he addressed the circumstances of Colborn and Lenk's discovery of Teresa's keys in Avery's bedroom.

"Lenk gets up, walks out the door, comes back a minute later and, oh, my gosh, lo and behold in plain view, look at this key. This magic key that no one ever finds before suddenly appears in plain view."

THIRTY-SEVEN

Judge Willis instructed the clerk to spin the tumbler. After five weeks of testimony from sixty witnesses—fifty-three called by the state and seven by the defense, almost 500 court exhibits, and a day and a half of closing arguments, it was finally time for the jury to decide. Sixteen jurors were seated at the beginning of the trial and now it was time to eliminate four of them. The clerk spun the tumbler and read off the names, and the four alternates stood up and silently left the courtroom. It was down to the twelve, six women and six men, who would decide.

The jury began deliberating at 12:54 in the afternoon and retired to their hotel at six that evening without reaching a verdict. But they had to pick a foreperson and wade through pages of complicated jury instructions first, so the lack of a verdict that night wasn't a surprise. They want to be careful, I told myself, a man's life is in their hands.

I went home that night confident that the jury would see through the now-discredited conspiracy theory and swiftly return a guilty verdict the next day, probably in the morning. Now that the prosecution had shown the blood vial defense for what it was, a desperate attempt to shift blame, I couldn't imagine how they could do otherwise. Other than the happenstance of Lenk and Colborn finding the keys, the defense had presented little of substance, and in light of all the rest of the evidence, even that seemed fairly harmless now. For more than a year, Buting and Strang had shouted "police conspiracy" to anyone with ears, but now I assumed the jurors had heard enough conjecture and were ready to decide.

But I shouldn't have been so confident. The jury resumed at nine the next morning, and after several more hours of deliberating without reaching a verdict, they sent Judge Willis a note—the jury wanted a magnifying glass. That's right, a magnifying glass.

Prosecutors squirm when deliberating jurors make a request or have a question they want answered by the judge because it usually means they're having serious doubts about the state's case. "Why did they want a magnifying glass?" I asked myself. "Was it to inspect the photograph of the RAV4? Were they buying the defense that the blood was planted and asked for a magnifying glass so they could take a look for themselves?"

It was impossible to say, but Judge Willis gathered the parties and brought in the jury. They are not to conduct their own investigation, with a magnifying glass or otherwise, the judge told them, they are to base their decision on the evidence in the record, and nothing more.

The jury resumed deliberating a few minutes later and then retired at six that evening.

Still, no verdict. They'd sat stone-faced through five weeks of testimony and there was no way of knowing which way they were leaning. It had me on edge, and I could only imagine how Kratz and the rest of the prosecution team felt—not to mention the Halbachs.

It wasn't long after the jurors began deliberating the next morning when they sent an even more distressing note to Judge Willis. They wanted to review the testimony from Sherry Culhane, and worse, they only wanted her cross-examination.

Jerry Buting had established two things during his cross-examination of crime lab analyst Culhane, which I assumed were now on the minds of the jurors. First, Steven Avery's DNA was not found on the trigger of the rifle that he allegedly used to shoot Teresa Halbach. And second, there was no blood on the rifle's barrel.

"The victim in this case was shot at close range, wasn't she?" Buting had asked. "And you would typically find blood spatter on a rifle barrel that was used to shoot someone at close range, wouldn't you? Yet when you examined the rifle that my client allegedly used to shoot the victim in this case, you didn't observe any blood spatter, isn't that right?"

Buting's assumptions weren't valid. A gunshot at close range doesn't always leave blood spatter, and the absence of the shooter's DNA on the trigger wasn't unusual. But thanks to *CSI* and other popular TV crime shows, jurors assume there's always physical evidence left at crime scenes, and now they almost insist on proof by DNA. Sherry Culhane had appropriately qualified her answers, but it didn't matter, Buting had sown doubt in the minds of some of the jurors.

Judge Willis called in the lawyers again, and after some prodding, the parties agreed that the fairest way to handle the jury's request was to read all of Culhane's testimony concerning the rifle, not just her cross-examination by Buting. So the clerk called in the jury and Judge Willis read the testimony out loud in its entirety. After deliberating a few more hours, the jury retired for the evening.

Two and a half days of deliberations and there still wasn't a verdict!

I fell asleep that night thinking about Teresa Halbach's parents. They'd sat stoically through the entire trial, expressing quiet confidence in the system that they hoped would bring justice to the man who murdered their daughter. No parent of a murdered child expects closure, but a guilty verdict would at least end the drawn-out legal proceedings against Teresa's killer. I thought how an acquittal would devastate them, how it would add insult to an injury that you'd think could be insulted no further. I knew that if anyone could handle such pain, it would be the Halbach family with their unshakable faith. But at the same time, I thought, hadn't they already suffered enough?

* * *

It was just after four-thirty the following afternoon when the bailiff made the announcement. After deliberating for three days, the jury had reached a verdict. The parties and a sizeable crowd assembled, and when everyone was in place, the clerk called in the jurors. They filed into the courtroom with their heads down—not a good sign for Avery, I thought hopefully.

"Has the jury reached a verdict?" Judge Willis asked in a calm but firm tone of voice.

"Yes, Your Honor," the foreperson replied.

"Please hand the verdict forms to the bailiff," the judge said.

The bailiff handed over the forms while the courtroom waited in silence. The judge had previously warned the spectators against outbursts, and after slowly reading through the forms, he announced the verdicts.

"As to the charge of party to the crime of first degree intentional homicide as charged in count one of the information, we the jury find the defendant, Steven A. Avery, guilty."

A sigh of relief swept through the courtroom, except for behind the defense table, where the Avery family was as shocked and devastated as the Halbachs were relieved. Judge Willis mercifully wrapped it up by announcing that the jury had also found the defendant guilty of being a felon in possession of a firearm, but not guilty of mutilating a corpse.

The sexual assault and false imprisonment charges were previously dismissed since they couldn't be proved without Brendan Dassey's testimony. But none of that mattered. With his conviction for murder, Steven Avery would never live another day as a free man.

* * *

Teresa Halbach never imagined that a video diary she made three years before she died would be played during a sentencing hearing for the man convicted of her murder. The voice and face of a beautiful, grace-filled, loving, and very much alive young woman filled the courtroom as Teresa told us how she loved hugs, her family, God, making people laugh, traveling, people giving her compliments, and music groups like the Beatles and No Doubt.

"I love knowing that I like who I am," she said. "I love taking pictures. I love holding a camera in my hand. I love kids. I love babies. I don't hate anyone. I love a lot of people. I feel loved."

"Let's say I died tomorrow," Teresa said into the camera. "I don't think I will. I think I have a lot more to do. I just want people I love to know that whenever I die, that I was happy. That I'm happy with what I did with my life."

Her family struggled to hold back tears as Teresa's voice filled the courtroom. She said if she dies early she wished she could have been a mother "because that's the one thing I've always known that I want to be—a mom. And I will be a good mom one day. I will. As long as I'm happy," she said with a smile.

We don't have the death penalty in Wisconsin, but if we did, Steven Avery would have been executed—at least that's what the prosecution would have sought. Instead of death, life imprisonment without the possibility of parole is the maximum penalty for murder in Wisconsin. Judge Willis could set a parole eligibility date that would allow Steve's release some day, say when he was ninety if he happened to live that long. But with a crime as deplorable as this one, nobody expected him to do so, and the judge didn't prove them wrong.

With the sentence nearly a foregone conclusion, there wasn't much to argue about, but the lawyers, being lawyers, argued anyhow.

Kratz briefly commented on the defendant's criminal history, including the cat burning incident, and then he recounted some of the most diabolical details of his most recent crime.

Strang said he didn't know what happened the day Teresa was murdered, but he believed in Steven Avery. "There's more good in this man than there is bad," he said.

When it was his turn to speak, Steven Avery said he felt sorry for Teresa Halbach's family and their friends, as well as his family and himself.

"It's hurting everybody," he said. He also said he would prove his innocence someday—just like the last time.

"Teresa Halbach, I didn't kill," he said. "I'm innocent for all of this, and I figure later on I'll prove myself innocent. I feel bad about it. I wish they'd catch the guy who did it, whoever did it, because I didn't do it, honest to God."

And then it was time for Judge Willis to hand down the sentence. After noting that Avery had committed a calculated premeditated murder, he addressed the defendant directly.

"You are probably the most dangerous individual ever to set foot in this courtroom," he told Steve. "From what I see, nothing in your life suggests that society would ever be safe from your behavior."

And then Judge Willis sentenced Steven Avery to life in prison without the possibility of parole.

✳ ✳ ✳

On the morning of June 4, 2007, twenty-one years after passing through them the first time and less than four years after walking out a free man, Steven Avery was escorted through the gates at Dodge Correctional Institute in Waupun. There were no smiles this time, no cameras, no klieg lights, and no pretty reporters asking for a moment of his time. The doors clanged shut, and for the rest of his life, barring any more shocking revelations concerning the murder of Teresa Halbach, the nation's most famous exoneree will unceremoniously be known as Wisconsin State Prison Inmate No. 00122987.

EPILOGUE

A few weeks after Steven Avery was sentenced, Jody, the kids, and I drove up to Neshotah Beach on the north side of Two Rivers. Summer had returned early to Wisconsin that year, and thanks to an early season warm front, temperatures had preposterously risen into the lower nineties. We popped open an umbrella and spread out a blanket in the sand while the girls splashed around in the fifty-degree water and the boys rode the waves back to shore.

Call it obsession, but I wanted to see if the poplar tree was still there—the place where twenty-two years earlier Gregory Allen lay in wait for his prey. So my son Tom and I started jogging north along the beach, making our way out of the park and into the wilderness, where fifty yards inland, the towering pines still kept watch over what was happening below.

We approached First Creek a mile into our run, where Allen had lunged out from the poplar tree and manhandled Penny Beerntsen over the dunes. But the tree wasn't there. A few measly shrubs struggled for survival ten feet from the shore, but they were far too small to have spent the last twenty- two years growing. Maybe high waves from a storm had washed it away.

But, in truth, I was glad it was gone. An injustice perpetrated upon the local court system had persisted for twenty-two years. Festering like a cancer, it let an uncharged assailant repeat his crime, this time in Green Bay, it temporarily turned Penny Beerntsen's life upside down, though Penny recovered and is now a major voice for criminal justice reform, and it turned Steven Avery into an even more dangerous monster than he was when he was sent to prison the first time. And when two highly skilled defense attorneys resurrected that injustice twenty years later to defend him in a murder trial, it nearly destroyed the local justice system and let a madman go free. But Avery's conviction destroyed the injustice once and for all, and if the waters of Lake Michigan had washed away another sign of the original crime, so much the better.

I'd worked up a pretty good sweat by the time Tom and I got back to the park, so I ran down the beach with a full head of steam and after a clumsy version of high-stepping over the waves, I dove into the water. When I opened my eyes and looked at the rippled sand on the bottom, all I saw was sunlight and water. I ran out as fast as I ran in and rejoined Jody, who was looking as beautiful as ever under the umbrella.

"Did you hear, sweetie?" I said, with my heart still pounding. "They're talking about putting the glass back on the dome."

AFTERWORD

By Keith Findley, University of Wisconsin Law School Professor and former co-director of the Wisconsin Innocence Project

Every exoneration of a wrongly convicted person represents both tragedy and triumph—the tragedy of the wrongful conviction and all it entails, and the triumph of vindication, of justice finally served. Every exoneration fits this description—except perhaps Steven Avery's. It's hard to find the triumph in this case, while the tragedies are obvious and nearly beyond comprehension. The victims of this saga are everywhere—from Penny Beerntsen, to the women who were victimized by Gregory Allen after he could have been stopped if law enforcement had not ignored him while fixating on Avery, to the criminal justice system itself, and most profoundly, to Teresa Halbach and her family.

The story need not be all tragedy, though. For every wrongful conviction—including this one—offers the opportunity for learning and improvement. Every wrongful conviction—like every airplane crash or train derailment—is a case study in system failure, offering insights about how to prevent such failures in the future. It is incumbent upon us all to seize those learning opportunities.

The system was in the midst of learning from this case when Steven Avery was convicted of murdering Teresa Halbach. The legislature had convened the Avery Task Force, and adopted its recommendations for reform on eyewitness identification procedures and electronic recording of custodial interrogations.

After Teresa Halbach's murder, the political appetite for reform in Wisconsin withered. The cause of guarding against wrongful convictions lost its appeal and even became a sort of political untouchable. Discussions of criminal justice policy reverted to the norm—a sad cycle of thoughtless efforts by policy makers to be tougher than the next on crime, simultaneously driven by and feeding an irrational fear of violent crime.

But this story shows us that things need not and should not be that way. This story reminds us not just of the tragedies of this case, but of the need to make sure the criminal justice system gets it right. This is a story of personal and professional failure by, among others, law enforcement and prosecution officials who were focused single-mindedly on getting Steven Avery, even when the signs were prevalent that he did not attack Penny Beerntsen. But the personal and professional failures of a few individuals should not over-shadow the fact that these failures occurred in a context—in a system that enabled those individual failures. We cannot lose sight of the fact that this is a story of systemic failure as much as, if not more than, individual failure.

The system, for example, permitted law enforcement to use a composite sketch that altered and biased Penny Beerntsen's memory of her attacker, to present a photo array to her after law enforcement told her they had a suspect in mind (thereby pressuring her to pick one of the faces, even though, as we now know, the true perpetrator was not included), to follow it with a live lineup in which Steven Avery stood out like a sore thumb, and was the only one who had been included previously in the photo array. And then Penny was given confirming feedback, which we now know from social science research can deceive victims and witnesses into being more confident in their identifications than they would have been otherwise. Under these circumstances, Penny never had much of a chance to get it right. No victims or witnesses should have to suffer through such practices, which set them up for error.

The system also permitted skewed presentation of the facts because police and prosecutors knew they could hide the facts pointing to Gregory Allen without much risk of ever being exposed. Limited discovery rules in criminal cases means facts that might mean a lot to the defense can languish in police and prosecutors' files, either because of malfeasance or because the competitive enterprise of litigating cases in an adversary system makes it difficult for advocates on one side to recognize the value of evidence to the other side.

The system permitted reliance on inadequate or misleading forensic science evidence. Most forensic sciences, it turns out—foremost among them, microscopic hair examination—rest on very little real science. As the National Academy of Sciences (NAS) reported in 2009, most forensic sciences, apart from nuclear DNA analysis, have not been adequately sci-entifically studied or validated, and have never been shown scientifically to be able to reliably match a piece of crime scene evidence to an individual source. Moreover, as the NAS also reported, the placement of forensic laboratories within law enforcement agencies itself inevitably compromises the objectivity and neutrality required for true scientific analysis.

And the system enabled a jailhouse "snitch" to come forward falsely alleging that Avery had confessed to him the rape and attempted murder of Penny Beerntsen. The system enables such false statements by allowing prosecutors to reward informants and snitches for such testimony, without imposing any safeguards or limitations on its use to guard against unreliability. Fortunately, the snitch in this case did not come forward until after trial and so he never testified, but the sheriff banked his statement for use in the future should it be needed. The case thus reminds us of the risks of such testimony when it is used in trials (as it often is).

Finally, once Avery was exonerated, the system did virtually nothing to ensure that he would transition successfully back into the community, after the wrongful conviction destroyed his life, depriving him permanently of his wife, children, home, and livelihood. The sad irony is that in most respects a guilty person released on parole gets more assistance from the state than does an innocent person released upon exoneration. If nothing else, this case should serve as a sober reminder that we all have a stake in doing better at helping exonerees get started again upon release.

This case was devastating to a lot of people. It certainly was to me. It was the most professionally and personally difficult episode of my life. And I know that my own devastation pales in comparison to the injuries suffered by the real victims in this case. It is my profound hope that the system can find a way to continue to learn from the tragedies in this case. Only then can we say that this case, like all other exonerations, truly represents both tragedy and triumph.

POST-SCRIPT

September 11, 2013

As I write this, it is exactly ten years since Steven Avery was exonerated, and more than a quarter century since the assault itself. My thoughts about him have had a complicated evolution. For the 18 years after I misidentified him, I wondered what had led him to become so violent at such a young age. During his lengthy incarceration I also tried to imagine what life was like for his wife Lori, raising five young children on her own. Were their children better off with Steve out of the picture? What was it like for them when they reached school age and every appeal in their father's high profile case was front page news, detailed for their classmates to read?

The day my friend, Janine Geske, broke the news that Steve was not my assailant felt infinitely more difficult than the day I was attacked. I was horrified that I had played an unwitting role in a terrible miscarriage of justice, with such far reaching consequences. Steven Avery was incarcerated from age 23 to age 41—crucial years in anyone's life—for a crime he did not commit. Every wrongful conviction is also a wrongful acquittal, and Gregory Allen remained a free man for ten years after attacking me. In 1995 he was finally convicted of the brutal rape of another Wisconsin woman. How many others became his victims between 1985 and 1995? I was consumed with oppressive guilt.

During Steven's incarceration I became involved in the restorative justice movement, both speaking on victim impact panels in prisons and facilitating victim/offender dialogues. Following the advice I always gave inmates—to accept responsibility for our wrongdoings—I immediately wrote a letter of apology to Steve. When I finished that letter, the refrain from Paul Simon's "Homeward Bound" went through my mind: "and all my words come back to me, in shades of mediocrity." No apology could unring the bell of this injustice.

Although I intellectually understood that Steven Avery was not my assailant, I still had a visceral reaction each time I saw his picture. Gregory Allen's picture, on the other hand, elicited no emotional response. He seemed like a phantom. The psychologist I had been seeing since the exoneration advised me that I would never be able to attach the negative emotions I had experienced for 18 years to Gregory Allen. I had to work, instead, on removing those emotions from Steven.

I had begun that process when I received an alarming call from Janine in early November of 2005. A young woman named Teresa Halbach was missing, and Steven Avery was a suspect in her disappearance. My first reaction was utter disbelief. Steve's civil attorneys had begun deposing witnesses for his wrongful conviction lawsuit. Why would he jeopardize the outcome by committing such a horrific crime? Besides, it just didn't seem possible that the soft-spoken man who was so gracious when I apologized could be the perpetrator of this monstrous act. However, as details of Teresa's murder became public I became convinced that Steve was responsible. The same DNA technology which exonerated Steve as my assailant would help prosecutors rightfully convict him of Teresa's murder.

If memory is malleable and perspective is molded by both time and experience, where do I find myself 28 years after my fateful jog on the beach? I have recounted my assault in so many presentations that the events of July 29, 1985, no longer haunt me. If only the same was true of the aftermath of that day, with its mind numbing twists and turns. It sometimes feels like I'm living in a parallel universe where the usual rules don't apply. And I'm acutely aware that I'm a lifetime member of a terrible group I never wished to join: victims who have misidentified their assailants.

Always in the back of my mind is the nagging, unanswerable question: "If I had identified the correct person, would Teresa Halbach be alive today?" Was Steve so filled with rage over his wrongful conviction, and angry with me as his female accuser, that he murdered Teresa?

The sadness I felt over Steve's wrongful conviction and lost years has been superceded by his atrocity. I did not know Teresa and have not met the Halbach family, but I cannot begin to understand or even imagine the magnitude of their loss. They experienced the singular horror I have always felt I could not transcend—the murder of one's child. From their public comments at the time of Teresa's disappearance and during Steve's trial for her murder, it is clear that their strength comes from an abiding faith.

I think of Teresa on an almost daily basis, and am haunted by the video diary she made three years prior to her murder, which was played at Avery's sentencing hearing. When I walked our daughter down the aisle at her wedding in 2008 I knew that Teresa's parents would never have the same joy filled experience. At the birth of our two granddaughters I remembered Teresa's words, "that's the one thing I've always known that I want to be—a mom. I will be a good mom one day."

Our oldest granddaughter Chloe is three and a half. She bounds out of bed each morning at an ungodly hour, raises the shade on her window and declares, no matter what the weather, "Look, it's a beautiful day!" Tim Halbach, in a moving eulogy to his sister, shared, "Every day with Teresa was a good day!" To me, these two women—one just beginning life and one whose life was cut short—have shared the quintessential: today is all we have. Perhaps making each day a good day is how all of us can best pay tribute to Teresa.

Penny Beerntsen

AUTHOR'S NOTES

In 2005, Steven Avery was the first exoneree in the United States to be arrested for a subsequent homicide. Unfortunately, he wasn't the last. Marlon Pendleton was convicted of raping a woman on Chicago's south side in 1992. He was released from prison on November 30, 2006 after DNA testing showed he was not the perpetrator. But on August 16, 2011, Pendleton was convicted of voluntary manslaughter in the beating death of his girlfriend, Dannette Adkins.

Eight months after Steven Avery's murder trial, seventeen-year-old Brendan Dassey was convicted and sentenced to life in prison for his role in the murder of Teresa Halbach. He will be eligible for parole in 2047 after serving forty years of his sentence, when he is fifty-seven years old.

An independent investigation conducted by the Wisconsin Attorney General concluded there was no intentional wrongdoing by the sheriff or the district attorney in Steven Avery's wrongful conviction, citing, instead, poor communication between law enforcement agencies. Any opinion expressed herein to the contrary is that of the author, and though shared by many, it is not shared by all.

The names of some persons portrayed in this book have been changed to protect their identities.

Index